CONFLICT AND CONSENSUS IN JEWISH POLITICAL LIFE

BAR-ILAN DEPARTMENTAL RESEARCHES
DEPARTMENT OF POLITICAL STUDIES

COMPARATIVE JEWISH POLITICS Vol. II

CONFLICT AND CONSENSUS IN JEWISH POLITICAL LIFE

edited by

STUART A. COHEN AND ELIEZER DON-YEHIYA

Bar-Ilan University Press

Sponsored by the Schnitzer Foundation for Research
on the Israeli Economy and Society — Bar-Ilan University

ISBN 965—226—061—4

CONTENTS

CONTRIBUTORS

Leah Bornstein-Makovetsky	Lecturer; Dept. of Jewish History, Bar-Ilan University
Stuart A. Cohen	Assoc. Professor; Dept. of Political Studies, Bar-Ilan University
Eliezer Don-Yeḥiya	Assoc. Professor; Dept. of Political Studies, Bar-Ilan University
Giora Goldberg	Senior Lecturer; Dept. of Political Studies, Bar-Ilan University
Ilan Greilsammer	Assoc. Professor; Dept. of Political Studies, Bar-Ilan University
Sam Lehman-Wilzig	Senior Lecturer; Dept. of Political Studies, Bar-Ilan University
Charles S. Liebman	Professor; Dept. of Political Studies, Bar-Ilan University
Emanuel Rackman	Professor; President, Bar-Ilan University
Anita Shapira	Professor; School of History, Tel-Aviv University
Ephraim Tabory	Lecturer; Dept. of Sociology, Bar-Ilan University
David Vital	Professor; Dept. of Political Science, Tel-Aviv University
Chaim I. Waxman	Assoc. Professor; Dept. of Sociology, Rutgers University

INTRODUCTION

This book surveys manifestations of conflict and co-operation in Jewish public life. It does not claim to constitute a composite methodological introduction to the topic of Jewish communal government; still less is it designed to provide a comprehensive chronological survey of its development. Our aim, rather, has been to investigate individual instances of Jewish communal discourse and to examine some of the consequences to which each gave rise within its own particular temporal and geographic context. It is hoped that the exercise will foster a wider understanding of some of the procedures and mechanisms of Jewish self-government. It might also contribute to the identification of some of the principal issues which have generated Jewish communal debate.

Let it be said at the outset that the articles in this book do not immediately permit the postulation of grand and synoptic hypotheses concerning the structures and processes of Jewish public life. On the contrary, to a large extent they can be said to underscore the difficulties inherent in the very attempt to do so. They indicate that, even within the confines of a topic ostensibly so delineated as communal co-operation and conflict, the fabric of Jewish society is (and always has been) too richly complex to permit an offhand formulation of a general typology of Jewish political behaviour. The reason is not to be found solely in the sheer length and breadth of the Jewish communal experience. That, admittedly, is a daunting consideration; put quite bluntly, no single volume of case studies could be expected to support the weight of anything more than informed speculation. But the articles in this volume suggest that size is not the sole inhibition; from a conceptual point of view, neither is it the most pertinent. Also worthy of attention are three other considerations, each of which merits exploration in and of itself. The purpose of this introduction is to highlight those considerations, and to indicate the manner in which they are implicitly — and variously — reflected in the presentations which follow.

I

First in methodological order is the need to discern the identity of the *dramatis personae* in any particular communal episode. There is more to this than the obvious requirement that the protagonists be identified and their alignments traced. What also demands examination is the precise communal position from which each person or group purportedly speaks, and for which they claim to stand. Co-operation and conflict, after all, are only portmanteau terms, the personal effects of which often require close investigation. Failure to undertake such an enquiry might obscure the nature of the connective tissue linking particular personalities with particular problems. It might also produce a lopsided reconstruction of the origins and course of whichever communal situation it is that results in either harmony or discord.

The need to clarify the identity of the protagonists is a general requirement, probably applicable to all organised societies. But it seems to be particularly acute in the case of many Jewish communal relationships, where dependence on the vagaries of personality is often pronounced. The articles which follow suggest that, even so, there exist at least two contrasting levels of possible analysis. One is derivative from the view that Jewish communal management invariably pertains to a restricted number of elite groups, each of which vies for as much authority as contemporary Jewish circumstances will allow. To a large extent, the relationships between these groups are accordingly akin to a three-legged race in which the parties, even though often out of step and not infrequently tripping each other up, seem generally to be heading in the same direction. In this view, then, the thrust of communal discourse is essentially about means, rather than ends. Contentions, when they arise, do not concern the goals of communal association (these, indeed, are more often than not taken for granted). Instead, they focus on the precise location of a communal prerogative and on the practical control over a specific lever of communal government.

An alternative approach seeks, where appropriate, a somewhat more expansive dimension. Only superficially, it argues, do Jewish communal politics concern the occasional gyrations of elite groups entrenched at the apex of pyramidal Jewish societies. At their deeper level, they are the expression of a symbiotic relationship between both the entirety of the "establishment" (be it local, national or international) and the mass of the Jewish public. Communal discourse, in this view, is not therefore always restricted to the boundary rights of individual demesnes — prominent though such squabbles usually are in the contemporary records. It can also be seen to address matters which affect the very texture of Jewish life and call into question the entire infrastructure of Jewish communal association: its composition, responsibilities, and attested goals. These are the issues which come to the fore in the heat of several inter- and intra-communal debates (such as that generated by the "Uganda" controversy, discussed below by Vital). Not the least important aspect of such episodes lies in their tendency to blur conventional alignments, often by generating the formation of novel camps and parties. These are not simply more recent expressions of older "in" and "out" factions. They also address (and sometimes create) a wider public, whose aspirations they claim to articulate.

Ultimately, it could be argued, a working hypothesis of the full gamut of Jewish communal co-operation and conflict requires the application of both approaches. Nevertheless, the methodological differences between them do seem to demand attention. Each requires recourse to different types of source material, and each results in the writing of distinct levels of communal analysis. As much is illustrated by a comparison of just two of the following discussions: that which describes communal structures in the Sephardi communities of the Ottoman Empire during the 16th and 17th centuries (Bornstein-Makovetsky); and that which analyses the far more recent cases of challenges to authority within the American Jewish community (Waxman).

II

Whether or not the differences between those two cases ought really to be attributed to the sharp variations in their separate historical milieus is a question to which we shall presently return. Prior consideration might be given to the separate issue of the differences in perspective and emphasis which they can be seen to illustrate. At its most basic level, this is very much a question of emphasis. If we are to attempt the formulation of a typology of Jewish communal relationships, is it co-operation — or conflict — which is to be preferred as the norm, from which all departures are to be deemed deviant? Put another way, are instances of communal co-operation to be examined against a background of more perennial conflict; or are cases of conflict to be analysed within the context of a predominant environment of co-operation? The evidence can be expected to provide clear guidelines only at the two extreme (and atypical) reaches of total communal harmony or utter communal discord. It is likely to prove far less tractable for the intervening gradations, which are entirely neither one nor the other.

Here, too, the available approaches cannot be easily reconciled. Implicit in that which focuses on inter-communal differences over means rather than ends is the assumption that the pendulum of communal relations is heavily weighted in favour of concord. Disputes, quite apart from being considered unseemly (and, given the fragile nature of much Jewish life, impolitic), are also at odds with the hallowed Jewish traditions of mutual responsibility *(arevut)* and communal fraternity *(ahdut)*. In this view, accordingly, the fact that dissent is usually contained within set (if unwritten) bounds of propriety is not exclusively to be attributed to either the lethargy of most protagonists, nor even to the absence of many serious matters for them to fight about. Instead, the reasons are principally to be sought in the sensitivity of most of the Jewish public, for most of the time, and in most places (a category which would today include Israel as well as the Diaspora) to the fissiparous consequences of a departure from the norms of unity embedded in Jewish political culture.

This approach might be contrasted with its alternative, which takes as its point of departure a situation of intrinsic communal discord, in which interests often clash and where differences of principle are seldom deemed reconcilable. Such tensions, it suggests, continuously rumble beneath the surface of all domains of Jewish public life. They are obscured only by the fact that the resultant conflicts seem often quotidian and routine. They are apt to erupt, however, especially at times of sustained structural changes or of protracted ideological debates. Examples of the former category are provided by the modern histories of French Jewry (Greilsammer) and of Anglo-Jewry (Cohen): instances of the latter are to be found in American Orthodoxy's efforts to accommodate Reform (Rackman) and in Israel's debate over "Who is a Jew?" (Liebman). As here described, all four cases gave rise to communal, or national, "crises". Under the circumstances thus engendered, the attainment of a spirit of co-operation seems to be dependent on the successful application of essentially transient attributes. One, possibly, is a determined and mutual effort at personal compromise (which was apparently lacking, at the critical moment, in the episode described by Rackman, but was achieved in the case of Anglo-Jewry). Another might be the subtle exercise of political manoeuvre. One successful manifestation of the latter is discussed in Don-Yehiya's analysis of the resolution of religious conflicts in modern Israel.

III

By any standards of Jewish political history, the contemporary State of Israel is, of course, *sui generis*. Insights attained from that particular case cannot, therefore, be easily applied to other Jewish communities, where political issues are different in scale and where political participation (especially of the kind described by Lehman-Wilzig) is different in kind. Quite apart from all else, Israel is a parliamentary democracy, in which it is conventional to attain co-operation and to resort to conflict through the accepted procedures of intra-party debate and inter-party dialogue. Arguably, these are mechanisms which reinforce the tendency towards incremental change often said to be inherent in the very structure of Jewish communal life. As Goldberg's paper on *Ḥerut* points out, even the results of the 1977 elections in Israel did not portend a sudden swing; rather, they were the outcome of a steady shift in national priorities and images. Nevertheless, precisely because Israeli communal relations operate within an exceptional ambience of Jewish self-government, their analytical affinity with its other expressions necessarily appears slight.

The argument that Israel is an exception which proves the rule, with the attendant implication that all other Jewish communities might therefore indeed be dragooned into uniform methodological categories, in effect only dodges the issue. Specifically, it minimizes the essential heterogeneity of the entire Jewish experience, which has itself contributed to the rich diversity of Jewish communal forms, both past and present. Herein, indeed, lies the third — and perhaps most crucial — of the requirements for the proposition of a theoretical framework for the analysis of Jewish co-operation and conflict. Different Jewish communities were, and are, the product of different conditions. Moreover, during the course of their histories they have adopted forms of communal management which have both reflected and reinforced the separate circumstances of their origins and the disparate degrees to which they have been able (or willing) to interact with their local environment. To concentrate on their similarities at the expense of their diversity is therefore to run the risk of fashioning a collage of dubious comparisons. This, in turn, might do violence to the contexts within which particular communal battles were fought and concluded.

The articles in this book suggest that the contextual issue itself raises two subsidiary considerations: one might be termed latitudinal, the other longitudinal. The first finds expression in those presentations which touch upon the influence exerted on particular Jewish communal debates by the politics and culture of the host milieu. The discrepancies between the mechanisms whereby Jewish debates were regulated in Britain, France and the U.S.A. (and, for that matter, the differences in the tone in which they were conducted) are obviously relevant to this issue. But they constitute only one category of the variable. "Host", it might be pointed out, need not refer exclusively to the predominantly Gentile world of the Diaspora; it might also describe the burgeoning Jewish world of the new *Yishuv* and the majoritarian Jewish environment of modern Israel. This is implicit in Shapira's account of the struggle over *Avodah Ivrit* and in Tabory's description of the fate and fortunes of the Reform and Conservative movements in Israel. Both underscore the possible varieties of context, even within the Jewish world *per se*. Patterns of thought and behaviour, they suggest, cannot be transplanted from one Jewish society to another without encountering wearing resistance *en route*.

To this must be added what is here referred to as the longitudinal facet of the contextual consideration — the degree to which patterns of Jewish com-

11

munal co-operation and conflict can legitimately be compared across the watersheds of distinct historical periods. This is especially difficult territory. For one thing, the exercise demands the temerity to traverse ground heavily criss-crossed with fences set up by schools of specialists carefully delineating the peculiarities of their separate allotments. More to the point, it also requires an ability to relate changes from one epoch to another by discerning the levels of influence which permeate intermittent historical materials. To achieve this, not only do the forums of Jewish communal debate distinctive to any particular period have to be distinguished, but also the various premises of discourse appropriate to different eras. Notoriously contentious in this respect are appeals to the modes of communal dialogue assumed to be embedded in the tenets of Judaism. Even when these are articulated in the sources, they cannot blindly be trusted. Legends apart, people do not always mean what they say or write (and communal leaders are no exception), and the fact that some materials do articulate traditional notions of Jewish communal discourse is no proof that they constitute their authors' sole frame of reference. Precisely the same code of metaphors might have conveyed quite different meanings at different periods, especially when expressed in different languages and addressed to different audiences.

As is well known, the respective shares of continuity and discontinuity of Jewish communal mores are particularly hard to assess across the ideological battleground of the 18th and 19th centuries. Although the terms do beg some serious questions, it is generally accepted that those were the years which marked the end of medieval Jewish communal life and the genesis of its modern form. Of particular relevance to our concern is the fact that they also witnessed the erratic course of the uneven and irregular process termed the Enlightenment and the first flush of the modern, political version of Zionism. Both phenomena did occasionally generate atavistic impulses. But, in general, they encouraged a dedication to pulling up roots put down by earlier generations, rather than to nurturing their continued growth. Certainly, the Enlightenment and Zionism were concomitant with the progressively marked decline in commitment on the part of most Jews (particularly, but not only, in the Western world) to the *halakhah*, a legal fabric which had hitherto been commonly accepted as constitutionally authoritative. What transpired, indeed, was a thorough re-examination of the nature of the Jewishness of Jews — what became known as the issue of "Jewish identity" — and a restructuring of the framework of corporate Jewish institutions.

In this volume, our own focus of attention is concentrated on the course and results of those processes, rather than their antecedents. Only one of the following papers (Bornstein-Makovetsky) describes a communal situation unaffected in any degree by the currents associated with Emancipation; most discuss issues which were either directly connected with Zionism or otherwise influenced by its progress. The emphasis on matters concerned with Israeli public life is particularly marked. Accordingly, we are in no position to determine the extent to which the cases here described are comparable with others, of a different time and place. For the moment, we can only pose these — and other — contextual questions. We do so in the cautious hope that they may yet prove amenable to generic analysis, of a type which befits their acute importance for an understanding of the dual qualities of sameness and otherness in Jewish communal life.

No collaborative work of this nature could possibly be produced without help and encouragement from many quarters. Thanks are due, in the first instance, to those of our colleagues from other departments and universities who responded to the invitation to contribute articles to this book. In so doing, they helped us to advance one stage further than our previous departmental volume (*Comparative Jewish Politics: Public Life in Israel and the Diaspora*, eds., S. N. Lehman-Wilzig and B. Susser, 1981), which was entirely an in-house production. Equally gratifying were the advice and judgements of our editorial board, and of the additional readers to whom we turned for assistance.

We have also benefited from considerable technical assistance, notably from Mrs. Shirley Shaiak, of the departmental staff, and from Mrs. Miriam Drori, of the Bar-Ilan University Press.

Last, and certainly not least, it is a privilege to add our name to the list of beneficiaries of the Schnitzer Foundation for Research on Israeli Economy and Society, Bar-Ilan, whose trustees made generous grants which defrayed the publication costs.

Stuart A. Cohen
Eliezer Don-Yeḥiya

Bar-Ilan University.

LEAH BORNSTEIN-MAKOVETSKY

COOPERATION AND CONFLICT BETWEEN THE RELIGIOUS AND POLITICAL LEADERSHIP

RELATIONS BETWEEN *PARNASIM* AND RABBIS IN THE COMMUNITIES OF THE OTTOMAN EMPIRE DURING THE 16th AND 17th CENTURIES

Jewish communities in the Ottoman Empire during the 16th and 17th centuries constituted a traditional society whose ways of life were governed by Jewish law, in accordance with fixed halakhic norms. In the communities of Germany and Italy of the same period, the institutions of Jewish law seemed to be weakening; but within the Ottoman Empire they retained their strength. As much is revealed by the very extensive surviving records of legal judgements composed by the contemporary scholars of those communities. These indicate that Ottoman Jewish society and its leaders maintained a genuine religious world view, and sought to establish religious criteria in public affairs, for all areas of life, in accordance with traditional Jewish patterns. In this society, the authority of the secular-political leadership depended upon the legitimization of the religious leadership.

Another characteristic of this society was the trend towards decentralization within the communities, which was itself the result of the influx after the 15th century of tens of thousands of immigrants, primarily from Spain, Portugal and Italy. This trend was reflected principally in the maintenance of separate congregations, in which each conducted fully autonomous lives as independent communities with separate secular and religious leaderships. The trend towards decentralization was also manifest in the absence of a central leadership and a chief rabbinate with country-wide authority, and by the fact that the leaders did not convene on a supra-communal level, as was customary in Western communities.[1]

This situation greatly enhanced the importance of the local leadership.

1 Leah Bornstein, *The Jewish Communal Leadership in the Near East from the End of the 15th Century through the 18th Century* (Dissertation, Ramat-Gan: Bar-Ilan University, June 1978) (hereafter, Bornstein, Dissertation); *idem*, "Tendencies of

Although most of the communities of the Ottoman Empire were dominated by an oligarchic secular leadership, their democratic tendencies were revealed in the manner whereby local leadership brought its communal ordinances and decisions before the public.

An examination of contemporary sources, both Jewish (primarily *responsa*) and Ottoman, indicates the complete independence of the Jewish authorities in the conduct of local communal affairs. This situation resulted from the broad autonomy accorded by the Ottoman government to the Jewish *millet*. The communities enjoyed religious freedom and were permitted to conduct an autonomous social life; to a large extent, they also maintained independent institutions, especially for judicial-religious concerns. The members of each congregation accepted the authority of the local congregational *parnasim* (lay leaders) and rabbis. Only on rare occasions — when the leaders were accused of corruption — did they lodge a complaint with the government authorities; and even then the initial action was an attempt to force them to resign by means of halakhic rulings and communal decisions.

As a rule, the Ottoman government itself did not interfere with the powers of the Jewish leadership unless asked to do so by the Jews themselves. Hence, the present essay will not address the question of relations between the government and the Jewish leadership. Rather, its aim is to examine the relations between the two domains of authority within the communities of the Ottoman Empire: that of the rabbis (religious leadership), and that of the *parnasim* (the secular-political leadership), and the division of functions between them. It will attempt to determine whether relations between *parnasim* and rabbis in the communities of the Ottoman Empire were well-ordered and based on the accepted norms of pre-emancipation and traditional Jewish society; it will also examine the manner whereby the frictions and controversies which developed between these two authorities fitted into this framework. Of course, it will only be possible to sketch general lines, since the balance of forces within the local leadership differed not only from community to community, but also from congregation to congregation. Moreover, changes occurred within the leadership of the various communities over the course of this extended period. Nevertheless, it is hoped that the present study might stress the uniqueness of the relations between the secular and religious leaders in the communities of the Ottoman Empire, as compared to the situation prevailing in Germany, Italy and Eastern Europe during this same period.

Separation and Unification in Greek Jewish Communities during the 16th and 17th Centuries," *Bar-Ilan Annual*, XX–XXI (1983), pp. 242–70.

The Ottoman Empire, as referred to in the present article, relates to the entire territory of the Empire, other than North Africa.

I

In general there existed an absolute distinction between the two domains of authority, and only on rare occasions did one intrude on the other's sphere.[2] The powers and functions of each domain were generally defined and recorded in letters of rabbinical appointment and in communal ordinances. Thus, the *parnasim* were charged with a variety of functions affecting communal finances and taxation, and negotiated with the Ottoman authorities, who regarded them as responsible for the actions of the community. Personal wealth was the primary criterion in the communities of the Ottoman Empire for judging the ability of an individual to serve as *parnas*. Many of the *parnasim* were in fact called *gvirim* (wealthy men).[3] The heavy burden everywhere placed on the shoulders of the *parnasim* led many to refrain from putting forward their candidacy for this post, which did not promise financial profit.[4] Others, however, did seek the position of *parnas*, and even tried to obtain it by force, either because it accorded them power and prestige, or because they were genuinely concerned about the proper functioning of the community.[5] The sources confirm that the *parnasim* consistently refrained from interfering in the affairs of other congregations and from prevailing upon them in any way.

In contrast to the role of the secular-political leaders, the rabbis — generally called *ḥakhamim* ("sages") — were concerned with matters of religion, law and justice in the congregation and the community. Only on rare occasions did they also engage in political and administrative affairs.[6] As a rule, the

2 On this distinction in Jewish society, see: E. Don-Yehiya, "Religious Leadership and Political Leadership" (Hebrew), *Manhigut Ruḥanit be-Yisrael* (Hebrew: Spiritual Leadership in Israel), ed. Ella Belfer (Jerusalem, Tel-Aviv, 1982), pp. 104–34.

3 See, for example: R. Isaac Adarbi, *Responsa Divrei Rivot* (Venice, 1587), Nos. 99, 224, 229; R. Samuel de Medina, *Responsa Rashdam*, Ḥoshen Mishpat (Salonika, 1595), No. 371; R. Samuel Kalai, *Responsa Mishpetei Shmuel* (Venice, 1599), No. 23; R. Solomon Ha-Kohen, *Responsa Maharshakh*, IV (Salonika, 1552), No. 14; R. Ḥayyim Shabbetai, *Responsa Torat Ḥayyim*, I (Salonika, 1613), No. 64; III (Salonika, 1722), Nos. 40, 102; R. Ḥasdai Peraḥyah, *Responsa Torat Ḥesed* (Salonika, 1723), No. 39; R. Joseph Molcho, *Responsa Ohel Yoseph* (Salonika, 1756), Oraḥ Ḥayyim, No. 9.

4 On this tendency, and on its practical applications, see: R. Solomon Ha-Kohen, *Responsa Maharshakh*, III (Salonika, 1594), No. 53; R. Elijah Ibn Ḥayyim, *Responsa Mayim Amukim*, II (Venice, 1647), No. 26. There is also evidence from the 18th century indicating that everyone evaded the office of *parnas*. See: R. Ḥayyim Abraham ben David, *Responsa Tiferet Adam* (Salonika, 1867), Yore Deah, No. 59.

5 See, for example: *Responsa Torat Ḥayyim*, II (Salonika, 1715), No. 39.

6 Leah Bornstein, "The Rabbinate in the Ottoman Empire in the Sixteenth and Seventeenth Centuries," *East and Maghreb*, I, ed. H. Z. Hirschberg (Ramat-Gan, 1974), pp. 223–48; *idem*, Dissertation, pp. 133–72; *idem*, "On the Power Struggle

local rabbis were forbidden to impinge upon the affairs of their colleagues in other congregations and communities. Nevertheless, in practice, many did try to assert themselves over other congregational rabbis and to intervene in the religious affairs of other communities. Renowned scholars exerted personal authority beyond the limits of their own community, but their super-communal leadership was based on their scholarship and on their personal prestige. It did not rest on any official institutional authority — and in the many Sephardic congregations throughout the Empire was not even buttressed by the certificate of ordination, as was customary in the congregations of the Ashkenazim and Romaniots. When famous rabbis ruled on the affairs of other communities, the *parnasim* thus affected did not generally question the validity of the procedure, which they viewed as a form of halakhic control over communal life.

Although the division of powers between the *parnasim* and the rabbis was fairly clear, infrequently — and on certain well-defined issues — both authorities jointly conducted the affairs of the community. One such case occurred in Tire (Anatolia), where an early ordinance dating from the 16th century was applied at the beginning of the 17th century as well, to the effect that all communal affairs would be determined by a majority decision of the persons of high rank and the teachers of *Torah*.[7] In Magnesia, near Izmir, in the 16th century, the *parnasim* and the rabbis were accorded the power "to supervise, to examine, to observe and to correct all the affairs and regulations of the city."[8] During the 17th century, an early ordinance in one community forbade Jews from serving under the *qadi* in a court of law without first receiving the permission of the *parnasim* of the community and of four scholars. One member of the community received such permission on four different occasions.[9] It should be noted that, in most communities, the two authorities cooperated in the appointment of prayer leaders, teachers, scribes, ritual slaughterers, *shtadlanim*,* etc.[10] Another area of cooperation was in the enactment of the ordi-

---

in the Jewish Community of Patras in the 16th Century," *Michael*, VII, ed. Z. Ankori and Shlomo Simonsohn (Tel-Aviv, 1981), pp. 9—41 (hereafter: Bornstein, *Patras*).

7   *Responsa Torat Ḥayyim*, I, 53; R. Joseph Trani, *Responsa Maharit*, II (Fiorda, 1768), Ḥoshen Mishpat, 101; M. Benayau, "Tirya Regulations," *Qobez Al Jad*, n.s. 4 (1946), p. 204.

8   R. Joseph Karo, *Responsa Avkat Rochel* (Salonika, 1791), No. 206.

9   R. Daniel Esterusa, *Responsa Magen Giborim* (Salonika, 1754), No. 42.

*   (Representatives of Jewish communities who interceded with high dignitaries and legislative bodies).

10 Bornstein, Dissertation, pp. 240 ff.

18

nances of the congregation, which were generally drawn up by the congregational rabbi together with the *parnasim*.[11] This practice, whereby the religious authority accorded its seal of approval to the constitution of the congregation, was common in all medieval Jewish communities, and was continued during the period under discussion.[12]

As a rule, the rabbis did not play organizational and political roles. The only exceptions were those special cases when they were asked to do so by the *parnasim* and the public, and even then care was taken to preserve the prerogatives of the *parnasim*. The political deputations to the seat of Ottoman government in Constantinople during the 16th century by a group of famous sages from Salonika — R. Moses Almosnino, R. Benjamin Halevi Ashkenazi, and R. Samuel de Medina — were undertaken on behalf of all the congregations of Salonika (thirty in number), and in total cooperation with the *parnasim*. The latter selected the sages concerned primarily because of their great scholarship, which was also highly respected by the Jewish courtiers in Constantinople, the most well-known of whom were all scholars (such as: Joseph Nasi, Moses and Joseph Hamon, Abraham Ibn Migash, Solomon Abenaes, and Solomon Ashkenazi), who could exert their personal charisma on the other courtiers and on the Ottoman authorities.[13] Similar considerations affected the selection of other sages who also fulfilled secular roles. One was R. Bezalel Ashkenazi, who in about the year 1587 assumed the leadership of

---

11 See, for example: R. Tam Ibn Yaḥya, *Responsa Ohalei Tam*, in *Tumat Yesharim* (Venice, 1622), Nos. 26, 213; *Responsa R. Elijah Mizraḥi*, No. 57; *Responsa R. Joseph Ibn Lev* (Maharival), I (Amsterdam, 1725), No. 47; R. Moses Trani, *Responsa Mabit* (Venice, 1629), Nos. 84, 264; R. Baruch Kalai, *Responsa Mekor Baruch* (Smyrna, 1659), No. 19; R. Samuel de Medina, *Responsa Rashdam*, Yore Deah (Salonika, 1597), Nos. 149, 150, 151; Ḥoshen Mishpat (Salonika, 1595), Nos. 236, 398; R. Isaac Adarbi, *Responsa Divrei Rivot* (Venice, 1587), No. 53; *Responsa Avkat Rochel*, No. 206; *Responsa Ralbach* (Venice, 1565), No. 38; Rabbi Abraham ben Joseph Leveit Halevi, *Responsa Ein Mishpat* (Salonika, 1897), Ḥoshen Mishpat, No. 40; R. Samuel Gaon, *Responsa Mishpatim Yesharim* (Salonika, 1732), No. 12; R. Abraham Alegre, *Responsa Lev Sameaḥ* (Salonika, 1793), Ḥoshen Mishpat, Nos. 13—14. On the legal aspect of the communal ordinances, see: M. Elon, *Jewish Law: History, Sources, Principles* (Jerusalem, 1978) (Hebrew), pp. 587–91.

12 See Jacob Katz, *Tradition and Crisis, Jewish Society at the End of the Middle Ages* (New York, 1961), pp. 88–9.

13 L. Bornstein, *Maftehot, Index to the Responsa of Rabbi Samuel de Medina* (Bar-Ilan University, 1979), preface, p. 10; *Responsa Rashdam*, Yore Deah, No. 55; Even Ha-ezer, No. 43; Yitzḥak Molcho, "R. Moses Almosnino Brings Freedom to the Community of Salonika in the 16th Century" (Hebrew), *Sinai*, 8 (1941), pp. 245–56.

the community in Jerusalem; amongst his attributes was his command of Arabic and Turkish, which enabled him to appear before the Ottoman rulers. Another was R. Ḥayyim Benveniste, one of the two chief judges of Izmir in the 17th century, who writes that he represented the Jewish community in the city "before the gates of the princes and the judges of the land."[14] However, such examples serve only to highlight the fact that the rabbis generally restricted themselves solely to their religious powers and functions, acting as the intellectuals of Jewish society in the 16th and 17th centuries.

II

The appointment of members of one authority by members of the other generally leads to the selection of appointees upon whom the appointers can bring influence and pressure to bear. In the Ottoman Empire of the 16th and 17th centuries, such appointments generally did not affect the independent functioning of the two authorities, and only rarely did they cause friction between the authorities. Other than in isolated instances, the appointment of new *parnasim* was entrusted either to the *parnasim* currently in office, or to the local elite, or to the entire community. It was not the function of the rabbis. This served to prevent conflicts between the appointed *parnasim* and the rabbis, and between the latter and the members of the local elite, from which most of the *parnasim* were drawn.[15] An exception is the report, dating from the 16th century, that the members of a community failed to reach agreement on the appointment of the next five *parnasim*, and asked the rabbi to make the choice. Following their appointment, the new *parnasim* were forced to accept the rabbi's demand for a slight raise in salary.[16] In contrast, the appointment of the rabbis was largely dependent on the *parnasim*.[17] Most of the rabbis earned their living from the rabbinate, and their salary (which few waived) was in most cases their sole income. Moreover, most rabbis were

---

14 R. Yom Tov Ẓahalon, *Responsa Maharitaz* (Venice, 1659), No. 160; R. Ḥayyim Benveniste, *Sheyarei Knesset Hagedolah*, I, Oraḥ Ḥayyim (Smyrna, 1671), preface by the author.

15 We have several reports on the appointment of *parnasim* by the local rabbis or on the participation of the latter in such appointments together with other authorities, for example: R. Samuel Vital, *Responsa Beer Mayim Ḥayyim* (New York, 1968), No. 38; R. Meir Melamed, *Responsa Mishpat Ẓedek*, II (Salonika, 1799), No. 29; *Responsa Avkat Rochel*, No. 206.

16 *Responsa Ralbach*, No. 38.

17 For example: R. Isaac Adarbi, *Divrei Shalom*, sermons (Salonika, 1582), preface; *Responsa Mishpat Ẓedek*, I (Salonika, 1615), No. 49; R. Ḥayyim Benveniste, *Responsa Baei Hayei*, Yore Deah (Salonika, 1788), No. 206; R. Mordechai Halevi, *Responsa Darchei Noam* (Venice, 1697), Yore Deah, No. 4.

appointed for a fixed period of time.[18] These two facts together might have rendered the rabbis constantly dependent on the *parnasim*. However, the available sources indicate that, following their appointment, the rabbis were not afraid that the *parnasim* would refuse to renew their appointments if they did not comply with their wishes. In general, the tenure of a rabbi was not terminated, but was automatically renewed on the basis of the rule that "we may promote to a higher grade of sanctity, but we must not degrade."[19]

The manner of their appointment possibly did deter many rabbis from entering into sharp controversies with the *parnasim*, particularly in small communities. As a rule, however, the rabbis enjoyed considerable freedom of action. This was especially true of those who had already served the congregation for many years, and of those who were famous for their scholarship.

Very little evidence survives of confrontations between rabbis and *parnasim* over the reappointment of the former, and it would appear that many rabbis voluntarily changed the localities in which they served.[20] There was also little friction between the rabbis and the *parnasim* on financial matters, as most of the rabbis did not deal with money. The most extreme example of a dispute of this type occurred during the 1560s in Jerusalem, between R. David Ibn Zimra, the judge of the community, and the community leaders, who refused to reimburse him for the bribes he was forced to pay to the government in order to avoid serious punishment.[21]

III

Equally instructive is evidence concerning the deposition of members of one authority by the other. There are few sources which speak of the deposition of *parnasim*. Those which do cite as reasons: the failure to fulfill duties, the misuse of powers granted to them, or a public sense of injustice.[22] A famous case was that of the seven *parnasim* of the Lisbon congregation in Salonika in 1570. Accused of tyranny, of the oppression of the masses, of discrimination

---

18 Bornstein, "The Rabbinate" (No. 6 above); *idem*, Dissertation, pp. 139–43.
19 *Responsa Mabit*, III, No. 200; *Responsa of R. Solomon Leveit Halevi* (Salonika, 1552), Yore Deah, No. 8; R. Solomon Amarillio, *Responsa Kerem Shlomo* (Salonika, 1719), Yore Deah, No. 21; R. Joseph Hazan, *Responsa Hikrei Lev*, Orah Hayyim (Salonika, 1787), No. 4; Yore Deah, III (Salonika, 1807), No. 100.
20 See Bornstein, Dissertation, pp. 145–6.
21 *Responsa Mabit*, III (Venice, 1630), No. 188; Bornstein, Dissertation, pp. 185–97; Amnon Cohen, *The Jewish Community of Jerusalem in the 16th Century* (Jerusalem, 1982) (Hebrew), p. 51.
22 *Responsa Divrei Rivot*, No. 224; *Responsa Mabit*, III, No. 32; *Responsa Lev Sameh*, Hoshen Mishpat, No. 3; *Responsa Mishpat Zedek*, I, No. 75; *Responsa Beer Mayim Hayyim*, No. 38.

against the poor, and of a lack of concern for the maintenance of an orderly social life, they were deposed by a majority of the community.[23] The action sent shock waves throughout the city, and is an exception in the sources of the period. In all such cases, the rabbis of the congregations and other well-known rabbis of the community intervened only *ex post facto*, when asked to do so by one party or both. They did not initiate the action. Even R. Isaac Adarbi of Salonika, who wrote a legal decision confirming the dismissal of the leaders of the Lisbon congregation, was not originally a party to the act.[24] The rabbis discussed complaints lodged by individuals against *parnasim*, related in general to financial matters and to taxation, but such complaints were relatively few in number. Even rarer are accounts of violence on the part of the *parnasim* towards the public.[25] One singular exception is recorded in the legal ruling by R. Daniel Esterusa of Salonika, dating from the first half of the 17th century, forbidding the appointment as a *parnas* of a man known to engage in intrigues and violence. (Moreover, this decision was written in response to an actual query posed by one of the communities of the Empire.[26]) There are also only isolated instances of public contempt towards the *parnasim*.[27] We can assume that there was a certain reluctance on the part of individuals to appeal to the courts against the *parnasim*. After all, in some localities the *parnasim* themselves wielded judicial authority; they generally enjoyed a strong position within the community; above all, they could count on the backing of the rabbis, as long as they did not abuse their office.[28] On the other hand, in several cases the *parnasim* exhibited a negative attitude towards the rabbis in various communities. The extent of this phenomenon cannot be established with any certainty; but it is reasonable to assume that this, too, was limited in scope and relatively uncommon, and that the rabbis were very sensitive to any slight and documented all such offenses. There seems to have been no worsening in the attitude towards the

---

23 *Responsa Divrei Rivot*, No. 224; Leah Bornstein, "The Character of the Social Structure in the Communities of the Ottoman Empire from the 16th to the 18th Century" (Hebrew), *The Sephardi and Oriental Heritage Studies*, ed. I. Ben-Ami (Jerusalem, 1982) (Hebrew), pp. 82—93.

24 Loc. cit.

25 For example: R. Elijah Ibn Ḥayyim, *Responsa Raanah* (Venice, 1610), No. 111; *Responsa Divrei Rivot*, No. 376; *Responsa Maharit*, II, Yore Deah, No. 16.

26 *Responsa Magen Giborim*, No. 10.

27 *Responsa Raanah*, No. 111; R. Solomon Ibn Hason, *Responsa Beit Shlomo* (Salonika, 1720), Yore Deah, No. 12; R. Ḥayyim Benveniste, *Knesset Hagedolah*, Ḥoshen Mishpat (Smyrna, 1734), No. 420, Tur No. 36; *Responsa R. Moses ben Nisim Benveniste*, MS, Oxford — Bodleian 2693, p. 37a.

28 On the legal powers of the *parnasim*, see below.

rabbis at certain periods, as was the case in the Jewish communities of Germany of the 15th century and the first half of the 18th century.[29]

It is certainly difficult to instance more extreme tensions. Thus, evidence of the dismissal of rabbis by *parnasim* is scarce. In general, the *parnasim* seem to have refrained from taking such drastic measures and preferred to restrict the functions of the rabbis and to limit their authority — and even here the evidence is meager.[30] The restriction of the rabbis' authority by the *parnasim* created tension between the two domains of leadership, and the rabbis firmly insisted on the implementation of all the provisions of their letters of appointment.[31] Moreover, the rabbis did not exercise self-restraint when they were offended — an attitude which seems to imply that their position was quite strong. Nevertheless, it was not impregnable. Some extant communal ordinances do define the manner and means of their dismissal.[32] The reaction, too, could be tense. Senior rabbinic authorities in the Empire who were asked by the *parnasim* to approve such dismissals did so only when flaws were revealed in the character and abilities of the deposed rabbis (such as an inadequate command of *halakhah*), or if they were found to be lacking in fear of God. Thus, R. Moses Trani of Safed approved the dismissal of the rabbi of the Arabized congregation of Damascus in the 1570s for having generated fear within the community, for having distributed public funds to gentiles, and for having himself resorted to gentile courts of law.[33] More consistent, however, was the tendency in the legal judgements of the rabbis of the Ottoman Empire to protect their colleagues against arbitrary attempts at dismissal. Typical of this category was the decision of three of the greatest sages of Salonika in the 16th century — R. Samuel de Medina, R. Abraham Di Boton, and R. Soloman HaKohen — against the community of Kastoria in Macedonia, which had deposed its rabbi, R. Solomon Mevorakh.[34] For these rabbis the above-mentioned principle that "we may promote to a higher grade of sanctity, but must not degrade" implied that rabbis could not be removed

---

29 M. Breuer, *The Rabbinate in Ashkenaz* (Hebrew) (Jerusalem, 1976), pp. 22 ff; A. Shohet, *Beginnings of the Haskalah Among German Jewry* (Hebrew) (Jerusalem, 1961), pp. 92—113.

30 For example: *Responsa Mishpat Ẓedek*, II, No. 4; *Responsa Baei Hayei*, Ḥoshen Mishpat, I (Salonika, 1788), No. 34; Bornstein, *Patras*; *Responsa Torat Ḥayyim*, I, No. 53.

31 M. Benayau, *Marbitz Torah* (Hebrew) (Jerusalem, 1953), pp. 68—83.

32 See regulations from the 16th century: *Responsa Rashdam*, Yore Deah, Nos. 89, 137; R. Abraham di Boton, *Responsa Leḥem Rav* (Smyrna, 1740), Nos. 68, 70; and below.

33 *Responsa Mabit*, III, No. 91.

34 *Responsa Leḥem Rav*, No. 227.

after their term of service if no fault was found with them.[35] The sages also tried to persuade the *parnasim* not to scheme against the local rabbi. As R. Levi Ibn Habib wrote in the 16th century regarding R. Benjamin, the rabbi of the community of Trikkala in Greece: "We know that, from the outset, you chose the great sage R. Benjamin to be the leader over you all. Therefore, as he was promoted, he shall not be degraded. He is responsible for the leadership of the entire town, for there is none comparable to him."[36] The rabbis of the Empire demonstrated their desire for the maximum independence of the rabbinate and minimum dependence on the *parnasim* and the local community. Thus, in 19th-century Jerusalem, R. Aaron Azriel (1819-79) wrote, reflecting a reality which probably existed in previous centuries as well: "We never heard in the cities of Turkey and Arabistan of the removal of the rabbis who instructed them in righteousness. And if by chance we heard of some city in which the rabbi was dismissed, who knows whether the hidden reasons were sufficient by law, or whether, God forbid, they acted contrary to law."[37]

IV

The major conflicts between the two domains of authority centered around powers which one tried to take away from the other. Particular among these were the right to excommunicate, to judge, and to impose punishment. As sources of tension, these deserve to be treated separately.

The right of excommunication in the communities of the Ottoman Empire was the exclusive preserve of the sages. In some communities the *parnasim* did seek to obtain this right; but documented instances of their success are very rare.[38] More common were attempts to forbid the rabbis to impose a ban unless *parnasim* shared in the decision. Thus, for example, an ordinance dating from the early 17th century in Patras (Greece), later renewed, prohibited a certain rabbi from imposing a ban without the prior consent of the majority of the local court and the seven leading members of the community.[39] As a rule, the sages opposed such attempts at limitation, and insisted that the rabbis alone should exercise excommunication authority.[40] Indeed, as early

---

35   See note 19 above.

36   *Responsa Ralbach*, No. 99.

37   R. Aaron Azriel, *Responsa Kapei Aharon*, II (Jerusalem, 1886), Yore Deah, No. 7,

38   Such as: *Responsa Mayim Amukim*, II, No. 69; R. Baruch Engil, *Responsa* (Salonika, 1717), No. 57; R. Meir di Boton, *Responsa* (Smyrna, 1740), No. 8.

39   *Responsa Mishpat Żedek*, II, No. 4.

40   See: R. Elijah Halevi, *Responsa Zekan Aharon* (Constantinople, 1734), No. 98; *Responsa Ralbach*, Nos. 30, 99; *Responsa Maharshakh*, IV (Salonika, 1652), No. 10; *Responsa Mabit*, III, No. 91; R. Samuel Kalai, *Responsa Mishpetei Shmuel* (Venice,

as the 16th century, R. Isaac Adarbi of Salonika had protested against the demand that the rabbis should not impose excommunications without the participation of the *parnasim*, and that a ban issued by the rabbi alone would be invalid. "There is no greater contempt of the *Torah* than that the ban of a sage should not be valid without the consent of some frivolous or irresponsible person."[41] Nevertheless, it is indicative of the relations between Ottoman *parnasim* and rabbis that these tensions rarely reached such extremes. On the contrary, the rabbis often found it expedient to provide strong backing to the act of excommunication by making the *parnasim* partners to communal bans — both in the enactment of communal ordinances accompanied by sanctions including excommunication, and in the ceremony of individual excommunication. Thus, for example, present at the excommunication of David, clerk to Joseph Nasi of Constantinople in the early 1570s, by the rabbis of the city, were all the *parnasim* of the various congregations and the members of the local elite.[42] Such cooperation prevented the development of the situation prevalent at this time in Italy, where excommunication was exclusively in the hands of the rabbis, and where, as a result, the rabbi of a congregation was increasingly obliged to impose bans whenever such action was demanded by the *parnasim*, and was generally unable to impose a ban without the permission of the *parnasim*.[43] The situation in the Ottoman Empire was also different from that prevailing in the communities of Germany where the early ruling from the time of Rabbenu Tam and the Tosaphists was applied — namely, the rabbi should not impose a ban without the permission of the community, and that no member of the community could be banned without the permission of the rabbi.[44]

More significantly, the two leadership authorities found themselves in a state of mutual dependence over the right to judge and to inflict punishment. In the communities of the Ottoman Empire these powers were accorded to the communal courts, which were almost always headed by the rabbis of the communities and congregations. In some localities, however, these powers were accorded to the local *parnasim* (this was especially so in small towns,

1599), No. 97; *Responsa Maharitaz*, No. 4; R. Moses Benveniste, *Responsa Pene Moshe*, I (Constantinople, 1664), No. 95; R. Joseph Almosnino, *Responsa Edut Be-Yehoseph*, II (Constantinople, 1733), No. 19.

41 *Responsa Divrei Rivot*, No. 295.
42 *Responsa Mayim Amukim*, II, No. 54.
43 Robert Bonfil, *The Rabbinate in Renaissance Italy* (Hebrew) (Jerusalem, 1979), pp. 45—51, 73—94.
44 S. Assaf, "On the History of the Rabbinate in Germany, Poland, and Lithuania" (Hebrew), *Reshumot*, 2 (1927), p. 53. Breuer, op. cit., p. 13.

but was sometimes also the case in established communities with an organized and well-established religious leadership). The authority universally accorded to the *parnasim* to execute sentences imposed by the courts and to punish offenders was not questioned. In all the Jewish communities of the period the *parnasim* were responsible for the execution of judgements by virtue of the power of enforcement accorded to them, both by the community and by the government.[45] However, serious questions were raised by the rabbis with regard to the power of the *parnasim* to judge. The rabbis complained particularly of those cases in which the *parnasim* failed to accord the local rabbi full judicial powers, or completely denied him this authority. A good example is provided by the community of Patras, where an early ruling from the mid-16th century stated that the *parnasim* were to exercise judicial authority, and would consult the rabbi only if they so desired. The *parnasim* exercised this authority, and imposed a ban on one of the wealthy members of the community. Subsequently a new ordinance was enacted, whereby each individual would be judged before the *parnasim*, who alone would impose fines and punishments; the rabbis were not empowered to deal in these matters at all unless the *parnasim* wished to consult them. Nevertheless, the rabbis of the congregations did play a role in local jurisdiction, and it is reasonable to assume that even the *parnasim* felt that they had adopted too radical an approach. There may also have been some public demand for the participation of the rabbis in judicial authority.[46]

Notwithstanding further evidence of cooperation between the rabbis and the courts of the *parnasim*,[47] the rabbis generally viewed the latter with reservations, as they judged cases not according to the law of the Torah, but according to their own personal judgement. At times, the rabbis even voiced their sharp criticism. Particularly caustic is the statement by R. Yom Tov Zahalon of Safed regarding the court of the Lepanto community in Greece during the first half of the 17th century, composed of *parnasim* who were not proficient in *halakhah*. He derided them as "compromise judges," "cowherds"

---

45 See, for example: R. Moses Amarillio, *Responsa Devar Moshe*, II (Salonika, 1743), Ḥoshen Mishpat, Nos. 1—2; *Responsa Maharshakh*, I (Salonika, 1688), No. 107; *Responsa Beit Shlomo*, Yore Deah, No. 12; *Responsa Maharival*, I (Amsterdam, 1725), No. 56; *Responsa Lev Sameaḥ*, Ḥoshen Mishpat, No. 27; Bornstein, Dissertation, pp. 231-2.

46 Bornstein, *Patras*. See also: *Responsa Meir di Boton*, No. 36.

47 Such as: *Responsa Maharshakh*, IV, No. 10; *Responsa Mishpetei Shmuel*, No. 97; *Responsa Maharit*, II, Ḥoshen Mishpat, No. 11; *Responsa Edut Be-Yehoseph*, I (Constantinople, 1711), No. 43; II, No. 19; *Responsa Meir di Boton*, No. 36; *Responsa Pene Moshe*, I, No. 95; R. Aaron Ha-Kohen Peraḥyah, *Responsa Parah Mate Aharon*, II (Amsterdam, 1703); No. 67.

and "shepherds," and stated that they ruled contrary to the *halakhah*.[48] Similar epithets were used by R. Samuel Kalai of Arta in Greece.[49] Such courts of *parnasim* are also known to have existed in the communities of western and eastern Europe in the period under discussion. There, however, they generated controversies which were far more acerbic, principally because it was the expressed ambition of the *parnasim* in these communities in effect to limit the judicial powers of the rabbis as much as possible. Examples are provided by the 16th-century dispute over judicial powers in Padua, Italy, between Rabbi Samuel and the *parnasim*, who had won extensive judicial powers; and by the dispute which erupted in Livorno in 1680 when the *parnasim* of the community agreed to remove all civil cases from the jurisdiction of the rabbis. There, the government accorded the local *parnasim* authority to approve or to nullify the legal decisions of the rabbis. The sources convey the impression that the disputes over judicial powers did not lead to the polarization of relations between the *parnasim* and the rabbis in the Ottoman Empire, as they did in the European communities. It would seem that taking judicial powers away from the rabbis was ultimately a limited phenomenon in those communities where rabbis officiated, and the *parnasim* were generally accorded these powers when there was no alternative, namely, where there was no religious leadership. Neither do we find in the communities of the Ottoman Empire the distinction sometimes existing in the communities of eastern Europe, whereby the local *parnasim* dealt with criminal cases such as disputes, insults, quarrels, and beatings; while the rabbis dealt with matters of civil law.[50]

V

One basic cause for the relative moderation of the relationship between *parnasim* and rabbis lay in their generally prevalent attitudes of mutual respect. The *parnasim* did not treat the rabbis disparagingly, and turned to them for help on legal and public questions with which they wrestled. We can

---

48 *Responsa Maharitaz*, No. 242. The expression "compromise judges" (as it appears in *Bava Batra* 132b) signifies judges who were not familiar with the law, and who therefore accorded something to each party. The other meaning is: people who did not know the law at all, but whose judgements were nevertheless accepted by the litigants.

49 *Responsa Mishpetei Shmuel*, No. 25.

50 See: Daniel Carpi, *Minutes Book of the Council of the Jewish Community of Padua 1577—1603* (Jerusalem, 1973), pp. 43–5; I. Tishbi, "The Letter of R. Jacob Sasportas against the *Parnasim* of Livorno in the Year 1681" (Hebrew), *Qobez Al Jad*, n.s., 4(14) (1946), pp. 145–58; I. Sonne, "On the History of the Community of Bologna in the Early 17th Century" (Hebrew), *HUCA*, XVI (1941), Hebrew Section, pp. 35—98; Katz (Note 12 above), pp. 80–4, 94–7.

assume that many of the questions posed to the rabbis were addressed to them by the *parnasim* themselves, or through them.[51] As a rule, the *parnasim* displayed great respect for the rabbis, without haughtiness, while the rabbis treated the *parnasim* with respect so long as they fulfilled their duties honestly and with dedication. It is interesting to note that such well-known 16th-century rabbis as R. Moses Almosnino, R. Shem Tov Melamed, R. Solomon Leveit Halevi, and R. Aaron Abiob (all of Greece) all considered the figure who most closely approached the ideal qualities of a communal leader to have been Mordechai, one of whose most salient qualities, according to these rabbis, was his modesty.[52] R. Samuel de Medina appealed to R. Mattathias Zarfati of Thabes, Istifa (Greece) to reconsider his decision to retire from public service, comparing the ingratitude of the public in his time to that of Israel in the time of Moses: "This is the great award which awaits the *parnasim* of Israel, that they bend their shoulders to the burden."[53] Political secular leadership was generally perceived by the rabbis to be a voluntary and a meritorious deed.[54] This approach differs widely from the negative attitude of the sages of Poland in this period towards secular leadership.[55] In contrast to Poland, the rabbis of the Ottoman Empire do not speak of the haughtiness of the *parnasim*, or of corruption in the conduct of communal affairs; in effect, there is no in-depth discussion of the problems of secular leadership. The *parnasim* in Poland were also accused of trying to restrict the influence of the rabbis in religious affairs, and of refusing to submit to the authority of the religious leadership. In the communities of the Ottoman Empire the situation was completely different, and the activity of the rabbis is evident in almost all the affairs of society other than purely secular matters. Even the Jewish courtiers in Constantinople accepted the authority of the rabbis, and this too may have been an important factor in the unlimited influence which the rabbis enjoyed in all religious matters of Jewish society in the Ottoman Empire. The rabbis, who were aware that the *parnasim* were by and large not

---

51   *Responsa R. Elijah Mizrahi*, No. 82; *Responsa Zekan Aharon*, No. 17; *Responsa Mayim Amukim*, II, No. 55; *Responsa Mabit*, I, 41; *Responsa Mishpetei Shmuel*, No. 23.

52   Rabbi Moses Almosnino, *Meametz Koah*, sermons, No. 21, p. 169; R. Shem Tov Melamed, *Maamar Mordechai* (Constantinople, 1585), p. 21; R. Solomon Leveit Halevi, *Divrei Shlomo*, sermons (Venice, 1596), pp. 185b—186a; R. Aaron Abiob, *Shemen Hamor* (Salonika, 1596).

53   *Responsa Rashdam*, Yore Deah, No. 148.

54   Loc. cit.

55   See: H.H. Ben-Sasson, *Philosophy and Leadership* (Hebrew) (Jerusalem, 1959), pp. 194—228.

scholars, required of them only that they discharge their duties properly, and be "upright and worthy men, faithful to their service."[56] Both the sages and the entire public strongly opposed the appointment to positions of leadership of those found guilty of religious and moral transgressions. This principle was apparently observed in practice, and helps to explain the paucity of reported cases of corruption on the part of the *parnasim*, and the absence of any serious discussion of this issue in the sermons of the rabbis of the Ottoman Empire.[57] When the communities failed to prevent corrupt men from attaining positions of leadership they would appeal to the Ottoman authorities. Thus, in the 16th century, communal leaders in Irbil (Iraq) and in Sofia were brought before the Ottoman courts, having been accused by their respective communities of embezzlement and of tyranny.[58]

Another factor contributing to the generally good relations prevailing between the rabbis and the *parnasim* was the view of the majority of the rabbis that the wealthy class should decide on the leadership of the community — an attitude which accorded with the world view of the *parnasim*, most of whom were drawn from the local elite.[59] An important result of these good relations between the *parnasim* and rabbis was the salient fact that many well-known, leading scholars accepted the office of rabbi in their communities, and executed this office by virtue of their individual personalities — a process which elevated the stature of the rabbinate in the Ottoman Empire and contributed significantly to the shaping of Jewish society.[60] This situation must be contrasted with that prevailing in Italy during the Renaissance, where none of the great sages were appointed rabbis of their communities, with a subsequent erosion in the personal authority of the rabbis among the public.[61] Another consequence of this delicate balance of forces was the absence of

---

56 *Responsa Torat Ḥesed*, No. 31. Prior to entering into office the *parnasim* took an oath to behave honestly. See: *Responsa Rashdam*, Yore Deah, No. 227.

57 See notes 22—23 above. See also: *Responsa Mishpat Ẓedek*, II, No. 49; *Responsa Mishpetei Shmuel*, No. 39; *Responsa Pene Moshe*, II, No. 19; *Responsa Maharit*, II, Yore Deah, No. 14.

58 Mark A. Epstein, *The Ottoman Jewish Communities and their Role in the Fifteenth and Sixteenth Centuries* (Freiburg, 1980), p. 74, nos. 40—41.

59 See: E. Bashan, "The Attitude of the Sages of Salonika in the Sixteenth to the Eighteenth Centuries in the Confrontation over Oligarchical Rule" (Hebrew), *East and Maghreb*, II, ed. E. Bashan, A. Rubinstein, and S. Schwarzfuchs (Ramat-Gan, 1980), pp. 27—52. Bornstein (note 23 above).

60 Almost all the hundreds of authors of *responsa* in the 16th and 17th centuries served as rabbis of their communities and congregations, and many also served as judges.

61 Bonfil, op. cit., pp. 72, 93.

upheavals in the status and functioning of the two domains of leadership as they developed in the Ottoman Empire during the 16th and 17th centuries.

A final conclusion is that the strong influence exercised by the rabbinate and the religious leadership in the Ottoman Empire was derived to no small extent from the predominant religious world view and from the desire to establish religious criteria in all communal affairs. The integrity and unpretentiousness of the secular leaders also contributed considerably to the tolerant relations with the religious leadership.

ILAN GREILSAMMER

CHALLENGES TO THE INSTITUTIONS OF THE JEWISH COMMUNITY OF FRANCE DURING THE NINETEENTH AND TWENTIETH CENTURIES

Jewish political studies have made great strides during the past twenty years. Prominent amongst the many explorations in the field have been analyses of the Jewish vote, of Jewish "liberalism" and radicalism, of the implications of the concept of *brit* (covenant) in Jewish politics, and of the Jewish political tradition or traditions. Nevertheless, one area of research which seems to have received only limited treatment is the analysis of the institutional structures of Jewish communities and the manifestations of authority within them. Neglect of this area is paradoxical. If politics is, above all, the phenomenon of the exercise of power within any institutionalized society, an analysis of Jewish communal organizations should be undertaken in depth and systematically.

In Jewish institutions, as in any organized society, some people possess power and wish to retain it, while others challenge them in order to assume power themselves, to gain a share of the power, or to change its orientations. In Jewish societies this challenge is ambiguous in nature: on the one hand, those who mount it generally acknowledge a common destiny with other Jews and are often willing to collaborate, to a certain extent, with the institutions they are challenging; on the other hand, they criticize those institutions, their leaders, and their methods.

In the study of power struggles within Jewish communities, the case of France is of particular interest. First, it presents a well-defined time-frame. By 1808 Napoleon and the revolutionaries had completely wiped out the community's institutional past. During the course of the ensuing 180 years the community was assailed by successive waves of immigration which constituted a major ingredient in challenges to the existing authority. Second, French political culture, in which the community was throughout that period immersed, is particularly powerful (for example, the ideological split between right and left). Finally, there are few Jewish communities which have been confronted so brutally by the surrounding society, including manifestations of anti-Semitism and the denial of the right to be different.

The present article, which analyses challenges to authority within the Jewish institutions of France during the past 180 years, addresses itself to two primary questions.

1. Is it possible to identify continuity or permanence in the themes upon which those challenges were mounted from 1808 to the present day?

2. Were the challenges generated by themes central to the Jewish political tradition itself, or were they concerned with the major political controversies affecting French society at large?

I

ORGANIZATION

From the very first, the organization of French Jewry established by Napoleon [1] presented certain well demarcated characteristics. Some of these were accentuated with the passage of the nineteenth century; others were partially effaced, nevertheless leaving traces. The main features of the institution of the consistory have been presented in several works, but they have not yet been systematized and classified. To this end, seven of these features will be treated here:

(a) The consistories were a cumbersome and bureaucratic, but very solid, apparatus. Until the passage of the law separating church and state in 1905, the consistories underwent a series of reforms that considerably modified their organization.[2] Rather than noting those reforms, however, it should be emphasized that the consistorial system — as a system — remained virtually unshaken. If anything, the reforms tended to solidify it. The consistorial bureaucracy that developed during the course of the century easily surmounted every challenge.

(b) The consistories were not established spontaneously by the Jewish community in accordance with its own traditions; rather, they were founded by the government, which intended them to be a means for the administration, regeneration, and surveillance of the Jews.[3] Indeed, Napoleon sought to

---

1 The basic work on Napoleon's decrees remains: Robert Anchel, *Les Juifs de France* (Paris: J.B. Janin, 1946).

2 On these reforms, see Phyllis Cohen Albert: *The Modernization of French Jewry, Consistory and Community in the Nineteenth Century* (Hanover, N.H.: Brandeis University Press, 1977); idem, "Le rôle des consistoires israélites vers le milieu de 19e siècle", *Revue des Etudes Juives*, CXXX, 1971, pp. 231–54.

3 A good example of the anti-Semitic attitudes of Napoleon can be found in Zosa Szajkowski: *Agricultural Credit and Napoleon's anti-Jewish Decrees* (New York: ed. Historiques Franco-Juives, 1953).

develop the consistories as auxiliaries of the government: they were to compile lists of foreign and "undesirable" Jews; to ensure against the convocation of an unauthorized assembly of Jews; to inform the authorities of the names of those who had no means of support; and to provide the names of Jews to be recruited into the army.[4] With the fall of the Empire, such police functions more or less disappeared. What remained was the fact that the directors of the consistories frequently appealed to the government to exercise its power against "dissidents" within the community. The governmental origin of the consistories also extended the ambiguity of relations between the Jewish organizations (termed "officielles" — state-recognized — by their detractors) and the political authorities. The representatives of the Jewish organizations, during both the nineteenth and the twentieth centuries, always felt some doubt concerning the legitimacy of their right to express a collective political opinion in the name of the community. On that level no fundamental change took place until 1967.

(c) The consistory was an organization with centralist and monopolist tendencies, hierarchical in character and based in Paris.

Here too, the characteristics of the institution were clearly anchored in its origins. The broad outlines of the Decree of 1808 remained in force. The consistories have born the mark of the Jacobinism and centralism characteristic of the French administration in general. The very fact that from the first the institutions were organized within the departmental structure virtually ensured their faithful adherence to the broad outlines of French administration. The local consistories, in their subordinate relation to the Central Consistory, are reminiscent of the role of the departmental prefects *vis-à-vis* the government of the Republic.[5]

The consistories have progressively accentuated their centralized character. They have become more and more hierarchical, attempting to assume control over all aspects of community life. Phyllis Cohen Albert speaks of "the attempt to create a consistorial monopoly on Jewish expression and institutions." Towards 1862, while that monopoly was not yet absolute, it had been pushed to its extreme limits by a variety of methods: inspection by supervisory commissions, audits, and frequent appeals to the governmental authorities. Despite

---

4 See I. Alteras: "Napoleon and the Jews", *Midstream*, no. 26, June-July 1980, pp. 40–2.

5 On the decentralized characteristics of the Jewish communities before the French Revolution, see, for example: Beatrice Philippe, *Etre Juif dans la société française* (Paris: Montalba, 1979), particularly pp. 89–105: "Trois communautés, trois statuts: la vie à Bordeaux, à Metz et en Alsace".

this aggressive Consistory behavior, however, there were groups or even entire communities which managed to escape its control. Among the institutions which did so, if only partially, can be counted the Jewish newspapers, the Alliance Israélite Universelle, the mutual aid societies, and certain groups of worshippers.

(d) The consistories were an important factor in the integration and, to some extent, the assimilation of the Jews into French society.

Napoleon's aim was the "regeneration" of the Jews of France (by which he meant their rebirth after the elimination of their defects and vices) through their integration into French society. During the nineteenth century, the consistories accelerated this process in at least four ways. First, they sought to "disencumber" the Jewish religion of those of its distinctive outward features which were considered "too visible". Accordingly, a series of reforms rendered ceremonies in the synagogue more similar to those observed by the Christians. Second, they rejected every manifestation of Jewish nationalism, no matter how feeble, as soon as it appeared — and especially Zionism. Thirdly, and at the same time, they exhibited French patriotism of an increasingly extreme nature, especially after the defeat of 1870 and the loss of Alsace-Lorraine. Finally, they participated actively in the process whereby the Jewish community became increasingly bourgeois, facilitating the Jews' adoption of the values, customs, and ways of thinking of the French bourgeoisie and middle classes.[6] This acculturation was particularly visible in the behavior of the notables of the consistories towards the poorer classes of Jews. They wished to "transform" them by teaching them manual trades and apprenticing the boys, feeling that in so doing they were performing "good deeds".

These four consistorial orientations constitute the nucleus of what Michael Marrus, in his study of French Jewry at the time of the Dreyfus Affair, has called "the politics of assimilation".[7]

(e) The consistories adopted a passive attitude towards anti-Semitism. This feature is related both to the governmental origin of the institution as well as its policy of integration and assimilation. The consistories clearly chose a course of noninterventionism. Flagrant at the time of the earliest Napoleonic manifestations of anti-Semitism, the attitude of passivity continued through-

---

6   The adoption of the values of the French bourgeoisie is well described in Georges Wormser, *Français Israélites, Une Doctrine, Une Tradition, Une Epoque* (Paris: Editions de Minuit, 1963).

7   Michael R. Marrus, *The Politics of Assimilation, A Study of the French Community at the Time of the Dreyfus Affair* (London: Oxford University Press, 1971).

out the nineteenth century. As several studies have shown, it remained in force even when anti-Semitism reached its climax after the crash of the Union Générale in 1882, and with the publication of Drumont's writings. The period of the Dreyfus Affair (1894–1906) deserves special emphasis. The Central Consistory and the local consistories, faithful to their unchanging policy, took no action against the wave of anti-Semitism, and remained silent.[8] A single note in the *Archives Israélites* of 1898 mentions a protest against the demands of the anti-Semites. The Chief Rabbi of France, Zadoc Kahn, was criticized for having attempted to organize a small committee against anti-Semitism.[9] The Consistory did sometimes protest against certain discriminatory practices in the judicial and academic systems; but it did not even dare to think of creating Jewish self-defense organizations such as existed in Germany during the same period.

(f) At the heart of the consistories, influence was increasingly seen to reside with members of prominent families and affluent classes, who monopolized the leading positions by family tradition.

Initially, Napoleon himself desired the monopoly of the notables. He wished the positions in the consistories reserved for laymen to be occupied by wealthy Jews, who would possess an interest in upholding the established order. Subsequently, this domination was in part exacerbated by the weak representation of the "Jewish masses" in the consistorial elections: whereas, before 1849, the entire electorate of the French Jewish communities numbered only 900, after the reform their number had increased to about 15,000. Even then, however, participation in elections was quite restricted, and elections continued to be manipulated by the notables. The official list of candidates in a consistory was almost always elected without change. Co-option was quite common.

Another important reason for the preponderance of the notables can be pointed out: given the small size of the Jewish middle classes, the number of those who had the time and money to devote themselves to community affairs was necessary limited. Note must also be taken of the extraordinary respect and deference of the Jewish masses for their notables. As the recognized criterion of success was integration into French society, the wealthy classes remained the living symbol of Jewish success in France.

The prominent families of French Jewry were headed by a legendary "clan": the French branch of the Rothschild family, founded by Jacob (Baron James),

---

8 See Robert F. Byrnes, *Antisemitism in Modern France*, Vol. 1 (New Brunswick, N.J.: Rutgers University Press, 1950).

9 See: "Zadoc Kahn: le pasteur et la communauté", *Les Nouveaux Cahiers*, no. 41, Summer 1975, pp. 20–40.

the fifth son of the ghetto money-changer of Frankfurt. Jacob arrived in Paris in 1811 and maintained excellent relations with a succession of governments: the first Empire, the restored monarchy, Louis-Philippe, and Napoleon III. He extended large loans to the state and built France's first railroads. Until his death in 1868, he remained deeply Jewish, demonstrating his identification through his activity at the head of the consistory. His two sons, Alphonse and Gustave were, respectively, President of the Central Consistory from 1853 to 1905, and President of the Consistory of Paris from 1852 to 1911. The presence of a Rothschild at the head of the French Jewish community, which persisted after 1905 (indeed, still persists), had a somewhat mythical quality. The Rothschilds became a symbol as much for those who supported and admired them as for those who opposed them, and for the surrounding non-Jewish society.

(g) Finally, and parallel to the increasing importance of the notables in the consistories, the status of the community's "spiritual leaders", the rabbis, underwent a rapid decline. The process commenced with their compromise on matters of the "Great Sanhedrin" convened by Napoleon. It was reinforced by the way in which the first Chief Rabbi of France, E. Deutz (1810–42), perceived his functions.[10] Subsequently, the reduced prestige of the rabbis also reflected the growing lack of public interest in "theological" problems. The result was that the rabbis, trained at the rabbinical academy of Metz and then in that of Paris, were often quite respectable intellectually, but no longer spiritual leaders. Without any real juridical function within the community, their role shifted towards that of "wise administrators".

Given the characteristics of the consistory, and particularly the goal of integration and assimilation which it had set for itself, the decline of the rabbinate was in a way inevitable. It was also influenced by the "balance of power" between the lay notables and the rabbis, which throughout favored the former. The notables considered the rabbis to be mere executives. In fact, with only a few exceptions, the rabbis made little attempt to arrest their own decline. They generally accepted it, and resigned themselves to a situation which seems inconsistent with the Jewish political tradition.

---

10 Emmanuel Deutz (1763–1842) was rabbi of his native city of Coblenz. In 1806 and 1807 he was a member of the Assembly of Jewish Notables and of the Napoleonic Sanhedrin. After 1808 he sat on the Central Consistory. From 1822 until his death he was "Grand Rabbin de France". His son, Simon, converted to Catholicism at the age of 23 and adopted the name of Hyacinthe de Gonzague. On the organization and the orientations of the French rabbinate, see: J. Bauer, *L'Ecole Rabbinique de France (1830–1930)* (Paris: Presses Universitaires de France, 1931).

II

NINETEENTH CENTURY CHALLENGES

The criticism leveled against the consistories during the nineteenth century was, for the most part, quite feeble, especially when compared with the twentieth-century situation.[11] It is somewhat difficult to describe the inner tensions of French Jewry during this time, since they were not manifest. As several scholars have noted, alternative spokesmen for French Jewry failed to win power. It should also be emphasized that challenges of a "theological" nature to a certain extent offset class challenges. The wealthy classes tended to advocate reform, while the poorer Jews, especially in eastern France (Alsace and Lorraine), demanded stricter respect for the orthodox tradition.

Five types of challenges to French Jewish institutions can be identified during the nineteenth century.

(a) *The challenge of assimilation.*

Assimilation was unique neither to France nor to the period. It existed in every country where Jews were emancipated. Nevertheless, as is well known, the French climate was particularly favorable for assimilationism. The challenge became especially acute towards the end of the century. Encouraged by their social and professional success, certain French citizens of Jewish origin called for complete assimilation into French society and the abandonment of all Jewish particularism. It was from that standpoint that they criticized the official Jewish institutions. They considered that the mere maintenance of distinct structures was an affront to the welcome accorded to Jews by French society. A number of them converted, but assimilation in France primarily took the form of the enthusiastic adoption of scientism and free thought.

For several reasons, this challenge had little effect on the Jewish institutions. By definition, assimilated Jews generally evinced little interest in community affairs and consequently hardly bothered to criticize them. Second, the increase in anti-Semitism prevented the triumph of assimilationist views. Finally, the fact that the Consistory itself adopted a reformist and pro-integrationist attitude limited the attraction of assimilationist doctrines.

---

11 See Patrick Girard, *Les Juifs de France de 1789 à 1860. De l'Emancipation à l'Egalité* (Paris: Calman-Levy, 1976); particularly the third section: "La Communauté israélite, les institutions et les débats internes", pp. 170–244.

(b) *The challenge of reform.*

This challenge paralleled developments in other European countries: certain individuals, generally members of the affluent and urban classes of the community, criticized the consistories and the rabbinate for the "timidity" of their theological innovations. Anxious for these institutions to take the path of modernism more quickly and decisively, they wished to go even further than the proposals of the *Archives Israélites*, a review founded in 1840 which preached moderate reforms. It was in this spirit that a small group of liberals, grouped around Dr. Terquem of Metz,[12] demanded a basic reform of the Jewish religion as had been accomplished in Germany by the disciples of Mendelssohn and Jacobson.

Disarmed by the innovations and reforms of the consistory itself, this current remained relatively weak during the nineteenth century. However, in 1907, shortly after the enactment of the law separating church and state, it produced its own distinct institution: the ULI, l'Union Libérale Israélite (Liberal Jewish Union).

(c) *Orthodox criticism.*

In contrast to the reformist challenge, this challenge emanated from the leaders of the poor masses, especially those living in the eastern departments. They criticized the Central Consistory as a whole, the wealthy notables, the chief rabbis, and the consistorial rabbis for their reformist attitude. These Jews were deeply attached to their tradition, and presented a kind of "passive resistance" to the reformist decrees of the Consistory.

This challenge was manifested chiefly after the Paris rabbinical conference of 1856. Convened by Chief Rabbi S. Ullman, the Conference proposed several changes in order to "improve the condition of the religion". According to Chief Rabbi Klein, the most prominent orthodox figure of the time, "the honor of our religion was brought low, its glory was tarnished, and it was delivered as a prisoner into the hands of the consistory."

Among the most important members of the orthodox group were Abraham Créhange, editor of the newspaper *La Vérité*, and Rabbi Klein. The publication that propounded orthodox ideas, although of a moderate nature, was Simon Bloch's *Univers Israélite*, founded in 1846.[13] But the orthodox faction

---

12 See Tsarphati (Terquem): *Lettres d'un Israélite Français à ses Coreligionnaires sur* ... (Paris, 1821–37).

13 See Simon Bloch, *La Foi d'Israël, ses Dogmes, son Culte, ses Cérémonies, ses Pratiques Religieuses, sa Loi Morale et Sociale, sa Mission et son Avenir* (Paris, 1859).

lacked a coherent program: Klein emphasized theological issues and denounced innovations in religious practice; Créhange was especially critical of the passivity of the Consistory in response to the persecution of the Jews of Germany.

Throughout the century, the Central Consistory clearly regarded the orthodox opposition as the major challenge to its own power. It opposed the orthodox, sometimes applying police methods. Ultimately, the orthodox had no choice but, like the liberals, to secede. The orthodox communities continued to develop outside of the consistorial framework.

(d) *The challenge over the lack of democracy in the institutions of the Jewish community.*

The common denominator of the three challenges described above — assimilationism, reform, and orthodoxy — is that they can be found in almost any religious community groping towards emancipation. Neither was the challenge over the lack of democracy peculiar to the Jewish community; parallel developments are evident in the Catholic, Reformed, and Lutheran churches. However, this challenge was perhaps more specifically related to the Jewish political tradition. Indeed, during the nineteenth century it was principally articulated by the orthodox faction (although certain liberals such as Terquem were also associated with it).

The challenge was aimed at two targets. One was the omnipotence of the lay notables: the challengers demanded more democracy and equality and the distribution of positions and functions on the basis of merit rather than wealth. The other was the absolute monopoly of the consistories (which Bloch, in *l'Univers Israélite*, termed "l'absolutisme consistorial"), and their abuses of power. The challengers, Klein in particular, criticized the lack of communal autonomy and the centralized control which was both administrative and spiritual. Here, clearly, is evidence of a nostalgia for the autonomous/federalist tradition which harked back to pre-revolutionary times.

(e) *The challenge against nonintervention and passivity with regard to anti-Semitism.*

Throughout the nineteenth century, especially during its latter half, certain members of the community fought against the passivity of the consistories with regard to persecutions of Jews both in France and abroad. Criticism against noninterventionism emanated from three sources. One can be identified as liberal Jews. Faithful to the great principles of the French Revolution, and especially to the Déclaration des Droits de l'Homme of 1789 and the ideals of justice and equality, these persons decided to work for the emancipation and defense of Jews *outside France*. Thus, following the Mortara Affair, it was Adolphe Cremieux — and not the Consistory — who founded the Alliance Israélite Universelle in 1860. Similarly, it was that organization, and not the Consistory, which later intervened on behalf of the Jews of Russia and elsewhere.[14] As Graetz has shown, the predominant feeling at the time of the establishment of the Alliance was one of revolt combined with philanthropy and francocentrism. Nevertheless, the Alliance Israélite Universelle did not consider anti-Semitic activities in France as worthy of attention, even when these activities reached a paroxysm.

Once the first flush of activism had passed, the Alliance too became integrated into French society. Increasingly, its affairs were controlled by the notables and the body became institutionalized.

However, French anti-Semitism had meanwhile become the target of criticism leveled by certain orthodox circles, such as that of Créhange in Paris. His "Club démocratique des fidèles" frequently protested against anti-Jewish agitation in Alsace.

Furthermore, some individuals spoke out against the passivity of the consistory during the explosion of anti-Semitism surrounding the Dreyfus Affair.[15] Alexandre Weill, the poet, was one; Isidore Singer, another. But the most prominent of all was Bernard Lazare,[16] who waged a campaign in support of Dreyfus. His efforts were criticized by the community notables, who would have preferred him to keep quiet.

In conclusion, it must be emphasized that challenges during the nineteenth century were, on the whole, feeble; they possessed very few leaders, limited means, and little organization. They did not pose a serious threat to the omnipotence and virtual monopoly of the consistory or its principles. To the

14 See Andre Chouraqui, *L'Alliance Israélite Universelle et La Renaissance Juive Contemporaine: 100 ans d'Histoire* (Paris: Presses Universitaires de France, 1965); "L'Alliance Israélite Universelle, sa Doctrine, ses Realisations, son Rayonnement", *Les Cahiers de l'Alliance Israélite Universelle*, March–May 1953, nos. 71–73. See also Michael Graetz: *Changes in the Jewish Consciousness of French Jewry* (the Social and Intellectual Background of the Foundation of the Alliance Israélite Universelle from the 1820's to the 1860's) (The Hebrew University of Jerusalem, 1972).

15 See Michel Winock, *Edouard Drumont et Cie, Antisémitisme et Fascisme en France* (Paris: Le Seuil, 1982).

16 See Nelly Wilson, *Bernard Lazare, Antisemitism and the Problem of Jewish Identity in Late Nineteenth Century France* (Cambridge: Cambridge University Press, 1978). In 1896 Lazare published: *Une erreur judiciaire: la vérité sur l'Affaire Dreyfus*.

extent that they found expression, the challenges were linked to a Franco-Jewish political tradition predating emancipation, a tradition characterized by community, autonomy, and spiritual leadership accepted by the masses.

III

CHALLENGES: 1900–1939

It is striking that the three fundamental events of this period — the separation of Church and State in France, the First World War, and the rise of anti-Semitism and fascism during the 1930s — caused virtually no change in the characteristic features of the consistories.[17]

The 1905 Law of Separation transformed the consistories into voluntary "consistorial religious associations". The juridical structure did, of course, change; above all, the consistories lost a major source of funds: the salaries of the rabbis and the *hazanim* were no longer paid by the state. Otherwise, however, matters remained much as they were. The cumbersome bureaucracy was retained, the integrationist orientation was unaltered, and the power of the notables was unaffected. Moreover, the rehabilitation of Captain Dreyfus in 1906 appeared to justify noninterventionism; it seemed proof that French society was capable of correcting its own errors with regard to the Jews.

Nevertheless, the Law of Separation did impinge upon the centralist and monopolistic ambitions of the consistory: these no longer had any basis in law. In practice, the consistory (as it was still called despite its legal change in name) continued to be considered the spokesman of the community, by Jews and non-Jews alike. Moreover, the Central Consistory and its chief rabbinate remained the most important Jewish organization in France. Nevertheless, its virtual monopoly was ended. This was manifest in three domains:

First, the consistory was unable effectively to oppose the development of a distinct institutional network by the immigrants from Eastern Europe (the consistories fell, the financial resources of the Central Consistory were depleted, unable and unwilling to integrate the immigrants). Second, even among the native Jewish population, the consistory's power gradually declined. Its sphere of influence was already beginning to be limited to the area of "religion" (ritual and synagogues). Political, social, philanthropical, educational, cultural, and other organizations could now be freely established. Finally, even in the strictly religious area, the monopoly of the consistory was to be

17 See Paula Hyman, *From Dreyfus to Vichy: the Remaking of French Jewry, 1906–1930* (New York: Columbia University Press, 1979).

limited by the legal creation of the Union Libérale Israélite and the flourishing of small orthodox communities and prayer circles.

World War I dealt a harsh blow to the consistory. Membership in the local consistories fell, the financial resources of the Central Consistory were depleted, especially because of galloping inflation, the staff was cut, and its structures were disrupted. Moreover, the communities of Alsace-Lorraine which were returned to France were administered in accordance with the pre-1905 system (the salaries of their employees were paid by the state), and sought to retain a large share of independence.

Notwithstanding this situation, it remains true, as Schwarzfuchs notes, that: "the shock of the First World War, the necessity of replenishing the decimated staff of the community, the world economic crisis, did not arouse anyone (within the native community) to question the structure of the community." [18] The main impact of the war was felt among the younger generations of native French Jews, and would not become manifest until later, during the 1930s and World War II. According to Schwarzfuchs, the First World War became a generational barrier strengthening the self-consciousness of postwar youth as a group in conflict with the values of its elders. It was that generation which was to challenge the political and ideological assumptions of native Jewish leadership in the interwar years.

Meanwhile, not even the growth of the organizations of the extreme right and anti-Semitic propaganda, especially after the Stavisky affair,[19] served to shake the consistory in any significant manner. Its notables considered the anti-Semitism of the 1930s, like that of the nineteenth century, to be a passing aberration imported from Germany, an "un-French" phenomenon nourished by the economic crisis. The consistory, with the exception of a few public figures, continued to reject the legitimacy of any collective Jewish action to denounce anti-Semitism on the political level. There, too, it pursued its policy of nonintervention and neutrality.

Other than a small fraction of the native Jewish youth, it was the immense wave of eastern and central European immigrants which constituted the central source of challenge between the beginning of the twentieth century and 1939. In 1872 only 49,500 Jews lived in France (0.13% of the country's total population). However, between 1881 and 1914 approximately 30,000 Jewish immigrants arrived in France, most of them from Russia and Romania. The main

18 See Simon Schwarzfuchs, *Les Juifs de France* (Paris: Albin Michel, 1975), p. 284.
19 The Stavisky Affair (1934) was an embezzlement affair. It led to violent demonstrations of the extreme right in Paris, and to the development of anti-Semitic associations.

wave came from Russia after the Kishinev pogrom and the failure of the Revolution of 1905. After 1918, immigration greatly increased. Some 150,000 immigrants arrived between the two world wars, about three-quarters of them from eastern Europe, mainly Poland. In sum, between 1906 and 1939 approximately 175,000 Jewish immigrants arrived in France.

The challenge to Jewish institutions posed by the immigrants is directly related to the almost total contrast between that population and the native Jews.[20] Whereas the vast majority of the latter belonged to the petty and middle bourgeoisie, the immigrants were largely members of the proletariat and artisans.[21] Equally distinct were the two groups' perceptions of Jewish identity. Whereas the native community viewed Judaism as a religion, the immigrants had an ethnic and national conception of their Jewishness. Finally, they held contrasting views of relations between the Jew and the state. Whereas the native community aspired to integrate into French society and opposed any collective Jewish expression, the immigrants did not regard integration as the first goal to be attained. On the contrary, they believed in the need for Jewish politics, especially in the fight against anti-Semitism.

The attitude of the major Jewish institution, the consistory, towards the eastern European immigrants, took two forms: first, among certain notables, there was a partial effort to reject the immigrants (with more or less veiled attempts to exert influence on the authorities to limit immigration). Second, to the extent that rejection was materially impossible and unacceptable to a large portion of the native Jews themselves, a paternalistic attitude developed with respect to the integration of the immigrants: a mixture of condescending assistance and the refusal to share power in any way with the new arrivals.

A small fraction of the immigrants integrated themselves rather well into the communal institutions in the interwar period (it is impossible to give a precise percentage). It was principally the Sephardic Jews who fitted into the consistorial network, but also a number of Jews from eastern Europe. Many sent their children to the *Talmud-Torahs* (Sunday schools) run by the consistory; some also appealed to the charitable organizations dependent on the consistory (such as the welfare assistance bureaus). Social contact and intermarriage between the two groups also took place. However, most of the immi-

---

20 See David H. Weinberg, *A Community on Trial, The Jews of Paris in the 1930s* (Chicago: Chicago University Press, 1977); Michel Roblin, *Les Juifs de Paris, Démographie, Economie, Culture* (Paris: A. and J. Picard, 1952).

21 The socio-economic composition of the Jewish immigrants from Eastern Europe is well described in Charlotte Rolland, *Du ghetto à l'Occident* (Paris: Editions de Minuit, 1962).

grants were critical of the native institutions. Since they could not "reform" the consistory, they tended to develop their own institutional network.

It must be emphasized that the criticism voiced against the consistory by the immigrants of the twentieth century was not fundamentally different from that voiced by opponents and dissidents during the nineteenth century. The themes show clear lines of continuity. For one thing, the immigrants found fault with the monopolistic aims of the native institutions, accusing them of seeking completely to suppress pluralism. Moreover, the immigrants condemned the integrationist-assimilationist tendency which they detected in the orientation of the consistory: they found the native community to be lifeless, its publications uncommitted, and its institutions shallow vehicles for French culture.

Generally wishing to take their place in the state as Jews, the immigrants also condemned the noninterventionism of the consistory. What they criticized most was its passivity in the face of the rising tide of anti-Semitism. From the time of its creation in 1913, La Fédération des Sociétés Juives de Paris (the Federation of Jewish Societies of Paris), an immigrant organization, had assumed the goal of "defending the interests of the immigrant Jewish population rather than leaving that defense to the native Jewish population." This criticism increased during the 1920s and 1930s. On this issue, the immigrants found allies among the native Jewish youth, together with whom they founded the Ligue Internationale Contre L'Antisémitisme (International League Against Anti-Semitism; LICA), in 1928. This organization promoted activism and mass demonstrations. When twenty-three Jews were killed in Constantine, Algeria, the *Parizer Haynt* called upon the Consistory to "stop limiting its concerns strictly to religious matters" and to "put an end to its policy of silence."

The immigrants also criticized the notables. Their criticism was largely an extension of the protests previously noted against the lack of democracy in the institutions. But it was reinforced among the immigrants by a class element: the new arrivals generally belonged to the underprivileged classes and could not identify with the wealthy, assimilated men who held the communal reins of power. French Jewish notables were totally unwilling to share power in the communal institutions with Jewish refugees from eastern Europe. For a long time not a single consistory permitted its council to contain more than a certain percentage of foreign-born members, and many obstacles were placed in their path. When an immigrant was finally allowed to sit among the notables, it was more in the nature of a favor than the recognition of a right. In response to the virulent criticism voiced by the immigrants, the native notables consented to co-opt a few more immigrants in the late 1920s and

1930s, generally men of their own social class (titled immigrants, those belonging to the upper bourgeoisie, or at least financially and socially successful men). All the leftist and extreme left-wing Jewish organizations, composed almost exclusively of immigrants (socialists, Bundists, communists, leftist Zionists) criticized the monopolization of the community by a dominant class, symbolized by the Rothschild family. Their denunciation of the dominant Jewish class reached its climax in their refusal to maintain any contact with "bourgeois" community organizations (except at the time of the Popular Front).

Criticism of native institutions on religious grounds was also similar to certain criticisms voiced during the nineteenth century. That criticism was mainly orthodox in character, directed against the modernist reforms instituted by the consistorial rabbis, the synagogue style of the French Jews, and the limited religious instruction provided in the Sunday classes. In contrast, the immigrants expressed virtually no criticism from a reformist point of view and did not join the liberal community. In effect, the reform community continued to be comprised chiefly of wealthy, assimilated, native French Jews. Reform was largely foreign to the traditions of the immigrants.

But above all, many immigrants simply rejected the religious tradition completely, sometimes violently. Immigrant laymen, especially those who identified with the left and the extreme left, vehemently rejected religious institutions and condemned them publicly.

Prior to 1939, the immigrants did not manage to transform the native institutions. Primarily, this was because the consistories were still a perfect reflection of the sociological and ideological composition of the native French Jewish population. Until 1939 the latter considered the immigrants as foreigners with different conceptions, a different style of life, and a different kind of Jewish identity, and they saw no need to be influenced by them. Given this situation, the immigrants could either accept the conceptions of the native population and integrate themselves within the consistorial network without exerting any influence on it, or else create a separate and parallel network of institutions, in keeping with the principles of Judaism as they had known it in eastern Europe. The vast majority chose the second alternative. Several studies, among them David Weinberg's monograph on the Jews of Paris from 1933 to 1939, have shown that the majority of the institutions created by the immigrants were the *Landsmanschaften*, societies of immigrants from a given locality, which raised the funds necessary for the purchase of burial rights. Frequently a club grew up alongside the society, sometimes taking over the funeral rites. More than a hundred such *Landsmanschaften* soon existed, and they became the institutional scaffolding of the immigrant community. A framework for these groups was initiated in 1913, when A. Marmorek founded the Fédération des Sociétés Juives de Paris. This was strengthened in 1923, with the establishment of the Fédération des Sociétés Juives de France (the Federation of Jewish Organizations in France).

IV

CHALLENGES AFTER WORLD WAR II [22]

Despite the existence of the network of immigrant institutions, the *Consistoire Central* remained, in 1939, by far the most powerful organization of French Jewry. During the Second World War and immediately afterwards, three other groups of institutions appeared. Leaving the "religious" field to the Consistory, they assumed control over other basic areas of Jewish life.

(a) In 1943 the Conseil Représentatif des Juifs de France (the Representative Council of the Jews of France, CRIF) was founded as a clandestine organization.[23] Although it retained formal ties with the Consistory, it progressively achieved independent status. After the war, the CRIF became the foremost spokesman of the community in its political dealings with the state authorities.[24]

(b) The establishment of the State of Israel in 1948 stimulated the development of a variety of Zionist movements. The French section of the Jewish Agency, and not the rather weak Fédération Sioniste de France, provided a

---

22 We shall not deal in this study with the attitude of the Vichy government towards Jewish organizations. On this, see the basic work by Michael R. Marrus and Robert O. Paxton, *Vichy et les Juifs* (Paris: Calmann-Levy, 1981). On the destruction of the French Jewish community by the Germans, see Joseph Billis, *La Solution Finale de la Question Juive, Essai sur ses Principes dans le IIIe Reich et en France sous l'Occupation* (Paris: Serge et Beate Klarsfeld, 1977); Philippe Garnier Raymond, *L'Antisémitisme 1940–1944* (Paris: Brilland, 1975); Gerard Israel, *Heureux comme Dieu en France 1940–1944* (Paris: R. Laffont, 1975); Jean Laloum, *La France Antisémite de Darquier de Pellepoix* (Paris: Editions Syres, 1979); Centre de Documentation Juive Contemporaine, *La France et la Question Juive 1940–1944* (Paris: S. Messinger, 1981). A very controversial book has recently been published on the attitude of the major Jewish organization established during the war, the Union Générale des Israélites de France (l'UGIF): Maurice Rajsfus, *Des Juifs dans la Collaboration, l'UGIF. 1941–1944* (Paris: Etudes et Documentation Internationales, 1980).

23 The emergence of new clandestine organizations within the resistance movement is described in Jacques Ravine, *La Résistance Organisée des Juifs de France 1940–44* (Paris: Julliard, 1973).

24 Note also the existence of a French section within the World Jewish Congress; but even this recognizes the CRIF as the political spokesman of the community.

focus for those movements. The creation of the State gave real impetus to what had been only a marginal phenomenon in France.[25]

(c) Above all, in 1950, the Fonds Social Juif Unifié (United Jewish Social Fund, FSJU) was founded as a single organization for the collection and distribution of funds in the community. Although in theory the FSJU functioned in areas not dealt with by the Consistory, it nevertheless became its rival: the boundaries between the "religious" and "socio-cultural" spheres are not clearly defined, and a struggle for power developed between the two organizations. The FSJU was responsible for the reconstruction of French Jewry after the war, and was the main factor in the Jewish renaissance in France. If we add that fund-raising for the community and for Israel were united after 1967 in the Appel Juif Unifié de France (French United Jewish Appeal, AUJF) the following institutional outline emerged, remaining unchanged to the present time:

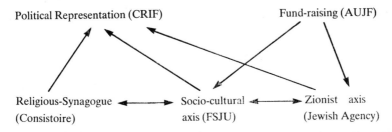

Although the institutional framework of French Jewry changed during and after World War II, the classical features of Jewish organizations partly persisted: a cumbersome bureaucracy, the centrality of Paris, a tendency towards the concentration of power, the influence of the notables, and deference to the government.[26] Between 1945 and 1967, however, challenges to the system were feeble. Of the several reasons for this phenomenon, primary seems to have been the need felt to rebuild the community. To this must be added the emer-

---

25   See the work of the former "Grand-Rabbin de France", Jacob Kaplan, *Judaïsme français et sionisme* (Paris: Albin Michel, 1975). On the new Jewish identity which developed after the war and the creation of the State of Israel, see Dominique Schnapper, *Juifs et Israélites* (Paris: Gallimard, 1980); André Harris and Alain De Sedouy, *Juifs et Français* (Paris: Grasset, 1979); "Juifs et Français, Juifs ou Français", *Les Nouvelles Littéraires*, No. 57 (2703), 13–19 September 1979, pp. 3–9; Yoshua Rash, "French, Foreigners and Jews", *Patterns of Prejudice*, no. 10 (1), Jan.–Feb. 1976, pp. 6–13.

26   See Yochanan Manor, "Réflexions sur le Judaïsme français", *Dispersion et Unité*, Vol. 18, 1978, pp. 177–89. For an example of the organization of a Jewish community in the provinces, see Monique Lewi, *Histoire d'une Communauté juive, Roanne* (Roanne: Ed. Horvath, 1974).

gence of a truly multipolar community (instead of the former consistorial monopoly or dominance), and the intermingling of all components of the community during the war. Finally, there was a perceived need to accord the large institutions legitimacy, in order to enable them to negotiate with the government and to deal with such matters as German reparations.[27]

The massive influx of 175,000 Jews from Morocco, Tunisia and Algeria did *not* provoke a challenge within the community prior to 1967.[28] The primary objective of the new arrivals was integration within French society and within the Jewish community.[29] Integration "without rocking the boat" was desired not only by the notables of the existing institutions, but by the north African immigrants themselves.[30]

Criticism of the major communal institutions did increase after 1967, and was expressed in two primary forms: challenges from within those structures themselves, and challenges which emanated from external sources. Despite the possible linkages between them, they will here be treated separately.

CHALLENGES FROM WITHIN

All the large institutions have been challenged from within, though in different degrees. On the whole, the role of the youth movements has been very important. But given the centralism of the institutions, and the power of the notables in Paris, the challenges from within were generally channelled, controlled, or suppressed. Thus, even during May 1968 — when France was otherwise in turmoil — the Consistory underwent only one small internal crisis. Its Paris offices were occupied by young people who demanded more orthodoxy in the

27 See David Weinberg, "The French Jewish Community after World War II. The Struggle for Survival and Self-Definition", *Forum*, no. 45, Summer 1982.

28 See, for example, Claude Tapia, "20 ans après, le Judaïsme Maghrebin en France", *Les Nouveaux Cahiers*, no. 59, Winter 1979–1980, pp. 51–61. For a good analysis of the demographic situation of French Jewry after the integration of the north African immigration, see Sergio Della Pergola, Doris Bensimon, "Enquêtes socio-démographiques sur les Juifs de France: Nouvelles Perspectives", *Dispersion et Unité*, Vol. 18, 1978, pp. 190–212.

29 The basic work on this subject is Doris Bensimon-Donath, *L'Intégration des Juifs Nord-Africains en France* (Paris: Mouton, 1971); see also Georges Levitte, "A Changing Community", in *Aspects of French Jewry* (London: Valentine, Mitchell, 1969), pp. 10–23.

30 Today, Jews from north Africa are rather well integrated in the community. However, Emeric Deutsch points out that two-thirds of the Jews in France have no link whatsoever with any community organization. See: "Radiographie d'une Communauté", *L'Arche*, no. 80, Sept.–Oct. 1982.

synagogue and the removal of the organ from the Great Synagogue on rue de la Victoire. But that event had no further consequences.

More significant were internal challenges of a different nature, here discussed under four principal headings.

a. *Internal Challenges in the Religious Sphere*

The religious sphere has been the scene of only "moderate" challenges. The consistory survived the postwar period and the arrival of the north African Jews with few serious problems (other than financial). It wisely granted some autonomy to the small communities which multiplied in the French provinces with the arrival of Algerian Jews.[31] These communities were free to choose their own form of worship, to appoint their own rabbis of local origin, and to govern themselves. The consistory very early accorded the *Sephardim* a role in the institutional leadership (these Sephardic notables were often affluent, and included few young people or women).

Above all, the "consistorial" type of Judaism, halfway between religious orthodoxy and moderate reformism, seems to have been perfectly suited to the Jews of north Africa, who, while respecting religious traditions, needed flexibility.[32] A decisive step in the identification of the north African Jews with the consistorial institutions came very recently, with the election in 1980 of the first Sephardic Chief Rabbi of France, René-Samuel Sirat. An intellectual, a university professor and an enlightened man, Rabbi Sirat owed his election to the votes of the wealthy *Ashkenazim* of the consistory, who understood the importance of such a nomination for the stability of their institution.

The small world of orthodox communities (called "de stricte observance", strictly observant) was also unchallenged. Given the independence of these small synagogues and *minyanim*, and the religious consensus reigning among their members, as much was to be expected.

Although not truly a "challenge", there have been currents of "renewal" and "neo-orthodoxy" in France. These, however, were located *outside* the established orthodox communities. On the intellectual level, it was Gilbert Bloch's Ecole des Cadres d'Orsay (in the suburbs of Paris) which injected some life into the world of orthodox Judaism and to the community in general. The young people trained in that institution, a kind of modern *yeshiva* open

---

31   For a description of the geographic distribution of these small communities, see Roger Berg, *Guide Juif de France* (Paris: Migdal, 1970).

32   See Doris Bensimon, "Pratiques et Attitudes religieuses en milieu juif parisien", *Dispersion et Unité*, Vol. 13, 1973/4, pp. 171–86.

to the outside world, under the direction of Rabbi Léon Ashkenazi (Manitou), acquired a traditional education, and some of them later found places within the community leadership. In Strasbourg, the Yechiva des Etudiants (Student Yeshiva), directed by Rabbi Eliahou Abitol, served as both a center of orthodox renewal and of challenge to the local community institutions. The Lubavitch movement, which has taken root in France by recruiting a large number of young *Sephardim*, has generally maintained its distance from the rest of the community.

Unlike the Consistory and the orthodox communities, the small reform movement was shaken by inner conflict. In the 1970s the rabbi, followed by young people, teachers, and the parents of pupils studying in the liberal "Talmud-Torah" (generally of Sephardic origin), criticized the old Union Libérale Israélite, founded in 1907. That challenge reached a crucial juncture, and the critics ultimately left the ULI to create a rival movement: le Mouvement Juif Libéral de France (French Movement of Liberal Judaism). Personal conflicts and the generation gap played a major role in the split, but emphasis should also be laid on the role played by young Sephardim who were attracted by Reform Judaism but wanted to be more active, more involved, more militant.

b. *Challenges within the Zionist Camp*

The Zionist camp, tightly controlled by the Jewish Agency, has experienced several crises since 1948, but has not been confronted by any real *inner* challenge (the major criticism came, as we shall see from without).

The Zionist camp underwent reform in 1970, when the old Fédération Sioniste de France was replaced by the Mouvement Sioniste de France. But the MSF was, on the whole, characterized by the ossification characteristic of its predecessor. Three months before the 1982 elections to the Zionist Congress, the MSF split and a new Fédération des Organisations Sionistes de France was established. But these developments reflected personal disagreements rather than real challenges within the Zionist camp. The absence of the latter must be attributed to the same causes adduced with regard to the orthodox communities. Like the latter, all the Zionist groups acknowledge a common goal and have a similar frame of reference. The orthodox communities bring together Jews who share an aspiration to safeguard the Jewish tradition founded on *halakhah*. Likewise, the Zionist camp brings together groups with the common goal of supporting the State of Israel (and, secondly, encouraging *aliyah*).

On the other hand, the monolithic character and ossification of the Zionist institutions of France are merely a reflection of the malaise affecting the entire World Zionist Organization. The delicate balance which characterizes the institutions of the latter can also be found in the various Zionist institutions of the Diaspora, and especially in France. Finally, the firm control exercised by the Jewish Agency is accepted by all the Zionist institutions. The Jewish Agency in France, as elsewhere, is averse to any major upset among the institutions it controls.[33]

c. *Challenges within the Political Representative Organization of French Jewry, the CRIF*

Criticism within the CRIF has been more vehement because that organization deals with fundamental political and ideological problems, and also because it includes almost all the Jewish institutions of the country. Within the CRIF the most severe criticism has been voiced by the Jewish communists, as organized in the Union des Juifs pour la Résistance et l'Entr'aide (the Jewish Union for Resistance and Mutual Aid, UJRE), and their Yiddish press. The communists have essentially been opposed to two things: the unconditional support of the CRIF for Israeli government policy, and unconditional support for the cause of Soviet Jewry.

Nevertheless, challenges within the CRIF have been very limited for several reasons. First, whereas the CRIF originally made all its decisions unanimously, it later adopted the system of a majority vote. This increased the marginality of communist influence, and reduced the impact of communist criticism of the CRIF leadership. Second, the CRIF defined itself as a federation of institutions. It expressed only the common denominator of its constituents, who were otherwise free to go their own way. Finally, particularly after 1967, there existed a general consensus regarding certain communal fundamentals: the need to defend Israel; to combat the resurgence of anti-Semitism; and to support Jews persecuted in the USSR and Arab countries. This general consensus, with the exception of small marginal groups, explains the feebleness of the challenges within the CRIF.

d. *Challenges within the Socio-Cultural Sphere, the FSJU*

Criticism within the FSJU, the primary socio-cultural axis of French Jewry, was much more vehement than in other communal sectors. The principal

---

33 Zionist youth movements do not constitute a challenge within the Zionist camp. See Yair Auron, *Les Mouvements de Jeunesse Juifs en France, Le Judaïsme Contemporain à travers le miroir de sa jeunesse* (Doct. Thesis) (University of Paris III, 1979).

crisis erupted in 1972, when the organization decided to erect a huge community center in Paris. The process whereby this decision was reached was severely criticized by the *Fonds Social*, especially since the huge sums involved would have tied up the budget and the future activities of the entire Jewish community for several years. A group of people, stimulated by academics, youth movement leaders, and some administrators of the FSJU itself, initiated a move to compel the leadership to introduce democratic reforms into the FSJU's 1966 constitution. After much preparatory work, the new constitution was adopted in November 1972.

The details of this complex reform need not be enumerated. It is sufficient to reiterate the conclusions reached by a study conducted in 1979,[34] which is still valid in 1985: the reform does not seem to have dismantled the structures of authority and power within this large institution. Despite the introduction of certain democratic measures, the notables managed to retain their power. The young challengers have been co-opted and "notablized", and very little has actually changed. As much was strikingly indicated by the Guy de Rothschild affair of February 1979. Rothschild, President of the FSJU, published an interview in *Lui* (a semi-pornographic magazine) in which he expressed a rather indifferent attitude towards Judaism and the Jewish people, and distanced himself from the State of Israel. The interview generated a revolt within the National Council of the FSJU. But all criticism was ultimately stifled, and the executive committee never expressed the slightest disapproval of its all-powerful president.

CHALLENGES FROM WITHOUT

Much more violent have been the criticisms expressed from *outside* the great institutions that form the basic framework of the community.

a. *Intellectual Criticism*

Jewish society, both classic and contemporary, as a matter of course bestows respect on the "intellectual", the scholar, the learned man, a respect which Laurence Fuchs relates to the importance of *limud*, traditional Jewish study.[35]

---

34 Ilan Greilsammer, "The Democratization of a Community: French Jewry and the Fonds Social Juif Unifié", *The Jewish Journal of Sociology*, Vol. XXI, no. 2, December 1979, pp. 109–24.

35 Laurence Fuchs, *The Political Behavior of American Jews* (Glencoe, Ill.: The Free Press, 1956).

In our particular case this characteristic has been reinforced by the special respect accorded to intellectuals by French society at large, where thinkers, writers and philosophers constitute a powerful and respected class of "intellocrates". Pierre Aubrey, in his study of *Milieux Juifs dans la France Contemporaine*, notes the influence of these two tendencies, and speaks of the "culture of intelligence" among French Jews. In his chapter on the criteria for social success in the Jewish community, the author emphasizes the "value placed upon studies". The *grandes écoles*, where entry is granted on the basis of competitive examinations, are an important criterion of success.[36]

Indeed, intellectuals occupy a special place in the Jewish community. Most of them meet on an annual basis, to exchange ideas in the Colloque des Intellectuels Juifs de Langue Française (Colloquium of French-speaking Jewish Intellectuals), organized by the French section of the World Jewish Congress.

Distinctions can be drawn between five categories of Jewish intellectuals in France. They are here listed in decreasing order of their influence in the community.

(a) Those who enjoy the widest audience are the graduates of the most elite *grandes écoles* (the Ecole Nationale d'Administration, the Ecole Normale Supérieure, and the Ecole Polytechnique), who have attained key positions in French society. In recent years, the prototype has been Jacques Attali, personal advisor to President François Mitterrand.

(b) Next were the Jewish "philosophers". These can be further categorized as either lay thinkers, such as the exponents of the "new philosophy" (for example Bernard-Henri Levy),[37] and the religious philosophers, who write about Judaism. Some of the latter, who are extremely popular in the community, have received universal recognition (such as Emmanuel Levinas[38]); others are rabbis (particularly Rabbi Ashkenazi). Each has his own sphere of influence, but, in terms of power, their impact on the community at large is quite important.

(c) A third category is made up of Jewish novelists or essayists. Some, such as Elie Wiesel, have long been influential in France; others, notably

---

36 See Pierre Aubery, *Milieux Juifs dans la France Contemporaine à travers leurs écrivains* (Paris: Plon, 1962).

37 Bernard-Henri Levy is one of the leading members of the group called the "New Philosophers". Among his works is: *L'Idéologie Française* (Paris: Grasset, 1981).

38 Emmanuel Levinas is one of the most famous philosophers of the postwar period. See *Difficile Liberté, Essais sur le Judaïsme*, 2nd ed. (Paris: Albin Michel, 1976).

Shmuel Trigano [39] or Alain Finkielkraut,[40] have gained importance in the past few years.

(d) A fourth category includes some famous university professors such as Richard Marienstras, professor of English literature and theoretician of "diasporism",[41] or the sociologist Albert Memmi.[42]

(e) Finally, mention must be made of the Jewish students, particularly those affiliated with the small Union des Etudiants Juifs de France (French Union of Jewish Students),[43] even though their influence is marginal.

The majority of Jewish intellectuals, perhaps 80%, accept the communal institutions as currently constituted; some might even be classified as "notables" within them. Some aspire to be included among the leaders, or at least the advisers of the Consistory, the CRIF, the FSJU and the Alliance, which they rarely criticize.

Those intellectuals who *do* challenge the large community institutions are found both within and outside these frameworks. The most critical totally condemn the large institutions, accusing them of corruption; of subjection to the notables and the upper middle class; of being unrepresentative; conformist; submissive to the government; and of unconditionally supporting Israeli governments. In sum, they call for the reconstruction of the Jewish institutional frameworks in their entirety. Typical of this approach was the attitude of Vladimir Rabi, a judge and literary critic. After a lengthy period of service within the community, Rabi totally rejected its institutional system, which he subjected to some devastating criticism. (Compare his *Anatomie du Judaïsme Français* [1962],[44] an attempt at a sympathetic description of the community's institutions, with the fierce criticism contained in his most recent book, *Un*

---

39 See Shmuel Trigano, *La Nouvelle Question Juive, L'Avenir d'un Espoir* (Paris: Les Presses d'Aujourd'hui, 1982).
40 See Alain Finkielkraut, *Le Juif Imaginaire* (Paris: Le Seuil, 1980).
41 Richard Marienstras, *Etre un Peuple en Diaspora: Mosaïques* (Paris: Maspero, 1975).
42 Albert Memmi, *Portrait d'un Juif* (Paris: NRF, 1962); La Libération du Juif (Paris: NRF, 1966).
43 It is difficult to identify the precise orientations of French Jewish students. An already outdated survey was conducted in the 1960s. See Georges Benguigui, "First-Year Jewish Students at the University of Paris", in *Aspects of French Jewry*, op. cit., pp. 24–96.
44 Wladimir Rabi, *Anatomie du Judaïsme Français* (Paris: Ed. de Minuit, 1962).

peuple de trop sur la Terre? [1980].[45]) Earlier, in an article on "La trahison des clercs", Rabi denounced the conformism of Jewish intellectuals and their compromising stand towards the notables and the community institutions.[46] Nevertheless, the impact of this phenomenon must not be exaggerated. The criticism voiced by Jewish intellectuals from outside the institutions has been undermined by the fact that several of them (the list includes Pierre Mendes-France, Pierre Vidal-Naquet, Alexandre Minkowsky and others), are not really involved in "Jewish" activities, whether in the area of religion, culture, or welfare.

In conclusion, the intellectuals have provoked a change more in the mentality of French Jewry than in its institutions. Their only institutional impact has been to channel the evolution of the FSJU into a slightly more democratic direction.

b. *The Challenge of the Left*

This criticism largely overlaps the preceding category: the majority of the leftists are intellectuals (with the exception of the communists of the UJRE, some of whom are, or were, members of the working class).[47]

A number of groups, once independent of each other, were recently combined in the "Collectif d'Initiative des Juifs de Gauche" (Collective of Leftist Jews) founded in 1980. This body represented several currents:
— The "culturalists" or "diasporists" (actually neo-Bundists) of the Cercle Gaston-Crémieux, led by Richard Marienstras. This small group of Parisian intellectuals criticized the orientations of the CRIF, of which it is not a part, and which it considers to be unrepresentative of the Jews of France. After the publication of the CRIF Charter (the political position) in 1977, updated in 1981, the members of the Cercle Gaston-Crémieux sharply attacked that organization. They consider the CRIF an authoritarian and anti-democratic organization, whose positions are too far from the left and socialism. It defines itself as non-Zionist and refuses to be represented by organizations which it considers to be aligned with the policies of the Israeli government. Finally, the neo-Bundists reproached the institutions for being insufficiently aware of

---

45   Wladimir Rabi, *Un Peuple de trop sur la Terre?* (Paris: Les Presses d'Aujourd'hui, 1980).

46   See Wladimir Rabi, "La Trahison des Clercs", *Les Nouveaux Cahiers*, no. 28, Spring 1972, pp. 2–9. See also "l'Establishment juif. Structures et Idéologie", in *Catalogue pour les Juifs de Maintenant, Recherches*, no. 38, September 1979.

47   On the existence of a Jewish working class in France, see Charlotte Rolland, "Un Proletariat juif à Saint-Fond", *L'Arche*, No. 13, January 1958, pp. 43–7.

the cultural diversity of the Jews, and for failing to work for the preservation of "minority" cultures and languages (Yiddish, Ladino).

— Representatives of the communists or "crypto-communists" of the UJRE. These number no more than the Cercle Gaston-Crémieux, since the vast majority of Jews who became communists have been completely assimilated, and have no interest whatsoever in a specifically Jewish organizational framework.[48] Unlike the neo-Bundists, they tend to be older and unaware of developments within the community. They ritually repeat the slogans of the communist party, and especially reproach the institutions for their support of Israeli government policies.

— Former communists who have broken with the party but have remained leftists. To these must be added members or supporters of the two non-communist parties of the French left, the Parti Socialiste and the Parti Socialiste Unifié.

— The Zionist left (holding views close to such Israeli groups as *Mapam*, *Ratz*, Peace Now, and former Black Panthers).

— Leftists, "survivors" of May 1968 who returned to Judaism.[49]

— Finally, the leftist current attracts a number of prominent Jews, some of them known for their anti-Zionism, or their hostility to Israeli policies.

The members of the Collectif challenge the "bourgeois" character of the institutions and the fact that the notables "use them to promote the interests of their own class". They all criticize the important role which religion plays in the socio-cultural institutions of the community and maintain that religious affairs should be relegated to a purely religious framework and left to the synagogues. But the main thrust of their attack is directed against the political orientation of the institutions. Prominent among their demands are the call for the institutions to align themselves with the positions of the French leftist parties, and for the denunciation of the foreign policies of the Israeli governments. More particularly, the Collectif is in favor of the recognition of "the legitimate rights of the Palestine people", and a majority of its members support an Israeli dialogue with the PLO.

48 See Annie Kriegel, "Les Communistes Français et leurs Juifs", in *Communismes au Miroir Français* (Paris: Gallimard, 1974); Etienne Fajon, "Les Communistes et la Population Juive", *Cahiers du Communisme*, no. 55(5), May 1979, pp. 58–67; Jean Ellenstein, "Les Communistes et les Juifs", *Cahiers Bernard Lazare*, nos. 61–62, Apr.–May 1977, pp. 19–29.

49 See Luc Rosenzweig, *La Jeune France Juive, Conversations avec des Juifs d'Aujourd'hui* (Paris: Editions Libres Hallier, 1980); C. Garson, "Le retour au Judaïsme des Soixante-Huitards", *L'Arche*, no. 238, January 1977, pp. 39–42.

c. Criticism by the Non-Institutional Jewish Press

Virtually the entire Jewish press in France is affiliated with or controlled by the community institutions. *L'Arche* is published by the FSJU, *L'Information Juive* by the Consistory (and previously by the World Jewish Congress), *La Terre Retrouvée*, by the Zionist movement, *Les Nouveaux Cahiers*, by the Alliance Israélite Universelle. Papers in Yiddish with small circulations are also affiliated in one form or another.[50] These publications may occasionally contain articles critical of their institutional publisher, but such criticism is very moderate. So too, are the sporadic attacks on other institutions. The Jewish press in France is *not* a focus of opposition to the establishment.

The single exception is the *Tribune-Juive Hebdo* published in Strasbourg by Rabbi J. Grunewald and Henri Smolarski. Once simply a bulletin published by the communities of the consistories of Alsace and Lorraine, the magazine became independent in 1968. It has since become one of the two or three leading Jewish newspapers of France, enjoying a large readership throughout the country. It is more original in character than the others, and takes a clear line on both religion and politics, with sympathies considered rather socialist. This orientation was demonstrated in the call for a "protest vote" against the right in the French presidential elections of 1981, and by some criticism of the *Likud* government. On the religious level it is rather traditionalist, and continues to be directed by an orthodox rabbi. *T.J. Hebdo*, as the magazine is generally called, has frequently and sometimes quite harshly criticized the large Jewish institutions — the Consistory, the FSJU, and the CRIF. It has attacked their lack of democracy, their upper-middle-class character, the power of the notables, and their lack of militancy. It reproaches the institutions for being divorced from the traditional sources of Judaism and, at the same time, for their indifference towards universalist concerns (the Palestinians, hunger in the world, the threat of nuclear weapons, etc.).

d. The "Activist" Zionist Criticism [51]

Since World War II the Jewish institutions of France have progressed from indifference or hostility towards Zionism to a sympathetic and favorable atti-

---

50 On the orientation of the Yiddish newspapers (*Unzer Wort, Unzer Weg, Unzer Stimme*, and *Neue Presse*), see Reine Silbert, "Le Yiddish est vivant et il vit à Paris", *Tribune Juive*, no. 721, 13 May 1982, pp. 11–15.

51 See Adam Loss, Jacques Attali, Annie Kriegel and others, "Juifs de France: Ce qui change", *L'Arche*, nos. 282–283, Sept.–Oct. 1980, pp. 59–111; "La Communauté juive de France vue d'Israël", *Sillages*, no. 3, October 1980, pp. 11–55; D. Landes, "The State of French Jewry", *Moment*, no. 6, Mar.–Apr. 1981, pp. 12–18.

tude towards the State of Israel. Support for Israel has, however, remained more a matter of form than of concrete action. This attitude of cautious timidity has been increasingly criticized since 1967, in part because of the increasingly pro-Arab policies of Pompidou and Giscard d'Estaing.

The *Likud* victories of 1977 and 1981 have had at least three effects on French Jewry:

— They served to strengthen those Zionist organizations affiliated with the *Likud*, which had hitherto been rather marginal;

— The *Shlihim* of the WZO and the representatives of the Jewish Agency in Paris have tended to more or less identify themselves with the policy orientations of the *Likud*;

— A large number of French Jews were galvanized by the incisive tone of the Israeli Prime Minister, Menachem Begin. The reaction of the public at large, especially the Sephardic community, has been sympathetic to the new Israeli government, and this attitude has been translated into greater Zionist activism, which was further reinforced by the hardening of French pro-Arab policies. The French President's lack of concern for Jewish sensitivities reached one peak in 1980, following Giscard's trip to the Gulf States, where he called for "the right of self-determination for the Palestinians", and another with the terrorist attack on rue Copernic to which the government displayed apparent indifference.[52]

The "activist" reaction found expression primarily in violent criticism of the passivity of the major community institutions. Young people, generally of north African origin, demanded that the institutions identify themselves totally with Israel. This militant pressure forced the large organizations to renounce their previous attitudes. The pressure from below was most clearly expressed in 1976, 1977 and 1980 in huge demonstrations (attended, in 1980, by 150,000 people) labeled "Twelve hours for Israel". These can be said to have revolutionized the traditional behavior of French Jewry.[53] The success of the "Douze Heures" in 1976 and 1977 encouraged the organizing committee, the Comité Juif d'Action (Jewish Action Committee), to form a pressure group known as Le Renouveau Juif (Jewish Renewal), in 1979. Renouveau undoubtedly presented one of the most significant threats to the power of the traditional institutions. On the one hand, it openly attacked the notables and community leaders, focusing explicitly on the Rothschild family during

---

52 Michel Wieworka: "Les Conditions de Formation d'un Mouvement Juif en France", *Esprit*, no. 4, April 1982, pp. 111–30.
53 See Ioav Tiar, "Crise de la Diaspora Française?", *Esprit*, no. 9, September 1980, pp. 57–78.

the "Douze Heures" of 1980; on the other hand, it was the first important Jewish group to call on the Jews of France to vote collectively against Giscard d'Estaing in the elections of 1981. The large institutions reacted forcibly. They expressed solidarity with the Rothschilds and bitterly attacked the Renouveau and the latter's demand for a "Jewish vote". Above all, the notables criticized the WZO representative in France, Avi Primor, for having orchestrated the Renouveau's actions, and arranged for his replacement.[54]

CONCLUSION

The first question posed in the introduction to this paper concerned the degree of *continuity* and *performance* in the themes upon which challenges were mounted against the Jewish community institutions in France. The evidence here reviewed attests to such characteristics. To say that is not to deny that these themes were expressed quite differently by such individuals as Rabbi Klein or Dr. Terquem in the nineteenth century, the eastern European immigrants in the interwar period, and the Jewish intellectuals today. The situations confronting French Jewry have altered greatly, and the composition of the community has undergone fundamental changes. Moreover, France itself has known ten different political regimes since the time of Napoleon I.

Nevertheless, three important themes do appear to recur: a) the power of the notables, b) the question of Jewish identity in France, c) the right to be different in a Jacobin/centralized society.

a) The entire period under study witnessed criticism of the concentration of power in the hands of a small elite, always composed of wealthy, mostly assimilated Jews. In the course of time, this group became somewhat more "open", but it remains a group of "notables".

b) The institutions have been criticized for *not* expressing Jewish identity in all its authenticity (or insufficiently so). It is not important here precisely which identity (religious orthodoxy, nationalism, universal prophetic messianism, etc.) serves as the basis of this criticism: the problem remains that of the fidelity of the institutions to Judaism.

c) Once they adapted themselves to French Jacobinism/centralism, the institutions were, at least until 1967, conformist, loyal to the system, and almost

54 "Juifs de France: Les Charmes peu discrets de la crise", *Tribune Juive*, no. 620, pp. 16–22, May 1980, pp. 4–9.

completely lacking in militance, both with regard to the situation of the Jews in France and elsewhere. The institutions have thus been criticized in the name of Jewish particularism, the right to be different.

A more qualified answer must be given to our second question: have challenges to the institutions focused on the major political themes of Judaism (or the Jewish political tradition), or have they been concerned with the central political controversies affecting French society? On the one hand, there does seem to be a certain link between the themes of the various challenges and certain major political problems posed by Judaism. Thus, the question of the "power of the notables" can be related to the tension between elitism and egalitarianism (a central political dilemma within Judaism). The constant criticism leveled against the institutions because of their "lack of Jewish authenticity" can be related to the tension between ethnocentrism and universalism; while the criticism voiced against institutional passivity and non-interventionism can be related to other important dilemmas of the Jewish tradition, such as revolution versus conservatism.

On the other hand, the challenges within the French Jewish community, during both the nineteenth and the twentieth century, are much more closely related to the great political controversies within French society. Thus the problem of the elite, of the "ruling circle" of notables, is one of the aspects of the ongoing debate on democracy in France. Throughout the period, France has been the focus of struggles for elimination of various privileges: those of the aristocracy, those of the rich, and most recently even the privileges of the "intellocrates", based on "knowledge" or science. Events such as those of May-June 1968 clearly show the depth and intensity of the controversy concerning privileges of all kinds. As for the struggle for "le droit à la différence", the right to be different, this has been a leitmotiv in a society so centralized, closed and nationalist as is that of France. Thus the challenge to the centralization of Jewish institutions has not been peculiar to the Jewish community. Rather, and together with other criticism, it has on the whole been an integral reflection of the political debate within French society at large.

STUART A. COHEN

SAME PLACES, DIFFERENT FACES: A COMPARISON OF ANGLO-JEWISH CONFLICTS OVER ZIONISM DURING WORLD WAR I AND WORLD WAR II

Anglo-Jewry can boast of very few historical milestones of the community's own making. Intellectually, as much as geographically, the community has generally found itself hovering on the periphery of the modern Jewish experience. Consequently, its members have usually reacted to Continental and trans-Atlantic currents in Jewish self-consciousness, rather than trying to shape them. Even to attempt to muster a historical roll of its intellectual and institutional achievements is to invite unfavourable comparisons with American and European counterparts. Its scholastic and political attainments too, although not entirely negligible, were more often derivative than original, contributing only marginally to the seminal forces of change which exerted such an outstanding effect on modern Jewish life elsewhere.

Only a survey of Anglo-Jewry's contribution to the course of Zionist history somewhat modifies this picture. Admittedly, in this case too the Jews of the British Isles cannot claim either unequivocal precedence or priority. Despite the prominence of both Jewish and non-Jewish philo-Zionists during the 19th century, the community was neither the first to advocate the cause of modern Jewish nationalism nor the most vigorous of its exponents.[1] Anglo-Jewish Zionists did, however, appear to play a particularly evident role at at least two crucial junctures of Zionist progress: during World War I and World War II. In the first period, when Great Britain emerged as the putative successor authority in Palestine, the early leaders of the English Zionist Federa-

---

1 The theme of Gentile British Zionism is outlined in Barbara Tuchman, *The Bible and the Sword; England and Palestine from the Bronze Age to Balfour* (New York, 1956). For the Anglo-Jewish background: Norman Bentwich and John M. Shaftesley, "Forerunners of Zionism in the Victorian Era", in *Remember the Days: Essays in Honour of Cecil Roth*, ed. J. M. Shaftesley (London, 1966); E. Orren, *Ḥibbat Zion be-Britanyah, 1878—1898* (Tel Aviv, 1974). The embryonic era of Zionist history is fully covered in David Vital's two works: *The Origins of Zionism* (Oxford, 1975) and *Zionism: The Formative Years* (Oxford, 1982).

tion contributed towards the formulation and timing of the Balfour Declaration; in the second period, when the British mandatory government's restrictive legislation regarding Palestine came under increasing attack, their successors helped to construct a communal platform for change. Neither development, of course, occurred in isolation. Both were prompted by the dual stimulant of both British official actions and the persuasion of other Jewries (notably that of Russia during World War I and of the United States during World War II). Nevertheless, in each case it was British members of the World Zionist Organization who found themselves occupying the centre of the stage and — from that unaccustomed position — helping to shape the destinies of Jews elsewhere than within their immediate geographical demesne.

This paper does not propose to retrace the effects of these episodes on relations between the British Government and the Zionist movement during the two world wars. Rather, it aims to concentrate on the separate issue of their impact on the history of the Anglo-Jewish community. This is an equally significant facet of the cases, not least because in both periods Zionist negotiations with the British Government took place within a climate of considerable anti-Zionist feeling amongst the Anglo-Jewish community itself. They thus provide singular instances of communal conflict over issues which were of other than insular concern. The purpose of this paper, accordingly, will be to compare and contrast the two episodes; in so doing, it will also attempt to analyse their affinities and account for their discrepancies.

I

Any comparison between the two cases must begin by noting their structural parallelisms. Anglo-Jewish debates over Zionism in both 1916-17 and 1943-44 were similar in at least three respects: their content; their tone; and their locus. During both crises, these co-ordinates largely determined the style and direction of communal discourse, thus exercising a major influence over their outcome and the manner of their resolution.

First, the issues of the debates: in both instances, the most prominent subject on the communal agenda was the need to formulate a statement of Anglo-Jewish opinion with regard to the future of *Erez Israel* — more precisely, with regard to the future government of the Jewish *yishuv* there. But, in neither period was debate restricted solely to the nuts and bolts of Jewish immigration and settlement. Rather, attention was concentrated on the wider question of the propriety of Zionism's ideological tenets. As all parties appreciated, this could be something of a Pandora's box. It implied — and necessitated — a wide-ranging investigation of matters as fundamental as the possible "dual loyalty" of British Jews; their fidelity to the "mission civilisatrice" of the

Mosaic faith; and their collective acknowledgement of the inherent irradica-bility of anti-Semitism in the western world. These were all important issues, and yet not subjects entirely germane to the formal matter on the table. At a purely theoretical level, indeed, it was possible to support the expansion of Jewish settlement in *Erez Israel* without necessarily subscribing to the political ambitions which the Zionists attached to that enterprise.[2] In practice, however, the distinction was somewhat difficult to maintain. Supporters of the thesis adumbrated by Herzl (who, although neither the first nor even the most intellectually distinguished proponent of the Zionist idea, was undoubtedly its most influential propagandist) were throughout blatant in their political declarations; they insisted — not least in their statements to the British Gov-ernment — that there was little point to "piecemeal" Jewish colonization in *Erez Israel* unless that endeavour was conceptualized in an avowedly state-building fashion. Their opponents found themselves forced to react in kind. Consequently, their presentations dwelt too (often at similar length) on the philosophical underpinnings of the anti-Zionist case, amounting more to a critique of Jewish nationalism in its entirety than to a comment on the details of its particular manifestations.[3]

Secondly, note must be taken of the common tone of the two conflicts. In both cases, the exchanges between the two sides were shrill and conducted in a highly-charged atmosphere which, at times, bordered on the passionate. Both debates, moreover, occasioned a highly publicized "battle of books", and thus deliberately broke the convention that Anglo-Jewish differences of opinion were best kept to the carefully circumscribed bounds of a moderate exchange within the community itself. In both cases, direct appeals were addressed to the "general public", non-Jewish as well as Jewish. Zionism became the subject of mass meetings, sermons, letters to the Gentile press, and an entire run of pro- and anti-Zionist articles and pamphlets. All attempted

2 Most obviously was this line taken by Claude Montefiore, President of the Anglo-Jewish Association and a principal spokesman for the anti-Zionist case, in his presentations to the Government; see 12 October 1917, Montefiore to Sir M. Hankey, War Cabinet Papers (Public Record Office, London), CAB 21/58. Leonard Stein, who was President of the AJA during World War II, similarly stated: "there is in fact no genuine alternative to Palestine as a field for large-scale Jewish settlement"; letter to Anthony de Rothschild, 11 August 1943, Files of the AJA (hereafter AJ; Mocatta Library, London), AJ 37/6.

3 See, e.g., the run of memoranda presented to the Government by Lucien Wolf in 1916 in Mowshowitch Collection of Wolf Papers (YIVO, New York), Nos. 5724–61; and Anglo-Jewish Association, *Memorandum on Palestine* (London, November, 1944).

to buttress their respective cases by marshalling a host of theological and political arguments. All also proclaimed the message that to adopt any course other than that they posited would be to court catastrophe for both the Jewish people and for humanity at large.[4]

Intensity of that degree is not attributable solely to the theoretical importance of the questions posed by the tenets of Jewish nationalism. Indeed, left at the level of a philosophical discussion, that particular debate might have promoted nothing more than an inconsequential exchange of doctrinal set pieces; highly interesting in its own way and undoubtedly of crucial relevance to a limited circle, but hardly the stuff out of which a communal rumpus need have been made. After all, strictly ideological debates were — as late as 1943 — limited to a few (albeit highly articulate) devotees. On the rights and wrongs of Zionist theories, the majority of the community remained persistently (and, given the intricacies of the subject, perhaps understandably) non-committal. Unless other catalysts are sought, therefore, the mere ventilation of the Zionist proposals does not adequately explain why all anti-nationalists should be described as "men who have no honour or decency & must be watched at every turn", and their opponents as "impertinent" and "upstarts".[5]

No single factor can explain why Zionism became a cause of such communal friction. It was not the only, nor the first source of tension to cut across Anglo-Jewish society during the twentieth century. Shifts, some of them dramatic, in the demographic and economic profiles of the community — together, of course, with the intrusion of the Palestinian issue itself — had all imposed serious strains on the institutional and managerial equilibrium which had largely characterized the community during the Victorian age. Nevertheless, the Zionist movement — precisely because it adopted an organizational form — does seem to have played a seminal role in the process of change. Inspired by the calculated theatricalism of the leaders of the English Zionist Federation, the organization transformed an idea into a cause and posited an agenda for communal action which was as revolutionary as its programme for Palestine. It proclaimed its determination to convert Anglo-Jewry to its cause, if necessary by displacing the incumbent communal leadership and by

4 Thus, in 1916–17, the anti-Zionists published an entire series of pamphlets entitled *Papers for the Jewish People*, many of which were reprinted by the Jewish Fellowship in World War II: Zionist counter-attacks were regularly published under the imprimatur of the English Zionist Federation during World War I and the Zionist Federation during World War II.
5 1 February 1918, J. Moser to C. Weizmann, Weizmann Archives (hereafter WA), Rehovot; and 19 November 1942, Sir R. Waley Cohen to S. Brodetsky, Archives of the Board of Deputies, London (hereafter DEPS), C11/7/3a/2.

embarking on the path of blatant communal "conquest". Through the medium of its various societies and organs, it also established the bureaucratic machinery which potentially made such a transfer of authority possible. In thus acting, the Zionists pitched themselves into a contest for communal power in its broadest sense; they placed themselves at the head of various popular parties of opposition to the entrenched patriciate ("The Cousinhood") which — quite apart from being staunchly opposed to Zionism — was said to regard communal government as its own private preserve.[6] Individual leaders of the English Zionist Federation (after 1929, the Zionist Federation) rose and fell with a regularity which gave their own organization the appearance of a collection of querulous prima donnas. Nevertheless, their underlying pose as the spokesmen for regeneration and reform across a broad institutional front changed hardly at all. What links the two world wars in this respect — for that matter, what remained constant between these two periods — was the theme that debates on Zionism were inextricably interwoven with a larger contest for communal control. Harry Sacher (of the EZF) put the matter bluntly in 1914:

> I should like to make clear the spirit and the purpose with which we approach your [anti-Zionist] friends. We approach them as one power in Jewry addressing itself to another power in Jewry.... If they oppose us we shall, however reluctantly, do what within us lies to destroy any authority they may claim in Jewry or beyond Jewry to speak for the Jewish people. We know we have the power to do it.[7]

Lavy Bakstansky (General Secretary of the Zionist Federation) spoke in much the same terms in 1943:

> We have not undertaken our campaign of opposition ... by accident, or merely on the caprice of any individual, it was the result of years of study and experience and accumulated bitterness at a system which was neither democratic nor effective. We feel very strongly on this matter, and if any attempt is made to undo the decision of July 4th [1943 — see

---

6 This argument is further developed in my articles: "'The Tactics of Revolt': The English Zionist Federation and Anglo-Jewry, 1895—1904", *Journal of Jewish Studies*, vol. XXIX (2), 1978, pp. 169–85; and "The Conquest of a Community? The Zionists and the Board of Deputies in 1917", *Jewish Journal of Sociology*, Vol. XIX (2), 1977, pp. 157–84. For a survey of communal developments in this period see: Vivian D. Lipman, *Social History of the Jews in England, 1850—1950* (London, 1954) and Chaim Bermant, *The Cousinhood* (London, 1971).

7 1 December 1914, Sacher to L. Wolf, DEPS, E3/204 (1).

below], we shall have no alternative but . . . to contest such a decision to the bitter end.[8]

It was this tone of the Anglo-Jewish debates on Zionism, as much as their content, which in turn determined their locus. In this respect, too, the similarities between the two instances are striking. Neither in 1916-17 nor in 1943-44 did the struggle between the Zionists and the anti-Zionists (and their respective fellow-travellers) take the form of an inter-institutional contest between organizations representing the two camps. Although such organizations did exist — and indeed tended to proliferate at moments of acute crisis [9] — protagonists on both sides preferred to conduct their battles in forums at which they could each claim representation. On both occasions, accordingly, it was the Board of Deputies and (to a lesser extent) the Anglo-Jewish Association which became the principle arenas of communal conflict; the Board — because it was recognized (by the British Government as much as by Anglo-Jewry's political public itself) to constitute the community's nearest approximation to a communal "parliament"; the AJA — because even though it was a far less representative body, possessed a distinguished record of overseas intervention and intercession on behalf of foreign Jewries. The fact that debates at both forums were regularly and prominently reported in the Jewish press [10] further augmented their value as worthwhile prizes. Equally crucial was the consideration that it was the elected leaders of these two institutions who comprised the Conjoint Foreign Committee (after 1917, the Joint Foreign Committee), Anglo-Jewry's unofficial "cabinet" and the body which claimed the greatest authority to approach the British Government on matters of international Jewish concern. That is why such great significance was attached, in both cases, to the communal disavowal of the declared anti-Zionist postures adopted by that Committee. The "communal revolution" of World War I was said to have been accomplished on June 17th, 1917, when the Board of Deputies voted to censure the anti-Zionist *manifesto* which the Conjoint Foreign Committee had published in *The Times* some three weeks

8 16 December 1944, Bakstansky to A. Krausz, Bakstansky Mss., Central Zionist Archives, Jerusalem (hereafter CZA), F13/417.
9 Particularly on the anti-Zionist side; its most notable institutional platforms were (during World War I) the League of British Jews and (during World War II) the Jewish Fellowship.
10 Especially by the *Jewish Chronicle* which, when reporting debates at the Board, adopted the British parliamentary formula of adding a member's "constituency" to his name. On the importance of the *JC* as a source see: [C. Roth], *The Jewish Chronicle, 1841—1941* (London, 1941), p. 115.

earlier, and when the President of the Board, who had appended his signature to the *manifesto*, was therefore forced to resign his position. The "victory" of World War II was deemed to have been consummated when the Zionists "captured" the Board of Deputies at the triennal elections of June 1943, and then forced the Board to dissolve its conjoint foreign arrangement with the AJA at its next meeting (July 4, 1943).

II

It is tempting to view these two episodes as connected links in a single chain, and to plot them as rising points along an axis of linear Zionist progression within the Anglo-Jewish community. Such, indeed, is the impression conveyed in Paul Goodman's celebratory house-history: *Zionism in England, 1899–1949* (London, 1949). Basking in the aura of triumph induced by the fortuitous coincidence of both Israel's victory in her War of Independence and the jubilee of the foundation of the English Zionist Federation, Goodman's narrative paints a picture of a movement inexorably marching towards the threshold of communal power. In his account, therefore, the censure of the Conjoint Foreign Committee's *manifesto* in 1917 marked a significant stage in the "capture" of the Board by the Zionists. As such, it emerges as a fitting prologue to Selig Brodetsky's election to the Presidency of that body in 1939 and to Lavy Bakstansky's electoral triumph in 1943. The conclusion suggested by Goodman's analysis is that not only were the two episodes comparable in form, they were also — indeed, perhaps primarily — causal in connection. The victory of 1943 was in many ways built upon the foundations laid in 1917.

This, it will here be argued, was not the case. A closer examination of the two episodes suggests that, notwithstanding their structural similarities, they were substantively different. Indeed, to project them as in some way organically connected is to ignore the fact that they revolved around different axes and — as a result — led in different rather than in complementary directions. Most obviously is this so in terms of their respective impacts. The principal achievement of the censure of 1917 was *diplomatic*. As has often been pointed out, the vote at the Board of Deputies in that year radically altered the delicate balance of the triangular relationship which had hitherto prevailed between the British Government, the Zionists and the anti-Zionists. At the very least, it eased the path towards the Balfour Declaration.[11] In this (diplo-

11 See, e.g., Isaiah Friedman, *The Question of Palestine, 1914—1918* (London, 1973), p. 240: "With the *ancien régime* coming to an end, the Foreign Office was no longer bound by a previous commitment and could move freely towards a closer association with the Zionists." Also Leonard Stein, *The Balfour Declaration* (London, 1961), pp. 442–62.

matic) sphere, however, the communal rumpus of 1943–44 had no such effect. Proceedings at the Board neither dissuaded the Government from its recent restrictive course in mandatory Palestine, nor did it gain the Zionists a better hearing at Whitehall. (As late as 1948 Clement Attlee, the Prime Minister of the day, was to inform Brodetsky — as President of the Board of Deputies — that no "useful purpose can be served at present by our engaging in a correspondence which will necessarily be of a highly controversial nature, since I can agree neither with your view of events nor with your interpretation of the principles involved".[12])

Equally significant were the different *communal* impacts of the two episodes — an aspect of both cases on which recent research has generally tended to lavish less attention. Baldly stated, whilst the Deputies' vote of 1917 caused a communal haemorrhage, polarizing the community and crystallizing the warring factions, that of 1943 exerted a comparatively salutary influence. As much is indicated by the contrasting institutional dynamics of the two cases. Significantly, it was only *after* the Board's vote in 1917 that the two sides began in earnest to muster their communal battalions, with each initiating the bureaucratic procedures necessary to the furtherance of their campaigns. The anti-Zionists constituted themselves into a "League of British Jews"; the Zionists into a fully-fledged "party" at the Board of Deputies.[13] The row which erupted in 1943, by contrast, witnessed no such fissiparous process. Once the dust of the debate had been allowed to settle, the subject of Zionism virtually disappeared from the Anglo-Jewish agenda; Jewish nationalists were raised to the ranks of the celebrants of a communal consensus, with their opponents being relegated to the status of a bunch of die-hards wistfully recalling happier days. That is one reason why the conjoint foreign arrangement with the AJA (which remained imperviously anti-Zionist throughout) was not then renewed. In 1917, when the parties at the Board itself had been almost equally divided (the Conjoint Foreign Committee's *manifesto* had been censured at the Board by only 56 votes to 51, with 6 abstentions), some form of umbrella organization was obviously called for if the community was to avoid altogether the pitfall of organizational disarray. By 1944, however, such an outward sem-

12 2 June 1948, Attlee to Brodetsky, DEPS C11/12/53.
13 See, e.g., Sacher to S. Marks, 12 April 1918, Sacher Mss., CZA, Z4/120: "We must form a Zionist party with Whips and endeavour to fill every vacancy with Zionists.... My idea about the party is that it should quite definitely declare that its organisation is not intended to affect the ordinary work of the Board or to introduce any kind of party vote but to create an organisation which would secure proper representation in full force on the Board when Palestine and related questions come up for discussion."

blance of co-operation was deemed entirely unnecessary. Not even the anti-Zionists themselves called for the institutional representation of their point of view.[14]

These differences cannot be attributed solely to the mere passage of time (as is implied by Goodman's teleological reconstruction of events). Neither can they be adequately accounted for by reference to the wider — albeit more specific — changes which took place during the inter-war period in the sociological composition of Anglo-Jewry's first- and second-grade leadership.[15] To say that is not, of course, to deny that both influences did play some role in the process of communal change. Arguably, the former view might find some support in the steady — although by no means spectacular — growth of popular support for Zionism between 1917 and 1943.[16] The second view might be buttressed by reference to such managerial transformations as were indicated by the rise to prominence of the B'nai B'rith, the Jewish People's Council and the British section of the World Jewish Congress. But these instances, although important to an understanding of the differing general contexts of the episodes, do not contribute very much to our knowledge of the specific mechanics which determined their separate communal impacts. These, it is here argued, might better be explained by a specific examination of the characteristics and motives of the protagonists involved.

III

At this level of analysis, prominence must surely be given to the differences which obtained between the personalities who played the principal roles in the two struggles. First, the case of 1916–17: a reading of the public speeches and private writings of the parties in this period leaves an impression of a duel between groups of inveterate antagonists. Each side was convinced, not only that its own position was intrinsically correct and just, but also — perhaps even more so — that its conflict with the opposing faction brooked no possible compromise. That attitude was bluntly expressed by Harry Sacher, Ḥakham Moses Gaster and Leopold Greenberg (of the Zionists) and by Claude Montefiore, Lucien Wolf and Edwin Montagu (of the anti-Zionists). All were sharply intelligent men and yet, once they had made up their minds on the central Zionist issue, stubbornly obtuse in the retention of their views. If anything,

---

14   See, e.g., minutes of the AJA Palestine Committee, 26 July 1944, 27/6/lb3.
15   Most specifically in Redcliffe N. Salaman, "Whither Lucien Wolf's Anglo-Jewish Community?", *Lucien Wolf Memorial Lecture, 1953* (London, 1953).
16   Details of which are supplied by Goodman, *Zionism in England*, pp. 46—51, 65-7, 73-4.

the more they got to know about the opposing viewpoint, the more adamant and extreme became their own positions. Gaster — altogether a prickly character — supplies one example. Only half a dozen years before the outbreak of World War I he had been prepared to concede the anti-Zionist point that: "The struggle for Emancipation was not one between Jew and Gentile; it was between right and wrong, between liberty and persecution, for the position which a Jew occupied in any country was the touchstone of its moral conception and political elevation".[17] By 1915, however, when he had begun to negotiate with the anti-Zionist Conjoint Foreign Committee on behalf of the Zionists, he was writing (in a book of essays edited by Harry Sacher) that "the emancipated Jew is, and always must be, an alien in the land in which he dwells; his efforts to assimilate himself to his surroundings deceive nobody but himself".[18] Montefiore, one of the most forthright and intellectually talented spokesmen for the other side, moved to comparable extremes. His initial reaction to political Zionism had showed traces of patrician disdain: Herzl and his followers were simply misguided. Twenty years later, however, he was far more aggressive. The Zionists, he had convinced himself, "want to make all Gentiles anti-Semites. . . . I think the Conjoint will sooner or later have to consider whether we are to sit silent at the awful things which the Zionists print. That Sacher book is *too* bad. . . . Are we to allow our whole position and the whole case of emancipation to be ruined & given away?"[19] Montefiore himself had no doubt of the answer. Accordingly, he and Wolf took steps to have published (in the Gentile press) a tract which claimed that Jewish nationalism was "a very dangerous movement . . . which, unless checked, may hinder emancipation in countries where this emancipation is yet to seek, and even imperil its continuance . . . in countries where that emancipation has already been attained".[20]

The hostility of the tone which infused such statements did not remain the preserve of a few individuals. It permeated all public and private discourse,

---

17 Speech at the Commemorative Dinner of the Jubilee of Jewish Emancipation, 30 November 1908, *Transactions of the Jewish Historical Society of England*, Vol. VI (1912), p. 98.

18 M. Gaster, "Judaism — A National Religion", in *Zionism and the Jewish Future*, ed. Harry Sacher (London, 1916).

19 11 July 1916, Montefiore to Wolf, DEPS C11/2/3/9.

20 "Zionism", *Fortnightly Review*, Vol. 100 (November 1916), p. 820. Publication was arranged by Wolf; see his lengthy negotiations with the editorial board of the *Fortnightly* in DEPS C11/2/9. Montagu had similar things to say, albeit more privately, in his rebarbative Cabinet memorandum: "The Anti-Semitism of the Present Government"; see Friedman, *op. cit.*, pp. 259–60.

and thus precluded all attempts at an understanding between the two sides both before and after the publication of the Balfour Declaration in November 1917. What is more, the venomous climate thus created affected the judgement of men whose temperaments were usually more balanced, leading them to commit blunders which their sense of political judgement and good taste might otherwise have helped them to avoid. It is this which explains why Lucien Wolf, the *doyen* of the community's diplomats and a man who prided himself (usually with good reason) on his caution, committed at least two uncharacteristic howlers: in 1915 he was goaded into accusing all "foreign Jews" of being essentially unpatriotic, their support for Zionism being merely the complement of their refusal to register for conscription; in 1917 he was hurried into ignoring Lord Cecil's warning to consult with the Government before publishing the Conjoint Foreign Committee's *manifesto*.[21] The first move generated a groundswell of popular support for Zionism amongst the poorer sections of Anglo-Jewry; the second seriously affected Wolf's own standing in official circles. Together, they probably did more than any other two individual events to banish all hope of a constructive exchange between the Zionists and their opponents and to force them into a situation in which a show-down became virtually inevitable.

The Zionists, for their part, were similarly affected by the atmosphere of dissent and committed *faux pas* of almost equal proportions. Most obviously was this so in the cases of Weizmann and Sokolow, the two men usually considered to be the most astute of the contemporary Zionist negotiators. At the outbreak of World War I both had determinedly set their sights on scoring a diplomatic triumph for Zionism by allying the movement to Britain's imperial interests. Neither, accordingly, relished a communal confrontation (for which, in any case, they did not possess the time or stomach). That is why Weizmann, from the first, resisted suggestions that the Zionists somehow "put the screws" on the Conjoint Foreign Committee and why Sokolow, almost to the last, sought to reach some "working arrangement" with Lucien Wolf.[22] Notwithstanding the authority of both men, however, neither was able to remain unaffected by the tide of invective which swept all around them.

---

21 Wolf's remarks concerning "foreign" Jews were widely reported in the *JC*, 7 April 1916 and *Di Tsayt*, 6 April 1916. On Cecil's warning, Friedman, *op. cit.*, pp. 235–7. In general, F. Hardie and I. Hermann, *Britain and Zion: The Fateful Entanglement* (Belfast, 1980), p. 41.

22 29 November 1914, Weizmann to Sacher and Simon, *Letters and Papers of Chaim Weizmann* (General Editor, Meyer Weisgal), Vol. 7 (London, 1975), pp. 58–60; and Friedman, *op. cit.*, p. 230.

Accordingly, each was tempted (although Weizmann faster and more completely than Sokolow) into taking up communal positions which were really irrelevant to their main, diplomatic purposes — and sometimes at odds with them. Sokolow, who had previously avoided the Board of Deputies, ultimately posed as its "kingmaker", proposing to dispose of the body's Presidency to whichever of the Zionists he deigned to favour.[23] Weizmann had even earlier showed himself equally insensitive to the feelings of rank and file Deputies. In May 1917, on the eve of the crucial debate at the Board on the *manifesto*, he had gratuitously offered to give the B'nai B'rith "caucus" the benefit of his advice as to how they should vote.[24] Here too, both moves backfired. They created the impression that the Zionists were not appropriate candidates for communal authority but a group of irresponsible communal mavericks, prematurely seeking a degree of power for which they possessed neither the necessary personal qualifications nor the required institutional backing. Even if the majority of Deputies were ultimately prepared to vote against the "establishment", they were not in the process willing to become Zionist lackeys. Accordingly, and much to Zionism's disadvantage, in June 1917 they took pains to declare that their vote must not "be strained to represent support for the principles of the Zionist Organisation". Equally bluntly, they subsequently rejected any of the Presidential candidates suggested by Sokolow, electing instead Sir Stuart Samuel — whose opinions on Zionist matters were known to be lukewarm.[25]

IV

A comparable examination of the leading figures in the debates of 1943–44 reveals an entirely different spectrum of individual characteristics and institutional aims. If the men of World War I might be described as determined combatants, their successors of World War II give the impression of being reluctant opponents; where the former seem to have relished the slings and arrows of communal confrontation (however brutal the consequences), the latter fought shy of the prospect. To that end, they attempted to keep open various avenues of communication, and thus to delay for longer than had once seemed possible a recurrence of the divisions which had been so flagrantly precipitated during the stormy days of 1916–17.

To say that is not to deny that spirits similar to those of World War I were

---

23 e.g. 4 July 1917, Sokolow to Lord Walter Rothschild, CZA, Z4/117.
24 Discussed in my: *English Zionists and British Jews: The Communal Politics of Anglo-Jewry, 1895–1920* (Princeton, 1982), pp. 274–5.
25 Ibid., pp. 292–3.

also abroad during World War II. On the anti-Zionist side, reference might be made for instance to the inveterate views and uncompromising actions of such men as Leonard Montefiore (Claude's son), Sir Robert Waley Cohen (the authoritarian President of the United Synagogue), and Neville Laski (Brodetsky's immediate predecessor as President of the Board of Deputies). Each of these members of the Anglo-Jewish establishment had declared his anti-Zionism before the outbreak of war; all reiterated their opinions during its course. By 1940, at the latest, they had together helped to draft an anti-nationalist statement which was to form the basis for the AJA's memorandum to the Government in 1944.[26] Even earlier (in 1939), they had persuaded Anthony de Rothschild to use his influence to block Brodetsky's candidacy for the Presidency of the Board of Deputies ("are [you] satisfied that he will have sufficient time at his disposal adequately to carry out such duties as fall to the lot of the President of the Board of Deputies. . . is [he] generally suited to take up that kind of work? Has he got sufficient knowledge and experience of the different aspects of communal life in this country or has he not rather concentrated his abilities in other directions?").[27] Even as late as 1944, by which time there could be no doubt of the extent of Zionism's hold on the popular Anglo-Jewish imagination, they were to insist on the necessity for the public expression of the opposite point of view; to that end they employed whatever resources they could muster within the framework of the anti-Zionist Jewish Fellowship.[28]

Some of the Zionists were similarly belligerent. Principally this was because they were led by a man of the calibre of Lavy Bakstansky, the General Secretary of the Zionist Federation. Altogether, Bakstansky could be frightening. His quick clear mind, staccato speech, decisive and forceful manner and steely determination to press home the interests of Zionism (as he understood them) overwhelmed whoever he dealt with — colleagues as well as opponents, nominal superiors as well as subordinates. The brain behind Brodetsky's presidential campaign in 1939, Bakstansky had directed his fellow Zionists to portray that incident as a tussle between two social classes, and not merely a clash of ideologies ("We shall fight this contest, and once and for all, the Anglo-Jewish democracy will make it clear. . . that we are no longer prepared to be governed by a clique from above.").[29] It was once that particular hurdle had been successfully negotiated that Bakstansky implemented the

26 See "Secret" minutes of meeting held at New Court, 9 September 1941, WA.
27 Anthony de Rothschild to Weizmann, 1 December 1939, ibid.
28 See, e.g., L. Montefiore's memorandum dated 12 July 1944, in AJ 37/6.
29 8 December 1939, circular (signed by S. Temkin of the Public Relations Committee of the Zionist Federation), S. Brodetsky Mss., CZA 182/9 (1).

remaining portions of his campaign to capture the Board in its entirety. The strict organization of the Zionist "Group" of Deputies; the electoral victory of 1943; the disavowal of the conjoint foreign arrangement with the AJA thereafter — all were based on the underlying premise that it was impossible "to persuade the AJA leaders to hold their hand or refrain from doing us harm. . . . On the basis of my personal knowledge of these people, many of whom are honestly convinced of the soundness of their views, I am certain in my mind that the opposition of these people to the Jewish State is so profound and so extreme that they will stop nowhere in their determination to prevent it from coming into being".[30]

It is difficult to avoid the feeling that, had they been left to their own devices, the factions represented by Bakstansky on the one side and Waley Cohen on the other might have repeated in 1943–44 some of the mistakes committed in 1916–17. That they did not do so must be attributed to the restraining influence exerted on the two sides by, respectively, Selig Brodetsky and Leonard Stein. It was they who injected into the World War II situation a brand of moderation and clear-headedness which had been lacking during World War I, and thus prevented a recurrence of the communal divisiveness which had characterized the earlier crisis.

Although Brodetsky and Stein stood on different sides of the ideological fence, they deserve to be treated in tandem — principally because they had so much else in common. Both had received an excellent education (Brodetsky, a Cambridge graduate, was Professor of Applied Mathematics at Leeds University; Stein, an Oxonian, was by profession a barrister); both had served their communal apprenticeships during the difficult inter-war years; and both had only recently (1939) been elected to their positions as Presidents of, respectively, the Board of Deputies and the AJA. These were commonalities which overrode the obvious differences in their social backgrounds (Brodetsky, who had come with his parents to the East End of London from Oliviopol in the Ukraine at the age of five, had a very different upbringing from Stein, who had been born into a native British middle-class family). From the perspective of communal management, what was important was that both men viewed and dealt with the numerous and extensive problems facing world-wide Jewry throughout the war in a remarkably similar manner. That is why they were able to establish the sort of personal *rapport* which had been so notably absent from the relationships between the antagonists of 1916–17. Their discussions, both agreed, "took place in an atmosphere of mutual respect and

30 15 September 1943, Bakstansky to Brodetsky, private and confidential, Brodetsky Mss., Mocatta Library, London.

goodwill . . . there was an endeavour by give and take to arrive at constructive suggestions".[31]

Fundamental to the attitudes adopted by both men in 1943–44 was the determination to avoid some of the worst excesses of 1916–17. Not surprisingly, therefore, references to the earlier crisis and its debilitating effects are scattered throughout their speeches and writings. They recalled the episode constantly, always harping on its structural damage rather than its ideological overtones.[32] Neither, of course, was prepared to renounce his own allegiance. Brodetsky, an active and prominent Zionist since his undergraduate days, remained a convinced Jewish nationalist wholeheartedly supporting (with only occasional lapses) the call for the establishment of a Jewish State.[33] This was a prospect which Stein adamantly opposed. Although a moderate Jewish nationalist in his youth, he had gradually changed his stance, objecting as much to the intemperate behaviour of the Zionists in communal matters as to the extent of their political ambitions in Palestine. Nevertheless, with the outbreak of World War II, both men had evinced a sincere desire to suspend their differences over such questions in an attempt to seek a common communal platform on a wider front. As Brodetsky informed his own colleagues, the catastrophic proportions of Jewry's contemporary crisis left them with little choice:

> It is all the more necessary that nothing shall be done which can only produce artificial separation in the community, with consequent harm to any efforts that might be made in connection with Jewish objects. I quite agree with you and Harry [Sacher], Bakstansky and others that the overwhelming view among the Jews of this country is in favour of our attitude and would be delighted to see activities undertaken without the obstacles presented in the past. I am not sure that the election of

31 6 November 1944, Brodetsky to Stein, DEPS B4/11. Brodetsky's personal esteem for Stein is also apparent in his *Memoirs: From Ghetto to Israel* (London, 1960), pp. 224–32, *passim*.

32 E.g. 1 April 1940, Brodetsky to Weizmann, WA and his "Confidential Statement" to the Zionist caucus on 8 December 1943, Brodetsky Mss.; also 8 July 1944, Stein to Brodetsky, DEPS B4/11.

33 One such lapse in his memorandum on "The Jewish Problem" to the League of Nations Union (dated 31 August 1942). Carefully side-stepping the issue of Jewish statehood, Brodetsky merely stated: "In the first place, the Jews have constructed their own economic life there, and rebuilt what may be described as the foundations of their national existence; in the second place, a great Jewish population in Palestine can be an effective means of the rehabilitation of the Middle East as a whole." (p. 11); Bakstansky Mss., CZA, F13/369(1).

officers in accordance with the desire of the Zionist group will be of real help, because I believe that the exclusion of the assimilationist group will make the success of the work more difficult. . . . You will understand that I look upon this matter not only from the point of view of a party, but from the point of view of responsibility for effort, and, if possible, achievement.[34]

It was with such thoughts in mind that Brodetsky both rejected many of Bakstansky's more flamboyantly aggressive initiatives, and deliberately launched some of his own. His part in initiating a series of round-table talks between the Zionists and anti-Zionists as early as 1940[35] was, in this respect, particularly noteworthy. So, too, were his persistent efforts — even after the Board had in 1943 voted to dissolve the conjoint foreign arrangement with the AJA — to keep open possible lines of communication with that body.[36] In terms of tactics, neither move served its purpose: no common communal platform with regard to Palestine was constructed, and the Board and the AJA eventually had to go their separate ways. But as a means of ensuring that the breach within the community should be contained within limited proportions — an end which, to Brodetsky's mind, had to be defined in terms of strategy — they undoubtedly must be considered successes.

For one thing, they helped to generate a remarkable degree of personal respect for Brodetsky amongst even the most inveterate anti-Zionists (as Waley Cohen put it: "Although I feel that owing to inexperience you have made a good many mistakes as President of the Board, nevertheless I do recognise the immense effort that you make to be fair to that large body in the Community who do not share your outlook on many political subjects that affect the Community").[37] What is more, they also contributed towards the prevalence of counsels of moderation within the anti-Zionist camp. Stein, in particular, responded with notable alacrity and whole-heartedness. He, too, sought an institutional arrangement which might "unite instead of splitting the com-

---

34   30 June 1943, Brodetsky to S. Marks, Brodetsky Mss.
35   23 June 1943, Brodetsky to Bakstansky, ibid.
36   On the 1940 initiative see 8 September 1940, Brodetsky to Weizmann, WA: on the later negotiations see the minutes of the "Consultations between representatives of the Foreign Affairs Committee of the Board and the A.J.A." in DEPS C11/1/7 and C11/1/9.
37   19 November 1942, Waley Cohen to Brodetsky, DEPS C11/7/3a/2. There were, however, limits: "There is no doubt in anyone's mind as to your own complete good faith — no one questions it. But equal confidence is, quite frankly, not felt in the [Zionist] caucus or ex-caucus group." 29 September 1943, Stein to Brodetsky, private, DEPS B4/10.

munity". Promising that he, at least, would "stand firm against anyone who may be spoiling for a fight" at the AJA, he was even prepared to enlist the help of Chaim Weizmann.[38] As late as November 1944 (by which time all hopes of a compromise on the political aspects of Zionism had receded) Stein attempted to convince both sides that their differences could henceforth be kept within reasonable bounds. Not even the publication of an anti-Zionist memorandum by the AJA need alter the situation. On the contrary, that document — he argued —

> was meant sincerely and in complete good faith to make it clear that the A.J.A., far from being lukewarm or indifferent about Jewish aspirations in Palestine, was warmly and actively sympathetic, and that the support which in 1917 was lacking in the circles represented by the A.J.A. was this time forthcoming in full measure. Believing, as I did, that in this way a service of some value could be rendered to the Jewish cause in Palestine, I took it for granted that a statement going so far in the direction you would desire would be regarded with satisfaction in Zionist circles, and warmly welcomed. I am most anxious that any misunderstanding which may exist should be dispelled.[39]

V

Ultimately, this is precisely what occurred. The Zionists did not, as Bakstansky had intended, conquer the community; rather, and as Brodetsky had hoped, it was Anglo-Jewry which conquered the Zionists.[40] Their enthusiasms, their energies and their organizational abilities (not the least of which was their persistent ability to raise enormous sums of money) were harnessed to other communal causes — in all of which the older patrician families continued to constitute essential vertebrae.[41] The benefits were mutual. On the one hand,

---

38 4 September 1944, Stein to Brodetsky, DEPS B4/11; no less significant is the fact that Weizmann accepted the invitation to address the AJA; see correspondence between Weizmann and Stein in April and September 1944 in WA.

39 5 November 1944, Stein to Weizmann, WA.

40 Compare Gideon Shimoni, "Selig Brodetsky and the Ascendancy of Zionism in Anglo-Jewry (1939–1945)", *Jewish Journal of Sociology*, Vol. XXII (2), 1981; and my "Selig Brodetsky and the Ascendancy of Zionism in Anglo-Jewry: Another View of his Role and Achievements," ibid., Vol. XXIV(1), 1982.

41 Thus, as late as 1955, it was possible to write: "Notwithstanding the status revolt symbolised by the change in power in the Board of Deputies, the old elite is still highly esteemed — for the part which they *do* play in the community, for their family status, and for their anglicised behaviour. Association with them is an active object of social aspiration." Howard M. Brotz, "The Outline of Jewish Society in London", in *A Minority in Britain*, ed. Maurice Freedman (London, 1955), p. 159.

Zionism became an acceptable component of the communal ethos, with the State of Israel benefiting (almost from the moment of its foundation) from the support of erstwhile antagonists as well as veteran enthusiasts. On the other hand, the Zionists were goaded into grasping the nettle of overall communal management, and in the process were themselves transformed into integral components of the class of communal leadership against which they had at one stage threatened to wield an ideological hatchet.

It was in this respect that the events of 1943–44 can be seen — over the long haul — to have benefited Anglo-Jewry in its entirety. They blended what had previously been rival factions into a composite (although not monolithic) society, whose leaders could perform their functions in relative harmony, whatever the residual difference in their basic philosophical assumptions. This was a substantial achievement, whose magnitude gains in force from a comparison with the aftermath of the events of 1916–17. Ultimately, it has here been argued, the differences in the two cases did not simply happen — they were fashioned. What is more, they were fashioned in accordance with the vagaries of personality. Gaster and Montefiore cannot bear sole responsibility for the fierce polemical assertiveness which so divided the community during and after World War I; neither, conversely, can Stein and Brodetsky be given exclusive credit for the recuperative repercussions of the comparable clashes of World War II. What has to be recognized, however, is that in the last analysis it was the individual contributions of these men which eventually determined the different textures of two conflicts which in other essentials were very much alike.

DAVID VITAL

THE AFFLICTIONS OF THE JEWS AND THE AFFLICTIONS
OF ZIONISM

THE MEANING AND CONSEQUENCES OF THE
"UGANDA" CONTROVERSY *

Whereas much in the history of the Jews is familiar and repetitive and much —
perhaps most things — fall into some sort of pattern or order, the advent of
modern, especially political Zionism represents a departure. Whatever the
future may hold for us in this country, it is surely evident that the condition
of the Jews as a collectivity — even, to be more precise, as a *set* of collectivi-
ties — has been transformed by the enlargement and consolidation of the
bridgehead established here 100 years ago and its equipment, in due course,
with the accoutrements and instruments of a fully-fledged state. It is therefore
in some sense ungenerous, in some ways unfeeling, to subject this extraordinary and dramatic and, indeed, triumphant change in the national condition to the sort of scrutiny which lesser topics by far are subjected by
students of history and society. And yet . . .

Bertrand Russell once said of the younger members of his family that,
having been born after 1914, they were incapable of "happiness". We may
say of ourselves that after 1945 we are incapable of happiness in something
like Russell's sense. Specifically, it is difficult to celebrate 100 years of Zionism
and the new *yishuv* without the nagging thought that somehow, somewhere
along the line, to some extent, the Zionists failed the people for whom they
claimed to speak. For after all, political independence came too late for the
majority of those Jews who would have been the first not only to enjoy but
to *need* it.

Of course, to speak thus of "people" and of the leaders of a movement —
any people, any movement — is to raise not only painful, but very difficult
questions. What might be the precise degree of responsibility the latter may

---

* This paper was originally read at a conference on "100 Years of Zionism" at Tel-
Aviv University (21–24 December 1981). An earlier version appeared (in Hebrew)
in *Ha-Tzionut: Me-Asef*, Vol. 9 (1984), pp. 9–20.

be said to bear for the former? To what extent can they be said to have been free to choose and act in the face of the great forces and events which were imperfectly understood at the time, yet overpowering in their immediate psychological and material impact? Still, the fact is that most great topics in recent Jewish history are necessarily discussed under the shadow of the wartime destruction of European Jewry; and the Zionist movement, its rise, development, and recent decline, cannot be an exception.

However, the question to which I wish to address myself here and now is of a somewhat different order from those to which I have just alluded. It concerns neither the moral right of the Zionists — specifically the Zionist leadership — to speak and act for some or all of the Jewish people; nor their deeds or misdeeds, their wisdom or otherwise, the validity or failure of their tactics. I am concerned rather with the frame of mind and the fundamental perspective in which the dominant strain within the Zionist movement, from its inception, tended to perceive the world and the place of Jewry within it: not with policy directly, but with what they conceived to be the proper order of priorities which should inform them in their formulation of policy. And my thesis is a simple one. It is that the matter was settled at a very early stage in the history of the movement. The debate on the ultimate purpose of the movement — whether it was to concern itself primarily with the Jews as living *individuals*, men, women and children, or with the Jewish people as a *collectivity* and with Judaism (whatever that might be taken to mean) as a culture — was held very early and settled firmly in favour of the latter with two crucial, interconnected, long-lasting results. Zionism as a rescue operation was diminished in favour of Zionism as national reconstruction in a particular way and a particular place; and what under one dispensation were seen — or could be seen — as tactical purposes, took on the aspect of absolute purposes under the other.

But before going on to show how ideology and policy came to be connected in practice and with what results, let me, by way of making clear what I have in mind, cite one, not very important, but suggestive example of official Zionist thinking in practice on the interconnection between Zionist policy and the fate of European Jewry in occupied Europe during the Second World War.

On September 13, 1944, a senior, accredited representative of the Zionist movement called at the State Department in Washington to meet members of its Near Eastern Affairs staff. The official, secret "memorandum of conversation" as recorded by the Department and relayed to American diplomatic and consular representatives in Cairo, Baghdad, Beirut, Damascus, Jedda, Jerusalem and London, was headed "Zionist Attitude toward Palestine". It reported *inter alia* two references to the rescue of Jews in occupied Europe which retain some interest today — although less for any practical effect the conversation may have had on either American or Zionist policy at the time, than for the *approach* underlying them. It is with the approach, the philosophy, if you will, that I am concerned — and that I am bound to emphasize. The first reference was to a proposal, then before the Congress, that temporary emergency shelters for Jews from Hungary be established in Palestine. The Zionist representative made it clear that he did not think much of it, partly because he distrusted the motives of those who had persuaded members of the Congress to put it forward and partly because he did not think Jews could succeed in escaping from Hungary anyway. But "in any case", he went on to say, "the Zionists were opposed to any scheme which would seek to place Jews in Palestine only temporarily and on the understanding that they would be sent elsewhere after the war".

The second reference was to the argument current at the time between the Colonial Office and the Jewish Agency on the final disposition of the 15,000 immigration certificates that still remained to be allocated under the terms of the 1939 White Paper. The Jewish representative had this to say (and I quote again from the State Department record of the conversation):

> The Colonial Office took the line that preference in the issuance of certificates should be given to those Jews, i.e. those in occupied Europe, who were in imminent danger of death. [However, while] the Jewish Agency could not deny the priority to which such persons were entitled ... it had argued that some provision should also be made for potential immigrants in such "safe" areas as Italy, North Africa and the Yemen.

The handwritten comments in the margin of the document [1] suggest that our representative's American audience could hardly believe their ears. But once again it is not my present purpose to discuss, or even to criticize, the political strategy and rationale that underlay such an extraordinary view of what the Jewish national interest required even so late in the war as September 1944. It is enough that it was so conceived and articulated and not in some confidential conversation at the State Department alone. What matters is its source, by which I mean the point in its history at which the Zionist movement — unwittingly — was set upon a course that should have led to such a position being taken and articulated in the first place.

---

1   Department of State, Near Eastern Affairs, Memorandum of Conversation, 13 September 1944.

Now it is, I think, beginning to be recognized that the point in time at which, in fact, such a course came to be set was in the immediate aftermath of what the textbooks still call "the Uganda affair". For the outcome of that great quarrel was the defeat of Herzl and his followers at the hands of what may be termed the "Hibbat Zion faction" in the movement. In a general way the argument may not be new, even if it remains unpopular. In any event, I want to go well beyond the simple — and, if I may say, vulgar — proposition that a certain, small part of modern Kenya could have been an effective substitute for Erez-Israel. What really mattered in 1903–05 and what remains of interest today are the ideological and conceptual differences between the two schools of thought, such that one school was willing, however reluctantly, at least to consider the East Africa project while the other dismissed it out of hand as a matter of absolute principle.[2] For what principle or principles were really at stake here? Was the debate only about territory: Erez-Israel, for or against? I think not. I shall try to show, at least in outline, that it ran far deeper and is not quite dead even today when the specifically territorial question has long been forgotten except as a curiosity of our recent past.

It may be said of the debate on the East Africa project as it proceeded within the Zionist movement from its beginning in the summer of 1903 to its formal conclusion some two years later that it was in every sense of the term *political*. On the one hand it reflected a struggle for leadership and authority. On the other hand, when all the surface layers of the quarrel have been allowed for — the genuine differences on strategy, the play of personalities and temperament, the private hurts, grudges and jealousies, the competition for place and influence, and the friction that could not but arise between men of different culture and social experience — there was here a clash of ideologies, of conflicting principles and incompatible prescriptions for the ills of Jewry. But far from mitigating the debate on ideology, the political fight for supremacy in the movement only intensified it — no doubt because in these, the formative years of the Zionist movement, ideology was all. The movement had no *material* power; it was a voluntary association within the larger society of Jewry that was itself devoid of any but the most tenuous centres of formal and truly enforceable authority. The influence and moral authority of Zionism were therefore functions of its power to move men's minds; and the source of such power as it had turned on the force and conviction carried by its

---

2 The crisis precipitated by the British East Africa proposal of 1903 and some other topics sketched in this article are discussed in detail in the present writer's *Zionism: The Formative Years* (Oxford, Clarendon Press, 1982).

doctrines. But its doctrines were (and have remained) very imperfectly defined. The Jewish national revival was devoid of figures comparable to, say, John Locke, or the American Federalists Hamilton, Madison and Jay; it had no great doctrinaire historian like Macaulay, no social and political theoretician of the quality of, say, Pareto — let alone Marx. The Zionists, it may be said, articulated their doctrine by stages, by trial and error, by periodic debate on matters of practical policy in so far as, and provided that, these forced them to consider fundamentals. And the unspoken rule was that action taken or action proposed led to the consideration and formulation of doctrine rather than that consideration of doctrine led to the taking of action. Hence the importance of this, perhaps the greatest of the movement's debates.

No doubt, on some points there was full agreement: that the Emancipation had failed to liberate the Jews; that, accordingly, the course of Jewish history must be reversed; that the *rule* of Exile must be ended and the Diaspora — all or most of it — wound up; and that, finally, by the setting apart of a defined territory into which the Jews would gather as a majority people, they would begin to govern themselves. This much was common ground for virtually all Zionists; this was the message and the prospect which they held out to their actual and potential adherents; and to argue otherwise was simply to put oneself outside any recognizable class of Zionists at all.

But these were very general propositions and, in practice, there were different schools, each with its distinct interpretation, none capable of squaring its differences with the others or redefining the common ground so as to minimize them. They could only fight their differences out, or suppress the intramural argument in the common interest, or retire. But to fight, in such circumstances, was to fight to win; and to win support for a particular interpretation of the common programme or for a particular strategy for making that programme effective was, in effect, to win the leadership of the movement. This was what leadership of the movement *meant*; and there was no other way of winning it.

Two linked questions had always been at issue and were to the fore throughout the debate on East Africa; what was the true and desirable relationship between the Jewish people and other nations; and what was the true and desirable relationship between the Jews and their own historic past? The starting point for the Zionists' view of these matters had been the question of the *individual* Jew and on this there had indeed been loose agreement all along. Thus, all Zionists rejected assimilation — in part because it carried with it the taint of surrender and self-abnegation, but more significantly on the pragmatic grounds that the painless, lasting, and self-induced absorption of Jews in large numbers into the surrounding population was simply not feasible. But so far as what might be termed the *collective* assimilation of the Jews was concerned, namely, the absorption (or re-absorption) of the Jewish people as a whole and as such into the society of nations, the terms on which it would take place, and the problems it would raise, matters were otherwise. There was no clear or authorized doctrine here; nor had there been, except rarely, explicit recognition that there was here an issue with which the movement was properly concerned. Least of all was there anything like consensus.

Broadly, there were two schools of thought and their classic exponents were those two somewhat eccentric figures on the institutional fringes of the movement, Zangwill and Ahad Ha-'Am. Strikingly different in background and views, they had this in common that both were intellectuals of independent mind and independent prestige, whose thinking revolved consistently around general, relatively abstract categories, and who granted or withheld their support in the fulfilment of solemn acts of moral and social judgement. Herzl and his closest followers — Zangwill among them — had always taken it as a matter of course that Zionism would bring peace between the Jews and other peoples. The Jews would enter the ranks of the nations on a basis of equality and benefit for all. Like Pinsker before them, they had seen no reason to reject the non-Jewish world *as such*. Their criticism of non-Jewish society had been precipitated by, and then been formulated in, the particular contemporary context of the disastrous relations between it and the Jews. But the brunt of their social and cultural criticism was directed *inwards* at Jewry itself. And the particular force and originality of what Pinsker and Herzl and, later, Zangwill had to say, lay in the combination of these two logically distinct strains of criticism: for they argued for radical and linked changes both in the relations between Jewry and other societies and in the structure and nature of Jewish society itself. Indeed, their primary reference all the while was rather to society at large, as they understood it, than to Jewry or Judaism. Ahad Ha-'Am had good cause therefore to pounce on Herzl's fantasy *Altneuland*, and dismiss it on the grounds that there was nothing immediately recognizable as *Jewish* in it. Indeed there was not. If anything, it was Viennese. *Altneuland* was poor literature: crudely constructed, of wooden characterization, psychologically superficial. It was also politically and sociologically naive. It will be recalled, for example, that the immensely complex matter of the interconnection between Jewish religious orthodoxy and Zionism as the champion of a Jewish national political renewal is disposed of in four brief sentences: "The New Society was the last to favour obscurantism among its people", Herzl wrote, "even though everyone was allowed his own opinions. Questions of faith were definitely excluded from all influence in public affairs. Whether you prayed in a synagogue, a church, or a mosque, in a museum or at a philharmonic concert — it was all one to the New Society. How you sought to get in touch with the Eternal was your own affair".[3] What emerges most clearly, in any case, is that *Altneuland* is represented as a *new* society, one which had broken away from tradition, one in which the Jews are at last a people like other peoples in all significant respects, and in which the newly gained territorial concentration and political autonomy are the basis for an internal social revolution. And it is this which permits their collective assimilation into the general society of nations on terms of equality and no greater specificity than is commonly tolerated and generally understood by all its other members.

Of course, nothing could be further from this than the ancient and profoundly ingrained notion of the uniqueness of the Jews: of their being a people eternally set apart and of their being a people dedicated to the preservation of their special character and role as a matter of first principle and above all else. It is true that in Herzl himself and in those who modelled themselves after him most closely there is a certain ambivalence from time to time on this point, a lack of ease. Every so often there is a relapse, so to speak, into the set and traditional mode of thought in which particularity and specificity are celebrated as a matter of course.

In Zangwill, however, a man free of the political pressures to which Herzl was subject and more than anxious to follow his private inclinations wherever they might lead him and to set out his views in the clearest language of which he was capable, there is no ambiguity at all, and no reluctance to make a break from the traditional mode of thought. After Herzl's death, as the retreat from Herzl's positions gathered speed and force, Zangwill tried hard to block it. His starting point, as always with the Pinsker-Herzlian school, was the current scene, what he called "the vital needs of the masses of the Jewish people at the present time", the gross inadequacy of such machinery as existed for alleviating it and for dealing with the great stream of Jewish migrants from Russia, and the inappropriateness of customary attitudes to the problem. Except that the pain and gloom which infuse Pinsker's *Autoemancipation*, which the Territorialist manifesto so greatly resembles in its approach, are replaced by a note, deliberately struck, of brisk and even cheerful pragmatism. Territorialism, Zangwill proclaims, is "business-like in anticipation of the inevitable".[4] Again, unlike the more circumspect Pinsker and Herzl there is, in Zangwill, along with the pragmatism, a great undisguised impatience with the hopeless conservatism, the pathetic absurdities, the internal contradictions, the humiliations — in a word, with the failure of Jewish life, public and private. "It is eighteen hundred

---

3 *Altneuland*, part V, chapter 2.
4 M. Simon (ed.), *Speeches, Articles and Letters of Israel Zangwill* (London, 1937), pp. 231–233.

and thirty-five years since we lost our fatherland, and the period of mourning should be about over", Zangwill told his listeners when he launched his movement. "We have either got to reconcile ourselves to our loss or set about recovering it. But to choose clearly between one alternative or the other is a faculty the Jew has lost".[5] There followed a renewed plea for Zionism; and all Herzl's main arguments were rehearsed, except that since Erez-Israel was unobtainable and, on the other hand, "Zion without Zionism" (that is, a return to the small-scale methods and the humble purposes of Hibbat Zion) "is a hollow mockery", then "better Zionism without Zion". Better, said Zangwill, "a Provisional Palestine". "Any territory which was Jewish, (and) under a Jewish flag", he believed, "would save the Jew's body and the Jew's soul".[6]

Now it is plain that what Zangwill was after was not so much the end of the Jewish people, once and for all, even with dignity preserved, at high noon and with church bells ringing, as in Herzl's celebrated first fantasy, as the end of Jewry as a Peculiar People. If elements of the past could be preserved without too much trouble and, above all, without impeding progress towards Redemption through Normalcy, as it might be termed, well and good. On the other hand, whatever threatened to impede such progress had to be jettisoned; and this sloughing-off of ancient burdens could be done, he thought, with a good conscience, to say nothing of some unjustified relief. It is precisely this that the other school denied.

For the opposing school of thought these ancient burdens — the past itself — were, on the contrary, of the essence, central and indispensable to their national feeling. Perhaps not *all* of it was to be preserved *intact*. Here these Zionists, like all others, took their distance from the entirely wholehearted and uncompromising traditionalists of Jewish religious orthodoxy. Further, on what precisely was to be retained and what modified or discarded they were themselves divided when not merely vague. "We remain [in the movement] to defend Zionism", wrote Yizhak Gruenbaum in a typical protest against the Herzlian approach: "Not the Zionism of diplomacy and charity for the impoverished of the East, but the Zionism that is the full renaissance of the Jewish people in Erez-Israel".[7] But what was to become of the Jews of eastern Europe meanwhile if they were not to be the subject of what he called "charity", and just what "full renaissance" was to mean he did not (and perhaps could not) say. In any event, what *united* the anti-Herzlians was that they all thought that

---

5   Ibid., p. 198.

6   Ibid., p. 212.

7   Itshak Gruenbaum, *Dor be-Mivḥan* (Jerusalem, 1951), p. 36.

continuity was crucial. The Jewish society at which they aimed, however vague
and ill-focused their picture of it, had to contain within it the major elements
of the Jewish heritage — language, culture, history and (with reservations)
faith. Like the Herzlians, they wanted to reform Jewry and alter the Jewish
condition; but the target that presented itself to them was the Diaspora which
they distinguished in their minds from Jewry and Judaism in some proper,
unencumbered, pristine state. The Herzlians compared Jews and non-Jews.
The anti-Herzlians compared modern Jews with Jews in some former or some
ideal condition. They were nothing if not romantics. The original Odessa Lov-
ers of Zion, the Ahad Ha-'Amist moralists, the Ussishkinite settlement-first
men and the other sub-categories of the genus, each group in its way, were all
creatures of the *haskalah*. All looked forward to a reform of the Jewish condition, but at the same time backward for the elements out of which to recon-
struct it. And since the return to the cultivation of land was an essential part
of their prescription for the restoration of social health in the future, and the
Land of Israel specifically was of course central to past Jewish history and
belief, they ended by seeing Erez-Israel as the pivot on which all would turn.
To do without it was to lose an indispensable source of strength, a force for
renewal as powerful as it was indefinable.

Certainly there were difficulties. The true Zionists had always known, wrote
Ahad Ha-'Am, that the enterprise on which they had embarked would take
generations to accomplish and that they could only approach their target very
slowly and gradually. All true Zionists, Ahad Ha-'Am argued, "stood on a
common, rock-solid base: belief in the power of the historic bond between
the people and the land to reawaken our people to *self-recognition* and to stir
them to fight for strength until such time as the conditions necessary for their
free development had been established".[8] And this, of course, was why they
had never had any interest in plans to resettle the Jews elsewhere. However,
what had happened in 1903, Ahad Ha-'Am argued, was that Herzl and the
"politicals" had bemused the true Zionists by holding out the prospect of the
end being attained with speed, with relatively little effort or preliminary
preparation, but rather by a single, great and adventurous leap. The "politicals", who seemed to think that a nation-state for the Jews could be established
anywhere if only the necessary land and rights were available, might indeed
be proper Jews, perhaps even proper nationalists, but they could not be *Zionists*. Not, that is, in his sense of the term.

We can see, therefore, that in both schools' thinking diagnosis and prescription were inextricable. If you were prepared to "manage . . . affairs slowly" in

---

8   'Ha-Bokhim', *Kol Kitvei Ahad Ha-'Am* (Jerusalem, 1951), p. 337.

Ahad Ha-'Am's Hibbat Zion manner, and give the *yishuv* in Erez-Israel all the time it needed to develop organically; and if, above all, you accepted with more or less equanimity that the immediate, material problems of the bulk of Jewry could only be alleviated by other, i.e. non-Zionist, non-territorial means and *elsewhere*, i.e. in the Diaspora itself — then the proper concerns of the Zionists did, and not unreasonably, boil down to care for a small, very superior community in Erez-Israel, whose essential role within the nation was educative and inspirational, an example, rather than an instrument; and then the East African (or any other "territorialist") project was an obvious monstrosity, a perversion of the original ideas. And therefore, in practice, the effect on this school of the dramatic renewal of the pogroms in 1903 was less to spur them to a greater effort to rescue Russo-Polish Jewry, than to induce *concern* lest the Herzlians seek at all costs to "hasten the end".

And indeed the fact was that the hard-pressed Jews of eastern Europe themselves, and the rank and file of the movement among them, were *not* disposed to wait. They did wish to "hasten the end". They did believe — at all events, and as Ahad Ha-'Am and most of his disciples had always recognized, they *wished* to believe — in "a speedy Salvation" (*yeshu'ah kerovah*). And they had been drawn to Herzl because he appeared to offer — and manifestly he was working for — a rapid release for them from their intolerable situation.[9] The fundamental diagnostic question, therefore, was whether their situation allowed for delay. Just how intolerable was the present condition of the great mass of east European Jewry; and how intolerable was it likely to become in any foreseeable, let alone distant future? How *urgent* was the treatment? On this the followers of Herzl and Zangwill on the one hand, and the followers of Ahad Ha-'Am and Ussishkin on the other, were profoundly divided. It was this part-ideological, part-diagnostic issue that lay at the heart of the great debate — along with one other.

The two schools were as deeply divided in their fundamental approach to Jewish public policy. For Herzl and Zangwill and their school the question of what could constitute correct public policy for the Jews was an open one. It was not predetermined in any fundamental way, certainly not by the past. Herzl, in this respect, was somewhat less firm than Zangwill. He was more in awe of the past, more fearful of the inestimable, revolutionary consequences of cutting the historic umbilical cord, and more sensitive to the sensibilities of others on all these scores. Zangwill, as has been suggested, was less concerned about the inner life of the Jews, less repelled or intimidated by the imperfectly understood life and culture of the gentiles and, because even more

9   Letter to Bernfeld, 8 March 1899. *Igrot Ahad Ha-'Am* (Jerusalem, 1925), ii, p. 250.

offended than Herzl by the dualities and timidities which life in the Diaspora entailed, more anxious to break free of them, once and for all, and at whatever the cost. But for both tendencies, the moderate Herzlian and the radical Zangwillian, within what might be called the ultra-revolutionary party in Zionism, a great deal turned on what might and might not be accomplished in actual practice. And it was decisive for their attitude to the tradition. The tradition had its undeniable value, but, in their view, it was not to preserve the tradition, even a modified tradition, that the Zionists had formed their movement; and therefore it could not be made the touchstone, let alone the cornerstone, of policy. For if one did so, in the manner the anti-Herzlians had made their own, one had necessarily to re-adjust — in practice diminish — one's purposes; whereas for Herzl and Zangwill it was the purposes that were the true and necessary cornerstones of policy and whatever impeded progress towards them had to be jettisoned or circumvented. To the question what would befall the Jews who could not be encompassed by his "centre" in Ereẓ-Israel, Ahad Ha-'Am answered, essentially, with a shrug; in his view Ereẓ-Israel could hold out no salvation for them in any event.

Ostensibly, these antitheses were still unresolved at Herzl's death, much as the question of East Africa as a formal issue remained unsettled. But the reality was that Herzl himself, just before his death, at the grand confrontation at the Greater Actions Committee in April 1904, had already conceded crucial points to the opposition and so caused the balance to shift several months before his death. It is, of course, just conceivable, that, had he lived, he would have sought to restore his authority to the full. To that end he would have had to find fresh allies, probably to throw over the old guard of Hovevei Zion altogether. He might have appealed to the silent rank and file, to such people as had cheered him in Vilna and still looked to him to release them from their misery. It would have been in character had he done so and in accord with past precedent, as when, having failed to gain the support of the millionaire notables of western Jewry, he resolved on the creation of a popular movement. But if he had lived, he would still have been an extremely tired and disappointed man and possibly too weak in body to precipitate and carry through a fresh upheaval. Besides which, he himself had become increasingly uncertain and ambivalent in his own attitude to the tradition and had already assured the opposition that in certain respects he would uphold it. He was certainly always a man of his word.

In any event, Herzl's death rendered the shift irreversible. Zionism became identified exclusively with Ereẓ-Israel once more. And, by necessary extension, there ensued both a long retreat from true political action and a massive blocking-off of anything like that call for radical national renewal and reform which the East Africa affair had brought to the surface of public consciousness and, in a limited way and for a brief moment, into the arena of open debate. The further and grimmer consequence was the fixing of that frame of mind and that order of priorities to which I referred at the outset.

Let me try briefly to sum up. The outcome of the great debate on the East Africa project had little to do directly with East Africa. The immediate issue had been settled long before the Seventh Congress passed its final resolution on the matter. What the debate did determine — wherein its vast importance in the history of the Zionist movement — was the approach that would come to characterize most Zionists' handling most of the time of two key classes of issues: those which bore on the society at which they were aiming and those which bore on the actual, immediate fate of the Jews as individuals.

In the course of the debate most members of the Zionist leadership (I attempt a definition of the term and an investigation of its salient sociological characteristics elsewhere) discovered that they had very firm views on two great public questions. They did not often articulate their views with precision, but we, in retrospect, can see clearly what they were. First, they ascribed a higher priority to the internal rehabilitation and reconstruction of Jewry than to what might be termed its external rehabilitation, namely, the reconstruction and reordering of Jewry's position in the world at large and the establishment of relations between the Jewish people and other peoples on a fresh basis. Second, they would under no circumstances countenance progress towards either of these two fundamental Zionist goals where it entailed a radical break with the past. *Continuity had to be preserved*. To what degree and in what respects could be debated. But the principle of continuity had to be honoured as beyond debate, implicitly, if not explicitly. And Erez-Israel was its symbol.

In contrast, Herzlian Zionism had hinged on an attempt to look at the real world, all of it, as much that of the non-Jews as of the Jews themselves; and on an attempt to prescribe as best one could for those who were in greatest distress — moral, but also and particularly material. On the issue of continuity it was, as I have tried to suggest, ambivalent. It did not really require discontinuity for itself, as some charged. It did not actively seek it except in so far as continuity was judged incompatible with the primary goals of Zionism as these were understood. But it did certainly hold these primary goals to be of overriding importance and value. It did certainly want and welcome change and was neither embarrassed nor half-hearted about it. And how far and in what direction there would be change was, for the Herzlians, a pragmatic question, not one of principle. It is, of course, hard to do full justice to their outlook in such short compass as this. The matter is extraordinarily complex. Their views were not clear-cut. But it may be said, that they took the world as they saw it and understood it and thought the Jews must go far towards adjusting themselves to it for their own good and if they were to survive at all.

The effect of the demolition of Herzlian Zionism in the last months of Herzl's life and the two years immediately subsequent to his death was, in the first instance, to resuscitate Hibbat Zion; and the adherents of Hibbat Zion had always had a more limited perspective. The real world of harsh politics and cruel choices had long since revealed itself to them as one in which they could not hope — and perhaps did not wish — to function. They had long since accustomed themselves to the thought that the task of *rescue* was beyond their meagre powers and resources. And they had long since — in what one is tempted to call the classic Jewish manner — turned for preference inwards once more.

Henceforth, of course, the mind of the movement would be almost exclusively on the *yishuv* and Ereẓ-Israel. Henceforth the Jewish national principle would have both an acknowledged champion and a plan for its safeguard far stronger and much more strictly committed than ever Herzl and Zangwill and their followers had been. On the other hand, to the question how the Jews themselves in their great majority would fare, there were now none who would address themselves as firmly and single-mindedly as that vast and terrible problem required.

ANITA SHAPIRA

THE STRUGGLE FOR "JEWISH LABOUR" —
CONCEPT AND CONSEQUENCES

The ideological concept of "Jewish labour" (*Avodah Ivrit*) crystallized during the period of the Second *Aliyah* (1904–14). It was based on the premise that all employment generated by Jewish capital in Palestine was to be allocated exclusively to Jewish workers.

From the beginning Zionism had sought not only a national-territorial solution to the "Jewish Problem", but the creation of a model society, in which the socio-economic anomalies of Jewish life in the Diaspora would be amended. This meant, first and foremost, the creation of a broadly-based Jewish working class. The Zionist movement sought to accomplish this aim through the settlement in the country of large masses of Jews who were at the time living in distressed circumstances in the countries of eastern Europe. Their immigration and almost mandatory productivization would contribute to yet another Zionist aim: the eventual attainment of a Jewish majority in Palestine.

The economic realities of Palestine with the advent of the Second *Aliyah* were more complex than the theoretically logical assumptions of the movement.

The early Jewish colonies (*moshavot*), established in the last two decades of the nineteenth century by the First *Aliyah*, were based on a monocultural economy, first vineyards and then citrus plantations. Both required large numbers of seasonal hands, and the early settlers employed Arab workers from the neighbouring villages. Accustomed to hard physical labour, the Arab hands were able to provide a cheap work force while still cultivating and partially subsisting from their own farmlands. They were prepared to work for a wage on which a European-born Jewish worker, with no supplementary income, could not possibly survive.

The Jewish farmers preferred Arab workers to Jewish: the former were more easily available and more numerous; they were cheaper; and their productivity was greater. Conflict between the Jewish workers and farmers was inevitable. The workers viewed the settlers as "enemies of Israel" who, for the sake of a profit, were obstructing the realization of Zionism. Without productivization, immigration would fall; without immigration there could be no Jewish majority. The idealistic pioneers of the Second *Aliyah* were left without work. Animosity, disillusion and despair soon set in.

The Jewish farmers, for their part, considered the Jewish workers dangerous socialists and revolutionaries, who lacked any comprehension of the "facts of life", and who attempted to impose impossible wages and unacceptable work relations upon them. Their employment of Arab workers may have been motivated primarily by economics, but they also adduced political arguments. If Arabs worked in Jewish citrus groves, good neighbourly relations with the Arab villages would ensue.

The difficulty of competing with Arab labour generated the demand for the separation of the Jewish and Arab economies and, concomitantly, of the Jewish and Arab societies. Ostensibly, this separation aimed at avoiding the typical colonial structure: a European minority exploiting cheap, indigenous labour. But more to the point, it aimed at establishing an autonomous Jewish economy in which wages and working conditions were more appropriately geared to the needs of the European worker. It was also viewed as a prerequisite for consolidating a Jewish majority in Palestine. Together, these ideas lay at the root of the concept of *Avodah Ivrit*.

The slogan, which dated from the beginning of the century, became part and parcel of Zionist ideology; by the forties, on the eve of the establishment of the State of Israel, there was no Zionist who rejected it in principle. Even the original farmers and their sons came to accept the idea of Jewish labour as both proper and necessary, doubting only their ability to implement it. The idea permeated the dominant value system of the Jewish community in Palestine: children growing up in the thirties, forties and fifties were reared on the clichés of "worker martyrology" and the "malevolence and contemptibility of the private farmers". Agricultural settlements based solely on Jewish labour — *kibbutzim* and *moshavim* — were accepted as the symbol of freedom and progress, and contrasted with the so-called economic failure, decadence and "feudalism" of the old colonies.

The success of the ideology of *Avodah Ivrit* owed little to the merits of the socio-moral argument of the Second *Aliyah*, that Jewish settlement based on the sweat of Arab labour was untenable or that the creation of an Arab working-class vis-à-vis a Jewish exploiting class would distort Jewish society; or even to the view that Jewish workers had exclusive rights to jobs in the Jewish economy. It was rather the growing tension and estrangement between the two peoples which, for security reasons, compelled a closing of ranks. Particularly was this so once the political situation began to point to partition as the solution to the problem of Palestine; the idea of *Avodah Ivrit* then seemed to have exhibited foresight and political wisdom.

The victory of the idea should not be interpreted as meaning that Jewish labour was indeed predominant in non-cooperative Jewish agriculture. Prior to 1947 Arab labour in privately-owned Jewish fields and citrus groves remained an insoluble problem. There were simply not enough Jewish labourers willing to work in agriculture under existing conditions. The "prosperity" of the early thirties generated a constant flow of Jews from agriculture to occupations considered more remunerative or "better"; this pattern recurred during subsequent periods of prosperity. In times of economic depression (as from 1927 until 1932) agricultural labour provided greater economic security than irregular work in the city. However, the fear of economic depression was not enough to curb the flow of workers to the city nor to create a Jewish agricultural proletariat, ready to view agriculture as its permanent way of life.

Paradoxically, the Second *Aliyah* ideal of Jewish labour, which provided the ideological foundation for the workers' claim to hegemony in the Jewish community in Palestine, gained credence at the same time that the Jewish agricultural proletariat dwindled. The labour movement saw itself, in its ideological mirror, as shouldering the brunt of the national burden. But individual workers were inclined, as most people are, to seek their own best interests, even when these conflicted with the priorities of the *Yishuv*.

There was both tragic and historical irony in the fact that it was precisely the socialist element of the national Jewish movement — whose dream was of a better and more just world — that was forced by the specific problem of Jewish labour in Palestine on to the front lines against the Arab worker. From the very beginning, this issue produced a double bind: while socialist ideology demanded international solidarity and the brotherhood of men, the competition of cheap Arab labour led to increasing hostility and estrangement between the two peoples. Very little material exists which sheds light on the encounter between Jewish and Arab labourers in the settlements. The Jewish picket-lines were directed against the Jewish farmers, and propaganda on their behalf was aimed solely at Jewish public opinion. The Arab workers were passive agents, completely disregarded — even when they were involved in brawls with Jewish workers. We may well ask what passed through the minds of those Jewish workers as they prevented these down-trodden *felahin* co-workers from entering the citrus groves. The mass of documentary evidence on the issue of *Avodah Ivrit* does not supply an answer. Members of *Hashomer Hatzair* and *Poalei Zion* — the left-wing of the Jewish labour movement — occasionally tried to establish contact with Arab labourers, but these were isolated attempts which were not followed up. The vast majority of Jewish workers in the settlements, who encountered Arabs daily, were blind to their existence. It seems that the leaders of the labour movement and specifically those of *Mapai* (the dominant party within the labour movement which from 1933 on controlled the Zionist movement) displayed more interest in the Arab question and the issue of Arab labourers than did the workers themselves. The direct encounter between the two peoples resembled a meeting on two sides of a glass wall.

In the anti-Jewish disturbances of the twenties and thirties the employment of Arabs in the settlements was neither a contributive nor a preventative factor. Attacks and raids were perpetrated against both the collective settlements — which employed exclusively Jewish labourers — as well as those settlements employing mixed labour. Farmers on the coastal plain who employed Arabs claimed that during the Arab Rebellion (1936–39) areas of mixed Jewish-Arab labour were quieter than in the colonies of the Sharon Plain, where farmers employed only Jewish labour. But it is possible that this relative tranquillity arose from other factors, such as the density and contiguity of the Jewish population on the coastal plain and the relative sparsity of Arabs in the area. In the final analysis, it was the question of security which united the entire *Yishuv*, including the private farmers, and, in the wake of the 1938 riots, Arab workers were withdrawn from the Jewish colonies. Nevertheless, life in Palestine moved in a cycle of peace and unrest and the peaceful years predominated. As a result, even after the 1938–39 uprisings, the security threat could no more prevent the return of Arab labourers to the colonies than it had done after 1921, 1929 and 1936.

Relations with Arabs on the political level were not influenced by the problem of *Avodah Ivrit*, probably because the Arab leadership did not take an interest in the lot of the Arab working in the Jewish economy. But, as already mentioned, the issue did, to a certain extent, determine the character of partition as a political solution during the thirties. While Jewish labour was originally conceived and propagated for broad ideological reasons, during the thirties and forties it acquired justification primarily as a means to ensure jobs for Jewish immigrants. This simplification of the ideological basis of *Avodah Ivrit* reflected a more general process overtaking the central stream of the labour movement: the waning of the importance of ideology and the increasing significance of political-pragmatic considerations.

The emphasis moved from the ideology of *Avodah Ivrit* to the actual struggle for the dominance of the labour movement in the Jewish community in Palestine. Labour leaders had, of course, been speaking about "thirty years of fighting for Jewish labour" but, in fact, the real struggles began only in 1927. Before that, the workers had attempted to solve the problems on their own: by adjusting to the difficult work; by lowering their standards of living to that of the Arab worker; or by establishing cooperative and collective settlements where they did not have to compete with Arab labour. The labour

movement had also used public opinion to put pressure on the farmers. However, the struggle between workers and farmers — as two distinct political and
social entities, began during the Fourth *Aliyah* (1924–26), increased during
the slump after 1927, reached its peak in 1934 and continued — albeit more
moderately — until the collapse of the citrus market in the wake of the Second
World War.

The struggle of the labour movement was presented by the workers as a
combined national and class struggle. In the sense that it aimed at guaranteeing
immigrant absorption in the country, *Avodah Ivrit* was indeed a national problem. But the timing, character and aims of the actual struggle of the labour
movement were affected by its relations with the entrepreneurial sectors of the
Jewish community in Palestine. Furthermore, they were intensified by the
class values of the labour movement at the time and its place in the overall
political fabric of the country and the Zionist movement. The fact that the
worker, struggling for his livelihood in the colonies, was also fighting for
the Zionist cause bolstered the labour movement's strength, endowing it with
the moral right to demand preferential treatment in immigration and contributing to the consolidation of its hegemony both in the community and in
the Zionist Organization.

Events elsewhere in the world during the thirties inevitably influenced the
character of the struggle in Palestine. The increasing use of violence as a
political weapon in the class struggle and among the workers themselves
emerged against the background of events in contemporary Europe: workers
were fighting fascist and Nazi violence, and losing. A strong class identity
emerged among the workers in Palestine and strengthened those forces within
the labour movement for whom "class struggle" meant a relentless fight for
power. There were two groups in the Jewish community against whom the
struggle was waged bitterly: the farmers and the Revisionists, and with the
latter it took on increasingly brutal proportions. The same features, however,
characterized the struggle against both: the dehumanization of the enemy
and his representation as a public enemy and destroyer of national values;
an unwillingness to compromise; and the desire to win at all costs.

The struggle of *Avodah Ivrit* was reflected in two socio-political demands
made by left-wing movement members. The first was for the organization of
Arab workers against both the Jewish and Arab bourgeoisie; the second was
for the intensification of the trade-union struggle for improved working conditions in the colonies, without taking into account the vulnerable position
of the Jewish worker there. The problem was more complex for centre-
oriented *Mapai* members. A section of the party had traditionally opposed
class warfare in the settlements. Nevertheless, they were influenced by the

militants, as can be seen from their attitude towards the Sharon Plain farmers, who out of Zionist convictions had taken upon themselves the double burden of Jewish labour and *Histadrut*-unionized labour. In those colonies where Jewish labour predominated it was the *Histadrut* — the Federation of Jewish Workers in Palestine — which had organized the fight for unionized Jewish labour, aimed at ensuring its monopoly over the labour market as a means of guaranteeing jobs and of putting pressure on both employers and workers. The farmers were compelled to accept the authority of the *Histadrut* labour exchange and to agree to conditions which they claimed were economically unviable. Added to the low productivity of the Jewish workers, these conditions drastically reduced the ability of the Sharon farms to compete in the market. In the case of the Sharon colonies which employed exclusively Jewish labour, the struggle lost its national aura and emerged as a political class struggle alone. It is no coincidence that the fiercest battles for control of the *Histadrut* labour exchange took place in those places where Jewish labour became consolidated. There was truth to the argument used by the workers to justify their power-struggle — that the labour exchange alone could ensure the exclusive employment of Jewish labour. Indeed, the very fact that the argument was used in the Sharon and not in the Judean Plains, where there was a tradition of Arab employment, casts further doubts on its validity.

The relations between the labour movement's leadership and the Farmers' Association were an indication of the limited ability of the labour movement to compromise. Until 1936 the citrus growers of the Judean Plains, whose economic power did not derive from Zionist institutions and whose farms were based on export rather than the local market, scorned public opinion and disregarded the Zionist bodies. The Manufacturers' Association, in sharp contrast, was dependent upon local demand, and the Jewish workers comprised its largest market. It was further dependent on Jewish workers for its factories since Arab workers were not yet capable of working in industry. Thus, the animosity of the labour movement, both leaders and workers, towards the independent farmers of the old colonies arose out of its inability to pressure them into acceding to its demands. The vast majority of workers during the early thirties was incapable of rational compromise. They wanted victory, even if only partial, provided that it resulted from their pressure and coercion.

From 1924 onwards, with the arrival in the country of middle-class immigrants, the members of the labour movement apparently acknowledged that there would be privately-financed farms and enterprises. Their attitude towards them, nevertheless, remained as negative as it had been during the first years of the Mandate, when they believed that the country would be built entirely by pioneers and national funds and that the socialist utopia was just around the corner. Now they had to concede, however reluctantly, that private capital was creating the jobs which employed most of the Jewish workers. The change in attitude towards private capital coincided with the overall change that occurred in the attitude of the labour movement to class struggle in the wake of the economic slump of 1935. Now the *Histadrut* was urging the Zionist movement to save the citrus industry which was facing a dire crisis; such a demand would have been impossible to imagine just a few years earlier. At the 19th Zionist Congress held in Lucerne in 1935 Ben-Gurion called for "Peace in the Jewish Community". This led to an about-face in class relations, ushering in a drive for a national consensus and to the abandonment of the slogans and militant action of former years. It was the result, among other things, of the failure of both the class struggle and of the struggle for *Avodah Ivrit*.

During the thirties Jewish workers in the colonies proved that they were willing to fight bitter class battles against the farmers; they were not, however, prepared to fight with the same ardour for the national interest — the retention of Jewish labour — if their personal interests were not involved. Hence, during the slump until 1932, large numbers of workers picketed for Jewish labour because they were also fighting for their own workday. But in 1934, at the peak of prosperity, the strike in Kfar Saba failed, because the introduction of Arab labour into the Sharon Plain did not affect the workers' own livelihood. The labour leadership was hard put to channel the energy that the workers were willing to expend on their personal gains into matters of national interest, and their failure was one reason for the appeal for "Peace in the Jewish Community".

The Farmers' Association, for its part, also took up the cudgels of class war in the thirties. True, its aims were more modest and of a more defensive nature than those of the labour movement, but one cannot ignore its efforts to stymie the legitimate contest for hegemony by the labour movement through economic and political means. It hit back at the democratically organized and numerically superior workers through the issue of Jewish labour. It began to boycott organized *Histadrut* workers, even, in some cases, bringing in Arab labour in their place. Be this as it may, the main reason for the continued employment of Arab labour was still economic: higher Jewish wages and lower productivity. If we view *Avodah Ivrit* as a burden imposed upon the Jewish community by Zionism, then the price paid literally by the farmers was a not insignificant "national" tax. The workers, on the other hand, had nothing to lose and much to gain: a livelihood and the glory accruing to their "national" struggle. Certainly, living conditions in the colonies were intolerable, but the question is what alternative did they have and what did they relinquish when they agreed to work in the colonies. When they agreed, it was because they had no choice. When they had the choice, they no longer agreed, save for a handful of such idealists as the *kibbutz* members.

When the farmers became dependent on the Jewish community and its institutions at the time of the citrus marketing crisis, which began in 1936 and intensified with the outbreak of the War, they were forced to abandon their political class struggle against the workers. But this did not imply that the problem of Jewish labour was resolved. It merely lost its political complexion and again assumed its basic, practical aspect: was the agricultural economy of the country capable of supporting Jewish workers on wages which could guarantee them and their families a livelihood?

The problem could not have been resolved either through the class struggle, which economically crippled the citrus growers prepared to pay the price of Jewish labour, or through the constructivist programme of workers' subsidies. The cost of financing workers' housing, social benefits and contractual offices in the colonies was too high. During periods of prosperity the independent farmers had no reason to agree to the dictates of the workers' organizations. During periods of crisis the Jewish economy simply could not afford the "luxury" of Jewish labour. In the final analysis, the problem of *Avodah Ivrit* could only be resolved within the framework of a comprehensive governmental system of labour legislation.

Jewish labour was one of the problems faced by the Jewish community under the Mandate, and its solution demanded the sort of national authority precluded by the fact of British rule. The fundamentally contradictory economic interests of the workers and the farmers obviated a solution based on free choice. The absence of a sovereign Jewish power which would force farmers to employ Jewish workers, subsidizing them during slumps, created the complex dilemma of Jewish labour, with all its ramifications for the political and social structure of the community. Attempts to "nationalize" Jewish labour after the failure of the "struggles" could not succeed, as legal authority and sufficient finances were lacking.

No student of the period can fail to be impressed by the wealth of material connected with the issue of *Avodah Ivrit*. It appears to have been the critical question of the period, preoccupying both the public and the leadership. It was considered an issue fundamental to the Zionist movement in Palestine, and especially to the labour movement. Is this impression correct? It would seem that leaders from the Second *Aliyah*, and those who came under their influence, viewed Arab labour as a threat to the Jewish character of the colonies and a potential danger to the entire Jewish economy. Even during the Arab Rebellion (1936–39) they gave the matter a great deal of thought, despite the other burning issues of the time. The general public, on the other hand, paid lip-service to the issue of Jewish labour, as it was the ideological corner-stone of labour hegemony in Zionism, but they were in fact more interested in other matters: the rise of Nazism in Germany and Europe; the Revisionists; the murder of Arlosoroff; the partition of Palestine; the purges in the Soviet Union; the Spanish Civil War. Moreover, since only a small percentage of Jewish workers was employed in the colonies, for the great majority of urban workers Jewish labour was not a critical issue. Finally, the great majority of the population was composed of new immigrants for whom the problem lacked the dramatic significance it was assigned during the Second *Aliyah*.

With the growth of the Jewish economy the issue necessarily became increasingly marginal. Contrary to fears, Arab labour did not spread to other parts of the Jewish economy, either because of the dependence of the manufacturers on the rest of the community, or because of the technological backwardness of the Arab workers. Arab labour remained limited to citrus plantations, a fact which led to the progressive reduction of its importance within the expanding Jewish economy. It seems, however, that the Jewish leadership was unable to shake off its time-honoured ideological mantle even though its traditional animosity towards the farmers weakened somewhat towards the end of the pre-state period.

All of the above notwithstanding, it is finally impossible to measure to what extent concern with the issue actually prevented the spread of Arab labour to other branches of the economy, and this question remains open.

It would seem that the major value of the dramatic struggles for Jewish labour was not in ensuring Jewish labour in the citrus groves. It had, rather, enormous educational value by creating in the public mind the basis for accepting an ideology, whose political postulate was the separation between Jewish and Arab societies. It prepared the ground for the partition solution to the problem of Palestine by directing Jewish settlement to areas sparsely populated by Arabs and creating a territorial contiguity of Jewish settlement. Partition became the natural solution to a complex of capital and labour relations in a country where two standards of living and two civilizations existed.

CHAIM I. WAXMAN

CHALLENGES TO CONSENSUS IN THE CONTEMPORARY AMERICAN JEWISH COMMUNITY

The American Jewish community is frequently portrayed as a consensus community, in which virtually no serious conflict exists. There is much truth to this characterization. As Daniel J. Elazar suggests with reference to the oligarchical but, nevertheless, representative character of the leadership of American Jewry: "They are representative because there is a certain sameness in American Jewry."[1] Some of the reasons for this characteristic may be rooted in the minority experience of American Jewry; others may be traced to what Peter Y. Medding refers to as the "decline in authentic Jewish values";[2] and still others to American society and culture themselves, which as early an observer as Alexis de Tocqueville considered to be essentially homogeneous.[3] Be that as it may, this characterization is somewhat misleading in that it tends to minimize the multitude of sources of serious conflict within the American Jewish community in recent years. This article will explore what appear to have been the most significant issues of conflict which have challenged the organized American Jewish community since the beginning of the 1970s, and the ways in which the community has dealt with them. Nevertheless, as will be indicated, the strategies adopted for dealing with these challenges have enabled the American Jewish community to retain its essentially consensual character, even in the face of conflict.

During the second half of the 1970s there were a number of disparate groups, ranging from Jewish student activists to Rabbi Meir Kahane, founder of the Jewish Defense League, who decried the nature of American Jewish

1 Daniel J. Elazar, *Community and Polity: The Organizational Dynamics of American Jewry* (Philadelphia: Jewish Publication Society of America, 1976), p. 285.
2 Peter Y. Medding, "Patterns of Political Organization and Leadership in Contemporary Jewish Communities," in Daniel J. Elazar (ed.), *Kinship and Consent: The Jewish Political Tradition and Its Contemporary Uses* (Ramat Gan: Turtledove Publishing, 1981), p. 285.
3 Alexis de Tocqueville, *Democracy in America* (Garden City: Doubleday Anchor Books, 1969).

leadership and the structure of the organized American Jewish community. Their basic grievance was that the communal organizations and their leadership were undemocratic because the organizations were unrepresentative of broad segments of American Jewry, that they were deaf to dissent, and that their leadership consisted of a self-appointed and self-perpetuating elite. Kahane's strongest attack was on the Conference of Presidents of Major American Jewish Organizations, an umbrella group which focuses upon Israel-related issues. Kahane charged that this organization selects its constituents undemocratically, through "the rather ingenious trick of having as member groups, organizations that are themselves umbrella groups, thus in effect strengthening the membership of certain groups that are members of the Conference in their own right."[4] The Conference, he alleged, only accepts organizations and leaders who conform to its positions, and it is undemocratic, unrepresentative, and detrimental to the interests of American Jewry. Similarly, he charged the Council of Jewish Federations and the National Jewish Community Advisory Council with being undemocratic "tools of the wealthy."

Along the same lines, although from very different ideological bases, a Jewish journal published by members and former members of the Jewish student counterculture published a nine-point critique of American Jewish communal life. In an editorial in the journal, *Response*, Steven M. Cohen, a sociologist now at Queens College, in New York, asserted that Jewish communal leaders view democracy "as an impediment to efficient operation"; that Jewish life is exclusionary in that it encourages the involvement of "the financially well-to-do, the males, the middle aged, the businessmen," but discourages the involvement of "the middle and working classes, women, young people (40 and under), intellectuals, and others"; that the communal structures reward those who assent and contribute to the smooth-functioning of those structures and punish those who challenge it; that communal life is localistic, parochial, and informed by business and management philosophy; that American Jewish diplomacy is the hand-maiden of Israeli foreign policy; that "the bearers of Jewish morality are slow to condemn Jewish immorality": that "religious life is stagnant"; that "synagogues are mostly dull and cold"; that Jewish education is largely "insipid and uninspired," and that Jewish teaching is largely "a second job and not a career."[5]

---

4 An advertisement, under the heading, "Democracy in Jewish Life," which Kahane placed periodically in the Brooklyn-based weekly, *The Jewish Press*, and other publications, during 1975.

5 Steven M. Cohen, "On Our Minds," *Response*, Vol. IX, No. 3 (Number 27), Fall, 1975, pp. 3–5.

Although Cohen advocated the formation of a new movement, a "Lobby for Jewish Change," and although there were (and are) many within the American Jewish community who agree with some, if not all, of his charges, the organized movement to challenge the Jewish Establishment which he advocated did not emerge. Rather, there have developed a variety of interest groups, each of which is organized under a banner which acts as a lobby to challenge the established operating procedures of the American Jewish communal structure on one of the specific issues on Cohen's list. Before reviewing the activities of these organizations and movements, it would be instructive more carefully to examine the basic allegation concerning the non-democratic nature of the American Jewish communal structure.

What is democracy? Many definitions have been provided and, essentially, there is an ideological stance in each. One of the ideological issues involved is whether elitism is compatible with democracy. On the one hand, there are those who maintain that the only true democracy is "participatory democracy," in which

> ... decision-making is the process whereby people propose, discuss, decide, plan, and implement those decisions that affect their lives. This requires that the decision-making process be continuous and significant, direct rather than through representatives, and organized around issues instead of personalities. It requires that the decision-making process be set up in a functional manner, so that the constituencies significantly affected by decisions are the ones that make them and elected delegates can be recalled instantly, doing away with self-appointed elites whose decisions have a broad political impact on the society, but who are accountable only to themselves, or to interlocked groups of their peers.[6]

According to this conception of democracy, the American Jewish communal structure is clearly not a democracy. It is governed by a leadership of professionals and volunteers, some of whom are self-appointed, some of whom are appointed by closed boards, and some of whom are elected by the constituent members of the particular organization but not by American Jewry at large, even though those leaders claim to speak on behalf of and make decisions which affect the larger community of Jews.

On the other hand, there are other conceptions which allow for democratic elitism. Joseph Schumpeter, for example, defined democracy as "that institu-

6 C. George Benello and Dimitrios Roussopoulos, eds., *The Case for Participatory Democracy: Some Prospects for a Radical Society* (New York: Viking Press, 1971), pp. 3–9.

tional arrangement for arriving at political decisions in which individuals acquire power to decide by means of a competitive struggle for the people's vote."[7] According to this view of representative democracy, the constant participation of those affected by the decisions is not required (nor is it feasible); all that is required is that the power to make decisions be acquired through a competitive struggle for the vote. In fact, the Italian political scientist, Gaetano Mosca, and the German sociologist, Robert Michels, both argued that participatory democracy is unfeasible. Mosca argued that there will always be rulers and ruled, and that among the factors which support the rule of a small elite, or ruling class, is the simple fact that most people are too busy with their own daily personal needs to become involved in politics for any length of time.[8] Michels argued that there is an "iron law of oligarchy" which is inherent in all organizations. On the basis of his analyses of the labor and socialist movements at the turn of the twentieth century, he concluded that as organizations grow, there is an increasing need for leadership, and that broad-based participation in every decision becomes increasingly impractical. Both the rank and file and the elite are more than happy with the arrangement whereby the few rule, regardless of whether the organization or party was initially conservative or radical. Revolutions, according to Michels, are nothing more than the replacement of one minority-ruled organization by another. Organization, he argued, means oligarchy, or rule by the few.[9]

Any discussion of the allegation that the American Jewish communal structure is undemocratic must commence by emphasizing the voluntary nature of both the community and its constituent organizations. Understandably, therefore, the leaderships of most such organizations are selected exclusively by their memberships and their representatives. Indeed, were one to examine the leadership-selection process in most local and national Jewish organizations, from synagogues to such secular organizations as B'nai B'rith, the many Zionist organizations, etc., it would be very difficult to substantiate the allegation that they are undemocratic in terms of their operating procedures. On the contrary, they would pass the test of democratic procedures with high marks.

As has been indicated, however, criticism of Jewish communal leadership and decision-making involves much more than technical democratic pro-

---

7 Joseph A. Schumpeter, *Capitalism, Socialism, and Democracy*, third edition (New York: Harper & Row Torchbooks, 1962), p. 269.

8 Gaetano Mosca, *The Ruling Class* (New York: McGraw-Hill Book Co., 1939), pp. 281–6.

9 Robert Michels, *Political Parties* (Glencoe: Free Press, 1949).

cedures. An even stronger criticism is that the political process is exclusive, that it caters only to the affluent. Part of the reason for this lies in another of Mosca's explanations of how a small ruling class is able to maintain its rule over the large masses, namely, that most people have neither the time nor the money which would afford them the opportunity for extended involvement in politics. Jewish communal leadership is very time-consuming; it also makes other demands for which most people possess neither the time nor the inclination. As a result, to a large degree the affluent are the leaders by default.

But the criticisms of Cohen and many others are not directed simply and solely at the communal leadership. Perhaps even greater fault is found with the entire communal structure which has become conservative and exclusivist. One need not accept the radical conception of participatory democracy to be critical of exclusivism. Even those holding the more modest view of representative democracy adhere to the goal of the will of the people as manifested by their vote and, that to be truly representative, as much of the citizenry as possible should be included in the vote. While the leaders of American Jewish organizations claim to act and speak on behalf of American Jewry as a whole, without limiting themselves to their own organization's membership, there is a widespread sense among American Jews that the organized Jewish community has turned inward and that it does not reach out to the increasing numbers of Jews who, perhaps because of acculturation and assimilation, are not now affiliated with, or feel uncomfortable with, the communal institutions. Many also feel that the organized community is not responsive to them and their needs and desires. Although there has been no successful coalition of all of the segments of the American Jewish population who experience dissatisfaction with the organized community, a variety of social movements and organizations for change have emerged within the last dozen years or so, and some of them are having impact. One of the most significant of these is the *Havurah* movement.

It is difficult to assign a precise date to the birth of the *Havurah* movement because of its heterogeneity and the fact that it sprang from various sources in different places. First introduced into American Jewish life early in the 1960s via the publications of the Jewish Reconstructionist Foundation,[10] the notion of *Havurah* dates back almost 2,000 years. The term means "fellowship," and was represented by two models in the ancient Palestinian Jewish community which emerged in response to the widespread decline in piety among the Jewish masses. One model, created by the Essenes, was located in

---

10 Bernard Reisman, *The Chavurah: A Contemporary Jewish Experience* (New York: Union of American Hebrew Congregations, 1977), pp. 7–8.

the remote parts of the country, and consisted of small groups of Jews who subscribed to a rigidly ascetic Jewish lifestyle; the other, created by the Pharisees who rejected the idea of removing themselves from the community, was located within the Jewish main centers of population and strove to serve as a means for influencing the religious behavior of the larger Jewish community.[11] To some extent, both of these models are represented in the contemporary American Jewish *Havurah* movement. In part, it consists of those who have given up on the established community and, especially, its synagogue structure, from which they seek to remove themselves as far as possible. Others of its membership are establishing fellowships within the community and even within existing synagogues.

Essentially, a *Havurah* is a small community of like-minded families who group together as a Jewish fellowship for the purposes of providing each other with social support and in order to pursue their own participatory programs of Jewish study, celebration, and community service. *Havurot* are generally small, ranging in membership from ten to two dozen families who meet regularly (at least once a month), often in members' homes on a rotating basis.

The first unaffiliated *Havurah*, "Havurat Shalom," was founded by a group of dissidents from the Jewish counterculture in the Fall of 1968, in Somerville, Massachusetts. Most of the founders were young Conservative and Reform rabbis and graduate students in Boston, who "felt estranged from American society, as exemplified by the Vietnam war and mass culture, and from the Jewish community, as exemplified by what they considered to be its inauthentic, bureaucratic institutions."[12] Subsequently, several other similar *Havurot* were founded in New York City and Washington, D.C. Shortly afterward, Rabbi Harold Schulweis, of Temple Valley Beth Shalom in Encino, California, experimented with a synagogue-affiliated model which proved to be highly popular. During the 1970s there was a proliferation of both the independent and the synagogue-affiliated *Havurot*, and in the summer of 1980 the first National Havurah Conference was convened at Rutgers University in New Brunswick, New Jersey, in which more than 350 Jews from diverse backgrounds and denominations gathered to share their Havurah experiences.[13]

According to a study of *Havurah* members conducted by Bernard Reisman, the overwhelming majority are married, under age 45, have somewhat larger

---

11 Jacob Neusner, *Contemporary Judaic Fellowship in Theory and in Practice* (New York: Ktav Publishing House, 1972), pp. 1–10.

12 Reisman, op. cit., p. 9.

13 William Novak, "From Sommerville to Savannah ... and Los Angeles ... and Dayton ..." *Moment*, Vol. 6, No. 2, January–February, 1981, pp. 17–21, 57–60.

than average American Jewish families, tend to be more politically liberal than the average American Reform Jew, have higher than average levels of secular education and occupations, have about average levels of Jewish education as compared to other American Jews, are somewhat more religiously observant than the average American Jew, and tend to identify themselves as Reform or Conservative, with only a very small percentage identifying as Orthodox.[14] The reasons for the low rate of Orthodox involvement with the *Havurah* movement may be deduced from Reisman's analysis of the motivations of the members. He suggests that the movement is a response to the cultural conditions of American society which is characterized by loneliness, passivity, dependency and meaninglessness, and that the *Havurah* represents a quest for community, participation, authority, and ideology.[15] Since Orthodoxy stresses high levels of community participation, authority and ideology, it is not surprising that very few who identify as Orthodox feel a need to join a *Havurah*.[16] It should also be noted that Reisman's data indicate that, despite the movement's founders, for the overwhelming majority of its members the *Havurah* is not countercultural.[17] Most of those who join *Havurot* do so not out of an ideological opposition to the dominant American Jewish culture. Rather, they join because they do not find that the existing institutions and their patterns of participation serve their needs. For them, the *Havurah* represents an alternative, more meaningful and satisfying avenue of Jewish experience. It is, as Schulweis suggests, an attempt "to decentralize the synagogue and deprofessionalize Jewish living so that the individual Jew is brought back into a circle of shared Jewish experience."[18]

While most American Jews are probably not very concerned with the low level and quality of Jewish education in the United States,[19] some who are have grouped together and formed the Coalition for Alternatives in Jewish Education (CAJE). In 1976 this group issued a proclamation calling

> ... for substantive structural changes in our classrooms, in order to transform our schools into intellectually stimulating, open and joyful

14 Reisman, op. cit., pp. 65–74.
15 Ibid., pp. 26–59.
16 Chaim I. Waxman, "The Sabbath as Dialectic: The Meaning and Role," *Judaism*, Vol. 31, No. 1, Winter 1982, pp. 37–44.
17 For a recent and careful analysis of this concept, see J. Milton Yinger, *Countercultures* (New York: Free Press, 1982).
18 Quoted in Harry Wasserman, "The Havurah Experience," *Journal of Psychology and Judaism*, Vol. 3, No. 3, Spring 1979, pp. 180–1.
19 Chaim I. Waxman, *America's Jews in Transition* (Philadelphia: Temple University Press, 1983), Ch. 8.

learning environments for our children and for ourselves. We also encourage such non-classroom learning as study weekends and camping programs, youth movements and *havurot*, programs in Israel and lifetime education. We welcome the emergence of alternative and parentrun schools, as indications of the ferment which is necessary for creative change.[20]

While the hundreds who attend the annual CAJE conferences come from a variety of Jewish backgrounds, there is a consensus among the conference participants that Jewish education will fail unless it breaks loose from its conservatism and incorporates dynamic new ideas and methodologies which will interest and involve the students in their own education. At the Fourth Annual CAJE Conference, held at Rutgers University in the summer of 1979, the major emphasis of the workshops was on new ways of teaching, with considerably less emphasis on content.[21] The annual conferences have attracted considerable interest among educators, and are an indication, to some extent, of the validity of Cohen's allegation that Jewish education in the United States is largely "insipid and uninspired." Yet, it remains to be seen how much more successful the alternative teaching methods will be, given the fact that Jewish education is not compulsory. Moreover, one of the most serious problems in Jewish education in the United States today is that it does not attract many dedicated and competent professionals. It remains, in large measure, a second job. One indication of this crisis in Jewish education is the fact that, whereas the tuition in most of the other graduate programs at Yeshiva University costs many thousands of dollars per year, that in Jewish studies is considerably less expensive and, yet, there are relatively few students pursuing that program. Also, despite the high tuitions for children in Jewish schools, Jewish educators are not highly paid nor is the status of the Jewish educator very high in the American Jewish community. The best and the brightest, therefore, choose other professions which offer much higher incomes and/or higher status.

CAJE began as a movement for change which challenged the prevailing communal structure of American Jewry, at least its educational structure. However, the very popularity of the Conference inhibits its persistence as a challenge to that communal structure. Indeed, many of the leaders of the Jewish educational establishment in the United States have endorsed the objectives and methodologies of CAJE, which has become part of, or has

---

20 Quoted in Seymour Rossel, "Can We Make Jewish Education Better?," *Present Tense*, Vol. 7, No. 2, Winter 1980, p. 24.

21 Ibid., p. 23.

been co-opted into, the prevailing Jewish educational structure; it is now part of the Jewish organizational structure, rather than a challenge to it.

While the objectives of CAJE are relatively limited (and its prospects for effecting change even more so), the situation is vastly different with respect to the Jewish feminist movement. The 1970s witnessed a large degree of turmoil and struggle with the issues of the roles of women in the American Jewish community and in Judaism in all of its branches. Though it may not have been part of its agenda, the American feminist movement of the 1960s spawned a specifically Jewish feminist movement some years later. In part, this may have been a consequence of the fact that many of the leading feminists, such as Betty Friedman and Gloria Steinem, are Jewish. Also, young American Jewish women have achieved a disproportionately high level of education, which made them acutely aware of feminist issues. Some of them found themselves caught between two worlds, as was evident in a statement contained in the first issue of *Brooklyn Bridge*, a self-styled "revolutionary Jewish newspaper," in February 1971:

> Jewish daughters are thus caught up in a double bind: we are expected to grow up assimilating the American image of "femininity" ... and at the same time to be the "womanly" bulwark of our people against the destruction of our culture. Now we suffer the oppression of women of both cultures and are torn by the contradictions between the two .... While PhDs do make Jewish parents proud of their daughters, the universities are recognized as hunting-grounds for making a "good" marriage. Grandchildren assure the race.[22]

For those women whose consciousness involved an examination of their positions within religious beliefs and practices, the contradictions were particularly acute. Reform Judaism, which had by the 1940s lost its distinctive German character, had adopted the principle of sexual equality in the synagogue as far back as the nineteenth century with respect to having mixed pews and counting women for the quorum (*minyan*) necessary to conduct prayers. However, even within Reform, women's "proper" place was still regarded to be within the home. Despite official Reform ideology of sexual equality in all religious matters, it was not until 1972 that a woman, Sally Priesand, was ordained as a rabbi. Women were still not acceptable in the role of spiritual leaders. Priesand was not the first woman to study in one of the rabbinical

---

22 Quoted in Anne Lapidus Lerner, "'Who Hast Not Made Me A Man': The Movement for Equal Rights for Women in American Jewry," *American Jewish Year Book*, Vol. 77, 1977, p. 5.

seminaries of Reform Judaism; there were at least two others earlier in the century, but they were both refused ordination. Priesand's ordination at the now-merged Hebrew Union College — Jewish Institute of Religion, on June 3, 1972, was given wide publicity in the media, and the influence of the women's movement on her achievement was clearly evident. As she, herself, wrote, in 1975: "Ten years ago, women were much more opposed to the idea of a woman rabbi than were men. Since then, however, the feminist movement has made a tremendous contribution in terms of consciousness-raising, and women now demand complete and full participation in synagogue life." [23]

Even in Reform there is some resistance to change, as is reflected in the remarks of one Reform rabbi who let it be known that women would not be called to the Torah in his congregation, on the grounds that "the Torah service is the last frontier of male religious functions." [24]

The ordination of women in Reform Judaism can provide the necessary title, but it does not guarantee a job. Some women, after experiencing strong resistance, have chosen to work in areas of Jewish communal service other than the rabbinate when their attempts to secure pulpit positions ended with frustration. Apparently, social attitudes are even more difficult to change than religious practice in Reform Judaism. As Anne Lapidus Lerner observed:

> Clearly, if the Reform movement, which in many cases has abrogated such basic areas of Jewish observance as *kashrut* or the use of *tallit* and *tefillin*, has changed dates of holidays, has held Sabbath services on Sunday, and has been equivocal about intermarriage, has taken so long to ordain a woman, the impediment was not religious in nature.[25]

If the impediments to change were so strong within Reform Judaism, which is explicitly based upon an ideology of change and adaptation, it should not be surprising that the issue of women's equality in Conservative Judaism, which claims adherence to tradition, became volatile and threatened to split the movement. At the 1972 convention of the Rabbinic Assembly, the rabbinic organization of American Conservative rabbis, a delegation of women, belonging to a Jewish feminist organization, called *Ezrat Nashim*, issued a manifesto which included demands for the complete participation of women in religious activities.[26] This was not an impulsive action. In 1971 *Ezrat Nashim* was

---

23 Sally Priesand, *Judaism and the New Woman* (New York: Behrman House, 1975), p. xv.
24 Quoted in Lerner, op. cit., p. 71.
25 Ibid., pp. 18–19.
26 Ibid., p. 19.

founded in New York City by a small group of well-educated Jewish women from diverse backgrounds, who came together as a study group. They perceived Jewish tradition as having been progressive in the past, but as having stagnated in recent times. Their concern derived from a deep commitment to Judaism and, simultaneously, a sense of having been utterly shortchanged in the area of religious expression as well as in the Jewish community as a whole.

The impact of the *Ezrat Nashim* manifesto was loud and clear. Groups such as the Women's League for Conservative Judaism, The United Synagogue of America, the majority of the Committee on Jewish Law and Standards (CJLS) of the Rabbinical Assembly — as well as the faculty of the Jewish Theological Seminary of America — all responded positively to some degree and affirmed the need to recognize "the feminist demand for increased women's rights."[27] The decision of the CJLS, by a vote of 9 to 4, to count women equally with men for the *minyan* resulted in a front-page story in the *New York Times*. But, a heated debate continued over precisely which rights to accord women. The results of a 1975 questionnaire indicate that a majority of the Conservative synagogues which responded call women to the Torah and count women within the *minyan*.[28] The issue of the ordination of women within Conservative Judaism was even more complex than that of counting them for a *minyan*. After a difficult struggle (and, perhaps not coincidentally, only after the death of Professor Saul Lieberman, the revered Talmud scholar on the faculty of the Jewish Theological Seminary), the faculty of the Seminary voted 34–8, in October 1983, to admit women into their rabbinic program and to ordain them. The following year, there were several women in the program and the Rabbinic Assembly affirmed its commitment to accept duly ordained women rabbis as full members. A small minority within the Rabbinic Assembly which opposed the ordination of women has formed the Movement for Traditional Conservative Judaism. In addition to the religious-ideological and social bases for their opposition, some point to the sociological evidence in the finding of the study by Liebman and Shapiro concerning the future of Conservative Judaism.[29] That evidence derives from the fact that the most

27 Ibid., p. 20.
28 Ibid., p. 21.
29 Charles S. Liebman and Saul Shapiro, "A Survey of the Conservative Movement and Some of Its Religious Attitudes." Study released at the 1979 Biennial Convention of the United Synagogue of America, Nov. 11–15, 1979. Also see Charles S. Liebman, "The Future of Conservative Judaism in the United States," *Jerusalem Newsletter: Viewpoints*, No. 11, Center for Jewish Community Studies, March 31, 1980.

committed segment of Conservative Judaism, those whose children are most likely to continue to affiliate with the movement, is least concerned with the issue of the ordination of women. Among those who are most adamantly supportive of such ordination there is a much weaker probability that their children will affiliate with the Conservative movement; they are much more likely to affiliate with Reform or not to affiliate with any synagogue. Nevertheless, the Movement for Traditional Conservative Judaism has not as yet been able to demonstrate that it is a significant force within Conservative Judaism.

Even within American Orthodox Judaism, there have been loud calls for innovation and a reevaluation of the woman's role, both within the synagogue *per se*, and within religious life in general.[30] Although the issue has not been as challenging, on an institutional level, within Orthodoxy as it has been within the Conservative movement, both because there is a more firmly-based conception of sex-role differentiation and a much stronger tendency within Orthodoxy to submit to rabbinic authority, it seems reasonable to anticipate that the challenges to traditional modes will accelerate in the future. Since the levels of secular education and occupation are rising among Orthodox women, it is difficult to imagine that they will not internalize many of the prevalent American middle-class notions of women's equality, as will their male counterparts who are also increasingly acculturated in the educational and occupational structures. It seems inevitable that increasing numbers of Orthodox women and men will experience serious personal conflicts with respect to their perceptions of the position of women within Orthodoxy. Unless there are indications of sensitivity to those conflicts and a receptivity to accommodation within the boundaries of *halakhah* and practice, those women and men can be expected to challenge the prevalent Orthodox institutional arrangements.

The religious sphere is not the only area within Jewish life that Jewish feminists have challenged as sexist. They have also challenged the exclusive domination by males of virtually all of the decision-making positions within American Jewish organizations. As Daniel Elazar observed, in 1973:

> With some exceptions, women function in environments segregated from male decision-makers within the Jewish community. The exceptions are significant for what they reveal. Very wealthy women who have a

30 See, for example, Saul J. Berman, "The Status of Women in Halakhic Judaism," *Tradition*, Vol. 14, No. 2, Fall 1973, pp. 5–28; Chana K. Poupko and Devora L. Wohlgelernter, "Women's Liberation — An Orthodox Response," *Tradition*, Vol. 15, No. 4, Spring 1976, pp. 45–52; Blu Greenberg, *On Woman and Judaism: A View from Tradition* (Philadelphia: Jewish Publication Society of America, 1981).

record of activity in their own right, often in conjunction with their husbands, but sometimes even without them, are admitted to the governing councils of major Jewish institutions and organizations. So, too, are the top leaders of the women's groups, in an *ex officio* capacity which is sometimes translated into meaningful participation but frequently remains *ex officio*.[31]

In an effort to determine the extent to which this pattern had changed by the end of the 1970s, this author examined the listings of "National Jewish Organizations" in the 1979 American Jewish Year Book,[32] specifically with respect to the proportion of women to men among the chief executive officers of six categories of organizations: community relations, cultural, overseas aid, religious and educational, social/mutual benefit, and social welfare. In each category, specifically women's organizations were excluded, as it was assumed that their chief executive officers would be women. (Although it was discovered that even among the women's organizations there were some whose executive directors were men.) The findings indicated that seven of the twenty-four chief executive officers of community relations organizations, or 29.1 percent, were women; five of the presidents of thirty-two cultural organizations, or 15.63 percent, were women; two of the sixteen chief executive officers of overseas aid organizations, or 12.5 percent, were women; ten of the 137 executive officers of religious and cultural organizations, or 7 percent, were women; one of the chief executive officers of sixteen social/mutual benefit organizations, or 6 percent, was a woman; and three of the twenty-five executive officers of social welfare organizations, or 12 percent, were women. Comparing those proportions with those of 1969, it was found that the only category in which there was substantial difference was in community relations organizations. In 1969 there were virtually no female chief executive officers in that category.[33]

Undoubtedly, there will be those who will argue that the gross underrepresentation of women in decision-making positions within American Jewish organizations is not the result of sexism but, rather, due to the lack of professionally-trained women capable of filling these positions. Others will argue that the underrepresentation is due to the fact that women are much less career-oriented than men, and that women are much less willing than men to relocate to other communities when their careers so demand. However, these argu-

31 Daniel J. Elazar, "Women in American Jewish Life," *Congress Bi-Weekly*, Vol. 40, No. 13, Nov. 23, 1973, p. 10.
32 *American Jewish Year Book*, Vol. 79, 1979, pp. 302–42.
33 *American Jewish Year Book*, Vol. 70, 1969, pp. 469–90.

ments do not survive closer scrutiny. First of all, many, if not most of the men who occupy the key decision-making positions in American Jewish organizational life did not undergo specific professional training for their present positions. Rather, they came up through the ranks and gained most of their expertise on the job. Secondly, the results of a survey of women in Jewish communal service indicate that the majority of women who responded are very interested in career advancement and are willing to relocate when necessary.[34] The available evidence strongly supports the conclusion that the pattern of moving up the ranks into key positions is typical for males; it has been closed to women. To a large extent, this remains so even in organizations which publicly support equal rights for women, including career advancement. Given this pattern of exclusion, it may be anticipated that women who seek leadership positions will find them outside of Jewish organizational life, and that increasing numbers of Jewish women who may not, personally, aspire to high-level executive positions will, nevertheless, feel alienated from American Jewish communal life.

Of the three movements for change discussed so far, only CAJE has become institutionalized. Neither of the other two, the *Havurah* and Jewish women's movements, has become an organization. They remain social movements which have relatively wide appeal among American Jews and, to some extent, even have support among many individuals and organizations within the American Jewish "Establishment." Perhaps precisely because they have not formally organized, they have thus far avoided Michels' "iron law of oligarchy." While each challenges patterns within the established communal structure and provides for alternative modes of Jewish expression and activity, they are, by and large, viewed as legitimate subcommunal movements by the organized community, rather than as countercommunal, threatening movements. They do not challenge any of the most sacred values of the organized community, even though they may challenge specific institutional arrangements.

In contrast, there was another movement which emerged in the 1970s which, while it initially attracted many who were disturbed by what they viewed as the inflexibility and lack of creativity of American Jewish leadership with respect to the relationship between the American Jewish community and Israel, was resoundingly condemned and ostracized by the organized community. Organized after the Yom Kippur War, the movement called itself "Breira."

34 Sophie B. Engel and Jane Rogul, "Career Mobility: Perceptions and Observations (A Survey of Women in Jewish Communal Service)," *Journal of Jewish Communal Service*, Vol. 56, No. 1, Fall 1979, pp. 101–2.

In so doing, it highlighted its opposition to the dominant Israeli view of *ayn breira*, that "no alternative" exists to the policies of the Israeli government with respect to its relations with the Arabs in general, and the Palestinian Arabs in particular. Founded by a group of students from the Jewish students' movement, Breira soon became a national membership organization with a paid staff and, by 1975, a monthly newsletter, *Interchange*, appeared. It attracted many rabbis and intellectuals who favored a more conciliatory stance by Israel with respect to its Arab neighbors and the territories captured in the Six-Day War, and placed emphasis on the creative viability and autonomy of Jewish communities outside of Israel, especially in the United States, a perspective which challenged one of the core tenets of official Zionism. By 1977 the organization's newsletter expanded to include the publication of critical articles dealing with a wide range of Jewish issues, such as the future of the United Jewish Appeal,[35] the racially-changing neighborhood of East Flatbush, Brooklyn,[36] and Argentinian Jewry.[37] The major focus, however, remained: an interlocking sympathy and empathy with Palestinian Arabs, a critique of Israeli policies toward the Arabs, and a critique of the American Jewish leadership's support of those Israeli policies.

Despite its initial popularity and success in gaining wide support from among many American Jews who were dissatisfied with the leadership of the organized community, Breira was short-lived. Its demise may be attributed to external and internal forces. Externally, the more right-wing Zionist forces within the American Jewish community launched a powerful attack upon the organization and portrayed it as an enemy of Israel. For example, an organization called "Americans for a Safe Israel" published and widely distributed a pamphlet by Rael Jean Isaac, a political sociologist and Zionist Revisionist, in which she alleged that Breira supported the political program of the PLO, and that a number of the founders of Breira had direct involvements with the PLO and anti-Zionist activities.[38] Much of the English-language Jewish press in the United States, especially one of the most widely-read American Jewish weeklies, *The Jewish Week*, published many of the same allegations. Given the priority of Isarel's security in the American Jew-

---

35 Milton Goldin, "The UJA: Losing Its Appeal?," *Interchange*, Vol. 2, No. 8, April 1977, pp. 1ff.

36 Elizabeth Koltun and Neil Schechter, "Whatever Happened to East Flatbush?," *Interchange*, Vol. 2, No. 7, March 1977, pp. 1ff.

37 Eugene F. Sofer, "Argentinian Jewry: What Do We Need to Know?," *Interchange*, Vol. 3, No. 1, September 1977, pp. 1ff.

38 Rael Jean Isaac, *Breira: Counsel for Judaism* (New York: Americans for a Safe Israel, 1977).

ish value system and the tendency to accept uncritically official Israeli government positions, it is not surprising that many of the initial Breira sympathizers quickly retracted their support of the organization.

Nor did many of the activities of Breira itself provide the assurance needed that it was, first and foremost, a Jewish organization dedicated to the well-being of Jews and Jewish communities both in Israel and throughout the world. As one of the founders of the organization was to subsequently observe, Breira frequently functioned in ways which left open the degree of its *ahavat yisrael*, basic love of Israel, land and people. As Alan Mintz put it: "The confident single-mindedness of the statements issued in the aftermath of the October War, ... seemed oblivious to the enormity of the trauma in human and spiritual terms."[39] Likewise: "The placards and statements distributed by Breira at the time of Arafat's speech at the UN, which read essentially 'Palestinians — Yes, Arafat — No,' were an example of a decent political sentiment vitiated by a miserable sense of timing."[40] Also, the credibility of the organization was suspect because it had "gone to lengths to court intellectuals who have hitherto had no connection with other Jewish causes."[41] The organized campaign by the Zionist right to discredit Breira and its own political ineptness was sufficient to bring about the disintegration of the organization. It would, however, be incorrect to assume that private dissent from establishment positions has disappeared among American Jews. On the contrary, it is as alive as ever, and seems to be reappearing in a number of recent efforts to build an organized movement for change. For example, many of those who were affiliated with Breira are now affiliated with what some view as its reincarnation, a more recently-founded organization called New Jewish Agenda, which is dedicated to most of the very same objectives as Breira, but which has a much more explicitly positive Jewish stance, even as it is critical of communal leadership and policies. The extent to which it can manage to avoid the fate of Breira remains to be seen. Or, to cite an even more recent example, the organization spearheaded by a small group of Jewish intellectuals who have records of extensive involvement in American Jewish organizational life, Israel-oriented affairs, and worldwide Jewish causes, which was formed following the Israeli operation in Lebanon during the summer of 1982. This organization was formed in protest at Israeli government policies, and seeks to provide an alternative to official avenues for American

---

39 Alan Mintz, "The People's Choice?: A Demurral on Breira," *Response*, No. 32, Winter 1976/7, p. 8.
40 Ibid.
41 Ibid., p. 9.

Jewish philanthropic funds raised on behalf of Israel, so that the Israeli government may not put those funds to use in carrying out policies opposed by many American Jews. The extent to which this new organization will succeed, thereby, in changing Israeli government policies is highly doubtful, especially in the short range, given the differences in the nature of the relationship between Israel and American Jewry.[42] On the other hand, because of the apparent strong stream of disagreement with Israeli policy within the American Jewish community, the prospects for this organization's success in changing the patterns of philanthropy within that community may be significantly stronger.

To return to one of the first issues raised in this article, namely, the democracy of the organized American Jewish community, it may be concluded that the answer is not a simple one. It is a democracy in that most of the organizational leadership is elected by the membership of the individual organizations or their representatives. The positions of the leadership probably represent those of the mainstream in the community, though not always, of course, uniformly so. However, there is a significant segment of the American Jewish population, consisting of many who are organizationally affiliated, and many more who are not, which is critical of the community leadership and structure and feels relatively impotent to effect meaningful change. Nor does the communal leadership feel the need to reach out to the elements of American Jewry, to bring them within the communal structure in a meaningful way, and to engage in critical analysis of established norms and possible need for change. It is this exclusive character of the communal structure and its leadership which poses the greatest challenge to the future of the organized American Jewish community.

42 Cf., Charles S. Liebman, "Moral and Symbolic Elements in the Politics of Israel–Diaspora Relations," in Daniel J. Elazar (ed.), *Kinship and Consent*, op. cit., pp. 345–54.

EMANUEL RACKMAN

POLITICAL CONFLICT AND COOPERATION: POLITICAL CONSIDERATIONS IN JEWISH INTER-DENOMINATIONAL RELATIONS, 1955—1956*

INTRODUCTION

In the history of the Jewish people there always were agreements and disagreements with regard to ritual and dogma. The disagreements precipitated sects during the Second Commonwealth, the Middle Ages, and even the early modern period, and these sects have been the subject of extensive research. The contemporary period, however, has received little attention, and more particularly the relationships between different groups within the so-called orthodox camp and, in turn, their relationships to non-orthodox groups. The views held by the different factions have yielded a rich literature but the position of each *vis-à-vis* its opponents still requires reporting and analysis.

For example, in the period between the two world wars two highly respected spokesmen of American orthodoxy articulated two directly opposite points of view. And American orthodox Jews followed one or the other of these spiritual leaders. The highly revered Rabbi Moshe Feinstein was asked whether it was halakhically proper for orthodox Jews to join with non-orthodox Jews in the formation of a community federation to raise funds for distribution to sundry charitable causes. (See *Igrot Moshe*, "Yoreh Deah" [1959] 296-9.) His ruling was that it is forbidden to do so unless those in charge of the distribution of the funds are orthodox Jews. Moreover, if any of the funds were to be used for the support of causes sponsored by reform and conservative Jews then orthodox Jews would offend against the *halakhah* insofar as their contributions would aid and abet the teaching of subversive doctrines to children by non-orthodox rabbis. The sin is a heinous one: "unless the participation of orthodox Jews (in the federation) would help orthodox causes to acquire more than the orthodox Jews gave. Under such circumstances it could be held that orthodox Jews were not helping the causes of heretics since they were

---

*   This article constitutes a personal memoir concerning an incident not yet subjected to scholarly treatment. During the period discussed (1955-56), the author was Vice-President of the Rabbinical Council of America (eds.).

diminishing the amount the heretics would be able to spend" (my own translation). Rabbi Feinstein also held that weddings at which reform rabbis officiated could hardly be deemed valid unless it was known that two observant orthodox Jews beheld the ceremony at close range and could thus be deemed competent witnesses. In the event of the termination of marriages solemnized by reform rabbis it may even be that no *get* (religious divorce) was required. (*Igrot Moshe*, "Even ha-Ezer" [1961], 177-80.)

These two responsa of Rabbi Feinstein are cited less for their relevance to the central theme of this paper and more for the point of view toward reform Judaism that they reveal.

By contrast, one can cite the view and practice of Dr. Samuel Belkin, the late president of Yeshiva University. He was very much committed to the unity of the Jewish people and the need for mutual respect amongst rabbis of the most diverse theological and halakhic positions. One way in which he justified his stance was to advance the proposition that in matters of policy the laity shall have a voice and, of course, in the overwhelming majority of instances, the orthodox Jewish laity wanted cooperation with non-orthodox Jews and, indeed, so deported themselves.

In his *Essays in Traditional Jewish Thought* (Philosophical Library, New York [1956], pp. 138–40), Belkin distinguished between "the problem of the authority of strict *halakhah*, and the problem of the authority of policy." With regard to the former, the great masters of the Talmud and Codes must render the final decision. But "how one should live in accordance with the *halakhah* is a different matter entirely." The controversy between the Mizrachi and the Agudath Israel was cited as one illustration of a "matter of policy" and "when questions of policy arise, the decision should not be made by one person or by one organization. Such decisions should be referred to the leading authorities in *halakhah*, members of the practicing rabbinate, and also to lay leaders who are concerned with the preservation of orthodox Jewry."

Not many years were to pass before the contrasting views of these men would find expression in an unfortunate chapter of American Jewish history, which this essay aims to describe and analyse.

The conflict was essentially non-ideological, and not even religious in the sense that differences in religious doctrine and canon law lay at the heart of the controversy. Instead the conflict was political in nature. Would one religious establishment risk the implication that a competing religious establishment was entitled to legitimacy? The conflict was political in the same sense that states often deny legitimacy to one political party or another — usually communist parties. It is for that reason that it merits consideration in a volume devoted to political conflict in the Jewish community and the Jewish state.

119

Furthermore, it was a conflict in which participants made decisions not because of their religious convictions as individuals but rather as defenders of establishment interests. It was neither one's creed nor one's conception as to what the *halakhah* requires that determined one's position, but rather what was best for the establishment of which one was a part. That, too, made the controversy political in character. And the result was disastrous — to the discredit of American orthodoxy, and a major cause of one of Israel's problems in the present.

Unfortunately it is difficult to document the facts. Most of the important meetings were held in secret; the principals met at midnight without the benefit of recorders of protocols; and what little is available in documents does not do justice to the lion's share of the negotiations, for which there must be reliance on the memory of those who played a part. Nonetheless, the tale should be told for the benefit of a perhaps wiser posterity in the future.

THE BACKGROUND

The Rabbinical Assembly in the United States — whose members are generally regarded as conservative rabbis and not orthodox — proposed to solve several pressing problems of Jewish family law by drafting a new *ketubah* — a new marriage contract which would be used in all marriages at which their constituents would officiate. The change was given considerable publicity and immediately evoked hysterical protests from the orthodox establishment. Some of the protests were based on halakhic grounds — the new *ketubah* might be deemed invalid as a marriage contract. Others, including myself, felt that it was too inadequate a correction for the existing evils in Jewish family law. Indeed, to undertake a "reform" which would do little good, was to place in jeopardy the chance for more radical changes. Many also felt that the suggested change would not be effective because the courts of the United States would not enforce it for constitutional reasons.

What became generally known was that the change had the approval of the late Professor Saul Lieberman, one of the greatest talmudical scholars of the century and a Jew whose orthodoxy was beyond question. However, he taught at the Jewish Theological Seminary, most of whose alumni were conservative rabbis, and consequently his proposal was deemed their proposal. What is more, it was commonly believed that Chief Rabbi Herzog of Israel had been consulted and had found no fault with the recommendation. Rabbi Joseph B. Soloveitchik's criticism was mild — he referred to one halakhic problem, clearly a minor one — which months later he admitted that he and Professor Lieberman could correct. Nonetheless, all hell broke loose! It was apparent that the conflict was not based on the merits of the proposal itself but rather on the unmitigated gall of a non-orthodox "establishment" venturing into a domain which had always been regarded as the exclusive preserve of the orthodox.

It was apparent from the start that establishment interests lay at the heart of the controversy and not religious concerns. And the danger that the division in the American Jewish community would be exacerbated was clear and present.

To prevent this, some of the leaders of the Rabbinical Council — the more progressive of the orthodox rabbinical organizations — began to talk with the leaders of the Rabbinical Assembly, and at the same time Professor Lieberman and Dr. Soloveitchik held secret meetings with each other. The time was ripe for some kind of understanding between the two groups with regard to Jewish family law in order that there be no split which would complicate the lives of American Jews, most of whom were prepared to abide by the *halakhah* in family law and wanted some kind of understanding between the orthodox and conservative leaders, all of whom were committed to the centrality of the *halakhah* in marriage and divorce.

From all of the talks, there emerged a very impressive plan which would have attained that unity. The plan provided for the following:

1. There would be set up in the United States a national *Beth Din* (court) which would be recognized as the official *Beth Din* of both groups — the Rabbinical Council and the Rabbinical Assembly.

2. Its members would be selected by Professor Lieberman and Dr. Soloveitchik, and the *Dayanim* (judges) would themselves provide for their successors in self-perpetuation.

3. Both rabbinical groups would delegate to the *Beth Din* exclusive authority to rule on all matters of Jewish family law and neither group would make any decision with regard to family law which was not approved by the *Beth Din*.

4. The *Beth Din* would be established as an independent corporation whose directors would be laymen responsible for the financing of the operation. They would not act as representatives of either rabbinic group.

5. When the *Beth Din* would be established, each rabbinic group would convene a national convention on the same day and simultaneously recognize the *Beth Din* as the exclusive authority in matters of Jewish family law.

121

6. Professor Lieberman and Rabbi Soloveitchik would together revise the *ketubah* projected by the Rabbinical Assembly so that it would have the approval of the *Beth Din* to be constituted.

7. The incorporation of the *Beth Din* would be entrusted to a law firm which enjoyed the confidence of both groups.

If this plan had been implemented, many important consequences for Israel would have ensued.

On Israel's problem "Who is a Jew?" both the orthodox and the conservative movements would have been united, for one *Beth Din* would have spoken for them. It would be unnecessary there to seek a change in the law adding the words "according to the *halakhah*." Reform Jews would remain a clear minority with only rare problems calling for resolution by the Israeli courts. The court cases would, most likely, involve only issues unrelated to *halakhah*.

In addition, the pressure of non-orthodox Jews on the government, the Jewish Agency, the World Zionist Organization, and their fund-raising arms would be entirely neutralized. It is only the combined pressure of the conservative and reform that makes the problem and the pressure so serious now.

The failure of the plan precipitated the alliance of the conservative and reform against the orthodox in the United States and in Israel. And the alliance is an "unholy" one. The reform reject *halakhah* — the conservatives are committed to it. What unites them, therefore, is only opposition to the orthodox. Consequently many conservative rabbis want to split their own movement. These dissidents feel that it is unfair to their point of view to make it appear that they are so close to the reform movement and so distant from the orthodox when, in fact, the opposite is true.

THE CAUSE FOR THE FAILURE OF THE PLAN

It must be obvious that once the plan had the approval of Professor Lieberman and Dr. Soloveitchik, it could not be impugned on halakhic grounds. The objection, therefore, could only come from the fact that orthodox rabbis were cooperating with non-orthodox rabbis. That such cooperation would advance the cause of *halakhah*, prevent abuses in Jewish family law, and even reduce the incidence of bastardy, was not sufficient to save the scheme. What mattered more was the political fact that a modicum of *de jure* recognition would be given to a non-orthodox group of rabbis. And this was one basis for the plan. However, the failure was dramatically linked with another historic event and a none too impressive face-saving justification by the

Rabbinical Council to rescue Dr. Soloveitchik from his understandably embarrassing situation.

At about the same time, a group of heads of *Yeshivot* pronounced a ban against the participation of the Rabbinical Council and its lay affiliate — the Union of Orthodox Jewish Congregations of America — in any federation with non-orthodox rabbinic and/or lay groups. The ban was also pronounced against membership by orthodox rabbis on boards of rabbis which included non-orthodox members. Rabbi Moshe Feinstein was one of the most celebrated signatories to the ban. Though requested to join him, Dr. Samuel Belkin, president of Yeshiva University, and Dr. Soloveitchik consistently refused. For Dr. Soloveitchik the refusal was emotionally more difficult. Nonetheless, for almost three decades he has held fast and though he incurred the unrelenting animosity of most of those who signed the ban, he remained the chairman of the Rabbinical Council's Halacha Commission and never ruled that the Rabbinical Council should withdraw from the Synagogue Council of America, which had representatives of conservative and reform synagogue and rabbinic groups as well as orthodox ones. Neither did he ever direct the Rabbinical Council to expel its members who were also members of mixed rabbinic groups.

The ban was widely publicized in the press precisely when the plan for the joint *Beth Din* was reaching its final stages of implementation. Indeed, the attorney had already prepared the charter for the *Beth Din*'s incorporation.

In that climate it was impossible to continue. While the plan did not call for cooperation, no one could have thought that anything other than a mutual understanding could have brought it about. On the face of it, the plan required no joint action by the two rabbinic groups involved. Their recognition of the independent *Beth Din* would be on the same day but by separate and independent conventions. The "myth" of separation was not violated. But only the stupid would have failed to sense that behind the separate and independent actions there was a "conspiracy" of cooperation. And so to avoid any possible misunderstanding that orthodox and conservative were engaged in a common effort, the plan had to be abandoned.

Yet how it was scrapped is also worthy of consideration. Even before the Executive Committee of the Rabbinical Council could consider it, the scheme required the approval of its Halacha Commission. The recommendation of the Halacha Commission would have ensured acceptance. Otherwise, rejection was inevitable. Rabbi Soloveitchik was chairman of the Commission and his firm stand for the plan was all that was needed. But the ban of nine heads of *Yeshivot* was too recent to be ignored, even if it went unmentioned. Consequently, while the Halacha Commission never approved the ban and to this day sanctions the participation of the Rabbinical Council in the Synagogue Council of America, and does not discipline members who are active in mixed rabbinic groups like the New York Board of Rabbis, nonetheless it rejected the plan for a joint *Beth Din* by a vote of seven to five.

One of the principal reasons given — and deemed significant by Dr. Soloveitchik — was the fact that the Rabbinical Assembly would not commit itself to discipline its members who would act in a manner that the *Beth Din* would find objectionable. The organization was prepared to commit only itself. It would take no action that would not have the *Beth Din*'s approval, but its members would be free to do as they pleased. In all fairness to the leadership of the Rabbinical Assembly it must be said that they did not rule out the possibility that one day such restrictions on the members might be approved. However, at that time it was too bold a step to take — the group still had many Reconstructionists who were less committed to the *halakhah* than the more recent graduates of the Jewish Theological Seminary.

Here again one finds that a political consideration, rather than a *halakhic* one, doomed a very significant plan which would have made the historic family law of Judaism the norm for the overwhelming majority of synagogue-affiliated Jews in the western hemisphere. It was not concern for the *halakhah* that determined the result, but the relationships between synagogue and rabbinic bodies.

THE SEQUEL

Sooner or later it would become necessary for the leadership of the Rabbinical Council of America, or at least its Halacha Commission, to rationalize why it did not yield to the ban of the *Yeshiva* "heads" while rejecting cooperation with the conservative movement in solving what many regard as the most painful and pressing problem of the *halakhah* in modern society — the problem of the *agunah* — the disadvantaged woman who cannot marry because of halakhic disabilities. Why did the view of Dr. Belkin prevail with regard to the ban and why did it fail in the area of family law in which the laity virtually begs for solutions?

The distinction was not long in coming and, in fact, there were early indications as to what it would be. When the Rabbinical Council considered participation with non-orthodox rabbis and congregations in religious services celebrating the three hundredth anniversary of the arrival of the first Jews to the United States, its Halacha Commission, led by Dr. Soloveitchik, ruled that there should be no joint services. However, it would permit such a joint non-sectarian observance where the non-Jewish community was to be involved. This was a preview of the now well established distinction between *klapei chutz* and *klapei pnim*. The former involved activity *vis-à-vis* the non-Jewish community. In such matters all Jews must act as one, and denominational or sectarian differences must be avoided as much as possible. However, within the Jewish community, the stance of separation must be maintained. And superficially viewed, Jewish family law involves only the Jewish community and consequently every group must go its own way.

Is the distinction based on halakhic principles, sources, authorities, precedents, or the like? None were ever cited and one has reason to doubt that any exist. The American Jewish situation is *sui generis* and history affords no parallel. Yet the fact that the distinction is an original conception does not warrant its dismissal. It may make good sense and constitutes excellent policy. But at best it might be deemed *Da'at Torah* — the wisdom that a Torah luminary would express and certainly revision may be called for in the light of experience. In this connection Dr. Belkin's suggestion that the laity have a voice was not heeded.

In many situations the distinction proved applicable. However, in many — perhaps most — it is not easy to determine what issue is of concern only to Jews. All Jews cooperate when their time-honored method of slaughtering cattle is threatened by non-Jewish government agencies. Indeed, with regard to all activity by the states and the federal governments, the Jews usually form a common front. However, is Jewish family law not an issue which one could have foreseen as involving the civil, non-Jewish, courts? Indeed, the very change in the *ketubah* which the conservative movement projected and which precipitated this sad chapter in American Jewish history, visualized the involvement of civil courts. Thus, no one should have been surprised when two decades later a number of matters pertaining to Jewish law were raised in the courts and not always to the credit of Jewish law or its fair name. Law journals and reviews began to take note. The "dirty linen" of Jews was exposed to public view. Alas, the first sin — the rejection of the plan — led to many more.

THE OUTLOOK

It is not suggested that the distinction between *klapei chutz* and *klapei pnim* be abandoned. However, in a society in which there are hardly secrets — everything that happens in the Jewish community is known by the world outside — every issue pertaining to Jewish equity and dignity involves more than the Jewish community. Consequently, almost every instance in which we have a divided house is to our detriment. Yet American Jewry had failed to take advantage of one grand opportunity to achieve a house united.

The *ketubah* which the conservative movement had revised and promulgated was considered by the highest court of the State of New York in 1983. This Court decided that the *ketubah* was a binding contract between the parties and the provision requiring the parties to appear before the *Beth Din* of the Rabbinical Assembly was enforceable. There is a possibility that a further appeal will be made to the United States Supreme Court since the husband raised a constitutional issue. He argued that the decision of the court violated the constitutional requirement of separation of church and state and alleged that the civil courts were being used to enforce palpably religious obligations.

At the present writing there is no way to predict whether the United States Supreme Court will entertain the appeal, and if it does, how it will dispose of the issue. It is the considered judgment of this writer that a civil court may even order a husband to authorize the writing and delivery of the *get* because the *get* is a totally secular instrument. It makes no reference to God or to His will; no reference to sacred sources; and contains no prayers or even exhortations. It contains date and place, the names of the parties, the fact of the divorce and the right to remarry. That Jewish law requires that it be written and delivered with many formalities makes the document no more religious than the formalities in yesteryear pertaining to a seal. That Jewish law requires that it be written exclusively for the parties involved enhances the dignity of the object as personally addressed invitations do in many other connections. Nor is God referred to in the process of the delivery of the *get*.

That it is a *mitzvah*, a divine commandment to give a *get*, makes it no more religious than the giving of charity, also a divine commandment, or the administration of justice, another divine commandment. The fact that a rabbi will not marry either party unless the earlier marriage is terminated with a *get* makes it no more religious than the fact that he will also not marry them unless they get a civil divorce. Does the civil divorce thus become a "religious" performance? The reference in the bill of divorce to the *dat* of Moses and Israel is not a reference to their faith. Only in modern Hebrew has the word *dat* come to mean religion. Originally it referred only to established custom.

There is no reason why courts should not specifically enforce any contractual commitment to give a *get*. What is more, they ought to order it in the case of any couple who were married by a rabbi because such a marriage — entered into with the consent of both — implies an obligation either to stay married or to cut the cord completely, and cutting the cord means ending the relationship with all that is required — in the United States, a civil divorce — and a *get*.

To comply with such an order, the husband is not required to subscribe to any religious beliefs and he does not have to mention God, soul, immortality, or any other words which imply a compromise of his convictions. He need only say that he instructs two competent witnesses to write and deliver a bill of divorce. And, as already indicated, the bill of divorce itself contains nothing more than the date and place, the names of the parties, the fact of divorce and the right to remarry.

That rabbinical courts in Israel have jurisdiction over divorces also does not make it a religious matter. These same courts once had exclusive jurisdiction in the matter of inheritance. Is the law of estates, therefore, to be deemed "religious"? These courts still have jurisdiction over child custody and the support of spouses. Are these matters, therefore, also "religious"?

However, the mere fact that the courts will be called upon to consider these matters reveals how questionable is the distinction between *klapei chutz* and *klapei pnim*. Non-Jewish courts are becoming involved in what a generation ago one would not have believed would be anything other than an issue within the Jewish community. If this could happen to Jewish family law, what area of Jewish communal activity can be securely withheld from the eye of the general community? And if so, is it the view of Rabbi Feinstein or that of Dr. Belkin that should prevail?

One inevitably asks: Shall it be conflict or cooperation hereafter? Separatism or accommodation?

SAM LEHMAN-WILZIG

CONFLICT AS COMMUNICATION: PUBLIC PROTEST IN ISRAEL, 1950–1982 *

1. INTRODUCTION

Public protest in Israel has been on the rise from the early 1970s and shows no sign of abating.[1] Whereas the first year of that decade was marked by fifty-six protests, 1979 saw two hundred and forty-one such events — on average two protests every three days! Indeed, viewed from another perspective, Israel ranks as the *most* protest-oriented polity in the democratic world today. In a poll conducted during December 1981, 21.5% of the Israeli adult population admitted to having participated in a protest event, far ahead of the previous

* This essay concludes a series of articles issuing from a large-scale project on Israeli public protest funded by the National Council for Research and Development (Grant No. 5095). I would like to thank the Council for its generous aid.

1 The first two decades of Israel's existence were relatively static, despite some year to year ups and downs. The 1950s averaged forty events per annum, while the 1960s averaged forty-three. The 1970s in contrast averaged one hundred and twenty-seven.

The methodology for data collection is explained at length in my article "Public Protest and Systemic Stability in Israel: 1960–1979," which appeared in the series' previous volume *Comparative Jewish Politics: Public Life in Israel and the Diaspora*, edited by Bernard Susser and myself. It can also be found in my other articles which are cited throughout this essay. Briefly, then, the main source for the data herein is the daily newspaper, *The Jerusalem Post* (*Ha'aretz* was used as a control). All protest events and/or instances of public unrest which entailed at least ten adults were scored along a number of variables (intensity, reaction of authorities, size, duration, organization, issue, level of authority protested against, locale, nationality, and type of protest). The following were not counted: economic strikes, Arab protest in the administered territories, regular conferences issuing a protest resolution, election rallies (unless they involved a public disturbance), and political pressure without a group physical presence (telephone campaigns, petitions, press conferences).

Attitudinal data were derived from a public opinion poll which I initiated (through the good offices of Dr. Mina Zemach — DAHAF Agency). The sample included 1250 adult Israelis, excluding the kibbutz and the Arab sectors.

record (11%) held by the U.S.[2] — and this some time *before* the reported 400,000 who demonstrated against the government's hesitancy to establish a Commission of Inquiry immediately after the Lebanese Sabra and Shatilla refugee camp massacres.

Given the fact that Israel's very existence has been under constant threat since its establishment, such a "world record" seems astonishing and puzzling. It is a virtual truism in political science that external danger tends to crystallize internal solidarity among all social groups, and the nation-state is no exception. Paradoxically, there is even strong evidence in Israel with regard to war years that such is the case along a multitude of non-political indicators.[3] Why, then, given the parlous state of the State, is protest frequency so high in Israel?

There is virtually no limit to the number of factors underlying social turmoil and public protest which have been advanced in the past by researchers from such disparate disciplines as psychology, sociology, economics, political science, criminology, cultural anthropology, history, and most recently socio-biology.[4]

2 Samuel H. Barnes, Max Kaase, *et al.*, *Political Action: Mass Participation in Five Western Democracies* (Beverly Hills: Sage Publications, 1979), p. 59.

3 Simha F. Landau and Benjamin Beit-Hallahmi, "Israel: Aggression in Psychohistorical Perspective," in *Aggression in Global Perspective*, ed. Arnold P. Goldstein and Marshall H. Segall (New York: Pergamon Press, 1982), pp. 261–86. See also G. Fishman, "On War and Crime," in *Stress in Israel*, ed. S. Breznitz (New York: Van Nostrand, 1983). From an economic standpoint, Amira Galin and Baruch Mevorach found that strikes decrease during war periods; see their "Al Politikah Ve'Sihsuhai Avodah," *Riv'on Le'kalkalah*, No. 108 (March 1981), pp. 35–42. The same phenomenon seems to hold for public protests, as my project indicates. No protests took place during the actual war period in 1967 and in 1973. 1982 presents a problem given the uncertainty (for the Israeli public and for the researcher) as to when the war officially "ended." The major battles ended within a month of the outbreak of hostilities. During this period there were virtually no protest events. However, opposition did build up through that summer and continued in force until June 1985, a period when Israeli soldiers were still dying in Lebanon as a result of hit-and-run attacks. Thus, in a broad sense, the 1982 War does follow the trend of its predecessors (no protest during major hostilities, a buildup of protest after their cessation), but technically 1982/3 could be considered a war-time protest period and, as such, a reversal of previous trends. In any case, regression analysis suggests that several intervening variables may be at work during the earlier war periods. See Sam Lehman-Wilzig and Meyer Ungar, "The Economic and Political Determinants of Public Protest Frequency and Magnitude: The Israeli Experience," *International Review of Modern Sociology*, vol. 15, No. 1 (Spring 1985).

4 To list but a few causes and/or facilitators put forward: relative deprivation, modernization, political culture, innate human aggression, mass communications, crowd psychology, frustrated expectations, territoriality, and anomie. For a useful introduction to the specific question of causality and to the whole field in general

All are reasonable, most are valid, but none can be said to be predominant — especially given the wide variations between nations from an institutional, environmental, and population standpoint. Thus, while several factors may be found in virtually all countries, the relative weight of each may differ considerably from society to society.

A close reading of the Israeli scene suggests three general categories under which might be subsumed most of the significant factors outlined by the vast literature. These are policy output, environmental conditions, and political communication. The first two are relatively straightforward since they lend themselves to statistical analysis (however sophisticated, cumbersome, and/or open to manipulation that may prove to be). The third is more difficult to deal with quantitatively and as a result is less "popular" as an explanatory variable. In the case of Israel this is particularly unfortunate because political communication may indeed be at least as important as the other two.

This essay, then, will devote most of its attention to delineating this third general factor, bringing to bear a number of peripheral quantitative studies which indirectly illuminate the nature of the problem. The predominant focus here on political communication, therefore, should not be construed as suggesting that it dwarfs the other two in importance; rather, it is an attempt to right an imbalance in previous works which have dealt with the cause(s) of public protest in general and Israeli protest specifically.[5]

see Ted R. Gurr, *Handbook of Political Conflict: Theory and Research* (New York: The Free Press, 1980), especially pp. 175–219 and its massive bibliography on pp. 501–53.

5 In a sense, I share part of the blame in this. My first article within this project — "Public Protest and Systemic Stability...," op. cit., virtually ignored the issue of political communication. Indeed, I began that article by declaring that the collected data supported my hypothesis of an increased protest pressure with the consequent weakening of formal political institutions, not realizing that the causal chain may have been the reverse. Later studies in the overall research project did begin to address this aspect, as shall shortly be seen. The same myopia exists in the general literature. In Gurr's review of the multifarious causal factors of protest and turmoil (*Handbook*, op. cit.), no mention is made of political (non)communication on the institutional plane. Indeed, "political communication" does not even appear in the volume's Index of Subjects! The closest thing to my argument is Huntington's modernization/institutionalization thesis: social modernization mobilizes the public to greater political participation; if political development lags, blockage ensues and aggressive modes of action occur instead. See Samuel P. Huntington, *Political Order in Changing Societies* (New Haven: Yale University Press, 1968). In a sense, my argument looks at the other side of the coin — what happens when political participation stays at relatively high levels while the formal political system *regresses* from a formerly open condition.

2. POLICY DISSATISFACTION AND ENVIRONMENTAL CONDITIONS

Policy dissatisfaction is the most obvious factor underlying public protest. Were one to ask virtually any Israeli protester why s/he was protesting, invariably the answer would be: "I'm against this specific law/policy." [6]

Given the very high level of political interest which Israelis display, it is not surprising that they are sensitive to the system's output. A poll taken in the late 1960s found 87% of the population to be "very" (61%) or "somewhat interested" (26%) in national security and foreign relations issues, with 85% discussing them "frequently" (55%) or "from time to time" (30%).[7] Eighty-six percent of the population read at least one daily newspaper; the most-watched TV show with the highest viewership is the nightly news report (*Mabat*). The country itself is relatively small and the government's role in daily life quite preponderant. Thus, almost nothing goes unreported and all public decisions have a strong impact on the citizen's social existence. As a result, Israelis react quickly and vociferously to what they consider to be policies harmful to their interests. In this they are qualitatively no different from most other democracies for, as Barnes and Kaase discovered in their massive project, "in all five countries, policy dissatisfaction has an impact on protest potential. In a broad sense, then, protesting is a response to dissatisfaction with specific societal goals." [8]

Yet, by itself, policy dissatisfaction cannot explain the phenomenon of Israeli public protest in its entirety. For one thing, wide variations in protest frequency over the years tend to indicate that more is at work here. The citizen does not live in a vacuum, reacting in reflex fashion only to stimuli from above. Rather s/he is a social being, and consequently is influenced by the general social, economic, and political environment. Thus, all things pertaining to political output being otherwise equal, significant differences relating to protest

6   This is not true of protest in many other — usually non-democratic — countries. A large part of the protest there is geared to toppling the government or even the regime. This motive is virtually nonexistent in Israel (excluding the extreme fringe on the Left and the religious fanatics on the Right). Protest against the continuation of the government has begun to increase recently, but is still usually as a result of specific policies. Israel has yet to see the "general strike" designed to topple the government.

7   Shlomit Levy, *Political Involvement and Attitude* (Jerusalem: The Israel Institute of Applied Social Research, Publication No. SL/530/E), Table 3, p. 22. On social issues the results were 67% ("interest") and 65% ("discuss"); on economic issues 69% and 63% respectively. The poll was taken in 1969.

8   Barnes & Kaase, *et al.*, *Political Action*, op. cit., p. 439.

frequency and other related aspects (e.g. intensity, duration, etc.) still manifest themselves as a result of differing environmental conditions.

A few of the most important such conditions should suffice to illustrate the point. Arguably, the central one is the economic mileu. Even here, however, the situation is complex. In a regression analysis which included virtually all the major economic variables and a few non-economic ones as well,[9] inflation exhibited the most consistent effect upon the frequency of protest. Less consistent, but still quite significant, was unemployment. It must be noted that in both cases this held true for protests on most *non*-economic issues as well (social, political, and religious). In other words, the fear of losing one's job and the frustration at seeing one's earning power eroded causes a general feeling of dissatisfaction, creating a mental set more predisposed to protest — even on issues not directly connected with inflation or unemployment themselves.[10]

Far more surprisingly, as GNP *per capita* increases and as the *rate* of such increase rises, protest frequency on all issue areas in Israel has gone up as well! The most probable reason for this is that *rapid* economic growth (a situation endemic to Israel for much of its history) leads to socio-economic dislocation. Relative deprivation can occur precisely when economic growth is at its peak, through a widening of the gap between some sectors and others.[11]

Another environmental condition, especially germane in the case of the State of Israel, is war. Until Operation Peace for Galilee in 1982 virtually no protest was to be found during hostilities throughout Israel's history. The immediate post-war periods display a more complex picture: social, economic, and religious protest is lower than "normal" for each respective period, while the frequency of political protest tends to be higher. This latter probably reflects the public's frustration with the government's inability to transform the fruits of military victory into any sort of permanent political achievement

9 Lehman-Wilzig & Ungar, "The Economic and Political Determinants of Public Protest...., op. cit. See too our article "Al Me'kha'ah Tziburit Ve'gormehah Ha'kalkaliim: Yisrael 1951–1979," *Ri'von Le'kalkalah*, No. 114 (September 1982), pp. 275–83, which comes to much the same conclusion although more limited in scope.

10 The consequences of inflation, especially, are both objective and subjective. Despite the most sophisticated system of linkage and indexation in the world, Israeli wage earners still suffer(ed) from salary erosion over the three- or six-month period until the next automatic raise. However, were this hole to be plugged up, the general disorientation of the consumer/worker/employer as a result of ever-rising prices may by itself be enough to cause profound social dissatisfaction. In addition, the steady devaluation of the national currency adds little to national collective self-respect, with its consequent political malaise.

11 For a fuller discussion of this see Mancur Olson, Jr., "Rapid Growth as a Destabilizing Force," *Journal of Economic History*, Vol. 23 (1963), pp. 529–52.

(not to mention peace *de jure*). Thus, for example, whereas in 1967 there were 9 political-issue protests, the following three years were marked by 20, 26, and 27 respectively (the number of non-political-issue protests actually declined relative to 1967). This dramatic increase is all the more remarkable given the fact that the years 1968–70 saw the first national unity government in Israel's history. Despite a virtual wall-to-wall government coalition of all the main-stream and non-radical parties, political-issue protest still rose precipitously (even above and beyond the pre-war period).[12]

One can point to a number of other environmental conditions which possibly influence protest. Some have been proven to be significant, others are more speculative. Of the former, government size, the existence of television, and election campaigns each correlate in some way to Israeli protest, and will be discussed in the following section. Political culture, on the other hand, is more nebulous — both definitionally and as a causal factor. One can point to the Jewish ethos of argumentation — in the social and educational spheres (the Talmud proceeds by dialectical argumentation almost throughout), as well as in the political sphere (numerous cases of "public protest" can be cited from the Bible alone: Exodus 14: 10–12; 15: 24; 16: 2–3; 17: 2–3; *Numbers* 11: 1; 14: 2–3; 16: 3, 13, 14; etc.).[13] Cecil Roth, the noted Jewish historian, described the Jew as the "Eternal Protestant."[14] Nevertheless, in the aforementioned public opinion poll, when asked "why do you think there is so much protest in Israel," the Israeli public placed the answer "in Diaspora the Jews always pro-tested against the authorities and continue this tradition today in Israel" — well below all others. Thus, if political culture does act as an environmental factor it is too subtle for the protesters themselves to be aware of it.

3. POLITICAL COMMUNICATION

Modern democratic institutions came into being about 200 years ago — more or less when political parties crystallized in their modern form. As a result, it was the political party which constituted the central component in the ongoing process of democratic political communication between the elected represen-tatives and their constituency. The party served as the chief source for inter-

---

12 For a detailed numerical rundown of all annual protest in Israel — by issue — see Lehman-Wilzig and Ungar, "The Economic and Political Determinants...," op. cit., Table 1.

13 See Abraham Kaplan, "The Jewish Argument with God," *Commentary*, vol. 70, no. 4 (October 1980), pp. 43–7.

14 Cecil Roth, "The Eternal Protestant," in *Personalities and Events in Jewish History* (Philadelphia: Jewish Publication Society of America, 1953), pp. 69–77.

esting and mobilizing the masses into some form of political activity, as well as constituting the actual channel for delivering political messages to the powers-that-be. In short, as Kaase notes, the political party is the "core mediating element between the governors and the governed." [15]

If anything, the pre-State situation in Israel was marked by the virtual supremacy of the political party in the political sphere. [16] The Labor camp, the dominant faction which held the key posts in the *Va'ad Leumi* (National Directorate) throughout the entire history of the Mandatory *yishuv* (the pre-State Jewish community), was considered in certain quarters to be indistinguishable from the government itself — a situation which continued for twenty-nine years after the establishment of the State of Israel. Party membership in proportional terms was high for all the major parties, in part as a result of the highly ideologized atmosphere, the multifarious services which the parties provided, and probably also in some measure due to the freeing of the Jews' political energies after two millennia of political quiescence in hostile and constricting surroundings.

The centrality of the party apparatus [17] with regard to the transfer of political messages from the public to the government was even further reinforced by the unique system of pure proportional representation in effect since 1920. No national representative is elected by a specific geographical constituency; rather, all enter national office [18] as part of an electoral *party* list. This has

---

15 Max Kaase, "The Crisis of Authority: Myth and Reality," in *Challenge to Governance: Studies in Overloaded Polities*, ed. Richard Rose (Beverly Hills: Sage, 1980), p. 17.

16 The same held true in the socio-economic sphere as well, since many if not most newspapers, sports teams, cultural clubs, publishing houses, banks and corporations, were party-owned and/or controlled. While this is a somewhat different matter, it does have bearing on our subject. One of its consequences was to stunt the growth of independent civic institutions which could have been used later as tools for lobbying and otherwise informally transferring messages from the non-affiliated public to the government.

17 Yonatan Shapira, *Ha'demokratia B'yisrael* (Ramat Gan: Massada, 1977), sees this aspect as being perhaps the most critical one in the development of Israeli politics:
    The transformation of Achdut Ha'avoda into a bureaucratized party was an event central to the understanding of the Israeli political system in its entirety. It constituted the dominant party and its internal organization became a model for all the others which arose thereafter. One cannot understand Israeli politics and the essence of the Israeli democratic regime without taking into account the behavioral patterns of these party bureaucrats (p. 102; translation mine).

18 Until 1978 the same held true on the local municipal level as well. Now, mayors are directly elected by the voting public; the city councils continue to be elected through proportional representation.

the effect of making all Members of Knesset beholden to their party first and to their (self-defined) constituency second, if at all.

As a result of all this, the formal channels of political communication all led through the same source. But as long as the party had a wide formal base, as long as it actively tried to mobilize new members,[19] and as long as it was willing to serve as the quasi-official conduit of public requests, demands, and even displeasure, to the formal political leadership, the political system as a whole could function with relative efficiency. However, this same overwhelming dominance would cause difficulties for the Israeli system as a whole were the parties to cease to function in their traditional manner. This is precisely what has happened over the past two decades.

The reasons for such party ossification and systematic hardening of the arteries are numerous, but an examination of those causes would lead us too far astray from the subject at hand. However, the post-1948 facts speak for themselves. As late as the early 1960s Gutmann could note that, despite some padding, "the incidence of party membership among Jews in Israel is certainly one of the highest in the world. At the time of the 1961 election almost one-third of the eligible voters of the eight major parties (excluding the Communists) were party members."[20] As a follow-up, in the 1981 poll the respondents were asked about their party membership and other political activity (Table 1). A mere 3.8% considered themselves active party members, a miniscule total *exceeded* by "active independents." Another 8.2% attested to being *in*active party members. Indeed, only 8.9% of the entire sample acknowledged being formally active in any way, shape, or form in Israeli politics, while, as earlier noted, the same poll showed almost two-and-a-half times as many (21.5%) having already participated in a public protest![21] It is little wonder that in an

---

19 For an illustration of the dominant party in the early *yishuv* successfully attracting a whole set of new immigrants, even at the expense of transforming the founders into a small minority, see Yosef Gorni, *Aḥdut Ha'avoda, 1919–1930* (Hakibbutz Hameuḥad, 1973), pp. 34–9.

20 Emanuel Gutmann, "Israel," *The Journal of Politics*, vol. 25, No. 4 (Nov. 1963), p. 704. Earlier, in his "Citizen Participation in Political Life: Israel," *International Social Science Journal*, vol. 12 (1960), he noted that: "At the end of 1952 it was reported by the parties themselves that about 300,000 persons, or a little over 20 per cent of the Jewish population of Israel, were organized into political parties. Three years later it was estimated that between one-third and one-fourth of all Jewish voters ... hold formal party membership" (p. 55). These fluctuating numbers notwithstanding, the general impression is one of far greater party membership a decade or so after 1948 than is the case today in the middle of Israel's fourth decade.

21 10.2% participated in one event, 5.4% in two, 2.5% in three, 0.8% in four, and 2.6% in five or more.

even more recent poll Dr. Mina Zemach found that a full 55% of the Israeli Jewish public believed that "the parties are not a critical component" of Israeli democracy.[22]

If the party's base has so shrunk that it can no longer function as a political communication intermediary, and the political system does not create or develop other institutions to take its place, one would expect a highly politicized public to take matters into its own hands. The dramatic rise in public protest since the early 1970s is precisely such a response to what Mueller describes as "constrained communication,"[23] and the Israeli protest data support this hypothesis in a number of ways.

First, an analysis of the differing levels of Israeli government against which protest has been directed shows a clear trend over the years away from the local authorities and towards the central government.[24] Whereas in the 1950s only 44% of Israeli protest was directed at the central authorities and 56% at the local authorities, by the 1970s the proportion had shifted markedly to 65% and 35%, respectively. On the face of it this is somewhat puzzling since there has been a slow but steady transfer of political authority to the local level.[25] If the mayor today has more power than yesteryear, why is the public directing its ire through public protest more and more to the central government?

Paradoxically, the proportional decrease in protest levelled at local government is a sign of its greater power — and the proper exercise thereof. Protest, after all, results from systemic dysfunction. If, on the other hand, the institutional channels of local government have changed and opened up to accept and transfer public input to the political leadership, then one of the main reasons for extra-parliamentary activity is negated. In the event, as Elazar has pointed out, it is "at the local level that the most innovative developments are taking place and local governments are far more advanced than the government of the state in institutionalizing the new democratic republicanism of

22 Eliyahu Chasin, "Ha'demokratia Ha'yisraelit '83 — Geshem Kashe 'Omed La'redet," *Monitin* (March 1983), pp. 149–51.

23 Claus Mueller, *The Politics of Communication* (New York: Oxford University Press, 1975), pp. 87–8.

24 For a full discussion of this specific subject see Sam N. Lehman-Wilzig, "Public Protests Against Central and Local Government in Israel, 1950–1979," *The Jewish Journal of Sociology*, vol. XXIV, no. 2 (December 1982), pp. 99–115.

25 The latest advance is, at the time of writing this essay (June 1985), a draft law supported by both major parties which does away with the requirement for the Interior Minister's approval of local authorities' by-laws (except for those involving the imposition of levies).

Israel."[26] Local committees, regional councils, independent (non-)party lists, direct mayoral elections, etc., have enabled the citizenry to participate and/or communicate with their local governments, thereby reducing the need for "direct action."

A second area of the protest data which indicates the importance of political communication is the period of election campaigns. As early as Hamilton and Tocqueville, it was noted that election periods raise the public's political temperature.[27] The same holds increasingly true for Israel. Yet of the nine Knesset election periods reviewed, seven were marked by *less* public protest *during* the two-month campaign period than in the same time frame immediately after the elections were over.[28] In fact, in most cases Israeli public protest is lower during the election campaigns than at any time over the ensuing two years. Why is this so?

In contrast to the trend of local government protest, here there are a number of possible (and complementary) answers. Psychologically, the public gets to hear what it wants from at least one potentially-governing source. From an economics standpoint, governments attempt to manipulate the business cycle so that prosperity coincides with the pre-election period.[29] Yet, to these must be added the element of political communication.

---

26 Daniel J. Elazar, *Israel: From Ideological to Territorial Democracy* (monograph — Jerusalem Institute for Federal Studies, 1978), p. 20.

27 "At the period which terminates the duration of the Executive, there will always be an awful crisis in the national situation" (Alexander Hamilton), in Max Ferrand, ed., *Records of the Federal Convention of 1787*, vol. 1 (New Haven: Yale University Press, 1966), p. 145. "The election becomes the ... all-engrossing topic of discussion. Factional ardor is redoubled, and all the artificial passions which the imagination can create ... are agitated and brought to light." Alexis de Tocqueville, *Democracy in America*, vol. 1 (New York: Vintage Books, 1954), pp. 140–1.

28 It should be noted that the same held true if six-month time frames were compared. For a full discussion of this specific subject and the data see Sam Lehman-Wilzig, "Thunder Before the Storm: Pre-Election Agitation and Post-Election Turmoil," in *The Elections in Israel — 1981*, ed. Asher Arian (Tel-Aviv: Ramot Press, 1983), pp. 191–212.

29 For the Israeli case see Yoram Ben-Porath, "The Years of Plenty and the Years of Famine — A Political Business Cycle?" *Kyklos*, vol. 28, No. 2 (1975), pp. 440–3. A more general analysis of the phenomenon, which provides some additional information on Israel is Edward R. Tufte, *Political Control of the Economy* (Princeton: Princeton University Press, 1978). It could be argued that such manipulation might have the opposite effect, since as mentioned earlier *rapid* economic growth can be destabilizing and thus lead to more protest. However, such rapid growth must take place over a relatively lengthy period of time in order for it to cause socio-economic dislocation. "Election prosperity," by the cycle's very nature, is short term.

Edelman points out how "election campaigns ... give people a chance to express discontents and enthusiasms, to enjoy a sense of involvement."[30] Since political communication through the act of voting is formalized, ritualized, and even sanctified during this period, there appears to be less need to resort to other modes of political intercourse. On the other side of the coin, this is also the period when the political parties tend most to listen to the public's desires (or at least give the impression that they do). In other words, it is perhaps the only time when the establishment opens up somewhat and some semblance of political dialogue between rulers and ruled is possible. As soon as the elections are over and the establishment no longer feels itself obligated to continue with this pseudo- (or at best quasi-) dialogue and thus withdraws into itself, the jilted citizenry — demanding a continuance of the dialogue — resorts to more direct means of informing their former suitors as to their disappointment and resentment.

A third independent variable which reinforces the "protest as communication" hypothesis is government size. In the regression analysis mentioned earlier it was discovered that the size of the government (number of cabinet ministers) is negatively correlated to overall protest frequency [31] (i.e. the larger the government the fewer the public protests). Expansion of the cabinet enlarges the opportunity for communication on the part of social and religious pressure groups with governmental patrons — especially in Israel, where large cabinets are usually the result of the dominant camp's need to co-opt fringe parties into the government due to its own relative electoral weakness. Thus, paradoxically, the weaker the governing party is initially, the less overall protest it has to contend with as a result of its forced broadening of the government's ideological representation.

Religious-issue protest in Israel affords a fourth perspective on the issue.[32] Such protest does not emanate from one source or group alone. Rather, there

---

30 Murray Edelman, *The Symbolic Uses of Politics* (Urbana: University of Illinois Press, 1964), p. 30.

31 See Lehman-Wilzig and Ungar, "The Economic and Political Determinants ...," op. cit. The only exception here was political-issue protest which showed a (relatively) less consistent positive correlation, perhaps as a result of the greater diversity of political opinions rendering decisive decision-making on political issues more problematical. It should be noted that no correlation was found with economic-issue protest.

32 For a fuller discussion of religious-issue protest see the first half of Sam Lehman-Wilzig and Giora Goldberg, "Religious Protest and Police Reaction in a Theo-Democracy: Israel, 1950–1979," *Journal of Church and State*, vol. 25, No. 3 (Autumn 1983), pp. 491–505.

are five different group-types who protest on religious topics, but two pre-dominate. One — a relatively small fanatic fringe group colloquially termed *Neturei Karta* ("keepers of the gate," but for our purposes including also all other anti-Zionist zealot communities) — accounted for a full 47% of all such protest over the thirty-year period. The second grouping, religious parties who work within the political system, is a conglomeration of the National Religious Party and *Agudat Yisrael* (i.e. pro-Zionist or at least non-anti-Zionist religious Jews). Together they accounted for only 40% of all religious-issue protest, despite the fact that numerically they constitute the overwhelming majority of Israel's religious Jewish community.

The disparity is to be explained, of course, by the fact that the latter parties are part and parcel of the political establishment (the NRP, especially, has been in the government for all but two years of the State's existence), and thus have access to the formal channels of political communication. The *Neturei Karta*, on the other hand, by far the most protest-oriented community in Israel relative to its size, has consciously eschewed such access; yet living within the physical jurisdiction of the Israeli government it does find a need to "communicate," to send a message to the Zionist Establishment, and the effective means of doing so is protest.[33]

Fifth and finally, if protest in Israel is in large measure a function of the public's need to communicate with the governing authorities, any introduction of new communication channels can be expected to reinforce the protest tendency. Such was certainly the case after the introduction of television in Israeli society. Given a time lag of approximately three years since its inception in 1968 (a reasonable period for a change — or further reinforcement — of societal norms), the 1970s were marked by a veritable explosion of protest events relative to the 1960s. Whereas the earlier decade averaged forty-three events per year, the 1970s were marked by an annual average of one hundred and twenty-seven.

Commenting on the American scene, Etzioni suggests that the relationship is a general one:

> The number of demonstrations in the pre-mass television decade (1948–58) was much smaller than the first television decade (1958–68) . . . television has played a key role in the evolution of this particular form of

---

33 It should be noted that such protests also serve internal purposes as well — fostering group cohesion or at times allowing one sub-group to display its holier-than-thou-ness *vis-à-vis* a rival sub-group.

political expression and in the increasing frequency with which this form is applied, in effect, in creating demonstration democracy.[34]

In other words, television is a protest facilitator and has several unique qualities which are particularly appropriate for protest as a mode of communication. Television thrives on "action"; public protest events (compared to the more sedate press conferences, petition signings, etc.) promise "action." Television by its very nature — limited time, need to concentrate resources — simplifies the message; protests, too, communicate simplistic ideas, demands, calls for action. In short, we have here a symbiotic relationship where both sides feed off the other to their mutual benefit.[35] In their need to communicate politically, Israeli protesters have gravitated to their "natural" partner, TV, significantly the *only* new institution for public communication established by the government since the early days of the State.

Taken one at a time, none of these five aspects are overwhelmingly persuasive in and of themselves. Different explanations can be (and in some cases have been) adduced to interpret the phenomena and the data. However, taken together they create a relatively coherent picture of protest as an act of political communication where other channels are blocked or do not exist. Still, they are all inferential; for the picture to be fully fleshed out it is incumbent to ask the Israeli public itself the reasons for their hyper-protest-activity.

As can be seen in Table 2, the respondents were asked the following question: "Compared to other countries, Israel has a high level of public protest. I [the interviewer] shall read to you a number of possible reasons for this. Choose up to three which you consider to be the most important reasons for the high number of public protests in Israel." Two answers (No. 1 and No. 4 in

34 Amitai Etzioni, *Demonstration Democracy* (New York: Gordon & Breach, 1970), pp. 12–13.
35 In facilitating protest it should be noted that the role of the mass media in general, and television in particular, functions on a different plane as well. As was mentioned earlier in this article, not only objective conditions but also the subjective perception of those conditions (e.g. relative deprivation) contribute to protest fomentation. Television does a marvelour job of bringing home the disparities of life — the opulent and extraordinary along with the destitute and mundane. This in itself can cause social disquietude. As Manoucher Parvin notes: "The more facts of a social condition are known by the people, the greater will be the likelihood that they will learn to dislike it more (or appreciate it less)." Thus, television acts as a protest facilitator not only as an effective transmitter of protest, but in addition actually may *cause* protest due to the "normal" messages it transmits. "Economic Determinants of Political Unrest: An Econometric Approach," *Journal of Conflict Resolution*, vol. 17, no. 2 (June 1973), p. 293.

the order presented) dealt with "political culture"; No. 3 represented the "policy dissatisfaction" factor; No. 5 was an "environmental conditions" answer; No. 2 and No. 6 were related to "political communication" (the former, "communication" in and of itself; the latter, "communication" as an instrumentality).

The response practically speaks for itself. Political culture, both past and present, is considered to be a weak explanation. The environmental factor fares somewhat better, as does policy dissatisfaction. Slightly stronger (42.2%) is instrumental communication ("whoever protests publicly achieves something; it is one of the few ways of achieving something").[36] But in first place by a significant margin (49.7%) the Israeli public chose the "pure" communications explanation: "the citizen does not have enough other means to express himself to the authorities." In other words, *insofar as the Israeli public is concerned, harsh environmental conditions and general policy dissatisfaction are less salient factors in fomenting protest than the lack of formal opportunities for political communication.*

This of course does not mean that the problem of political communication is the sole factor underlying Israeli public protest (after all, policy dissatisfaction and environmental conditions did attract some support). Nor does it mean that if the formal channels of communication were opened up once again, such protest would disappear (if not earlier in Jewish history, by now certain cultural patterns of public behavior have become normalized). But at the least, Israeli "democracy" — in the original Greek sense of the word: the rule of the people — would become more than a formal term, nowadays practically emptied of actual content in between the quadrennial ballotcasting. One might even expect a lowering of the political temperature as measured in the streets and a return to more orderly political communication between the governed and their representatives.

On a more general level, as the foregoing analysis suggests, protest *per se* is not an altogether negative phenomenon, although its high level of use does indicate a deep-rooted flaw in the political system.

There are several positive aspects to public protest. First, as Coser notes of societal friction in general: "Frequent conflict ... indicate[s] that a relatively high proportion of the membership actually is involved in the life of the group."[37] High levels of protest, then, are but another indication that the

---

36 Two other questions in the poll are relevant in this context. When asked — "do you think *legal* public protests in Israel are successful in achieving their goal?" — 5.8% answered "yes, always," 19.1% "yes, usually," and 40.2% "sometimes." When the question was changed to *illegal* protests, the drop was not all that substantial: 3.9%, 12.3%, and 33.3%, respectively.

37 Lewis Coser, *The Functions of Social Conflict* (New York: Free Press, 1956), p. 85.

Israeli public does care and would like to be more involved. No "Silent Generation" here. Second, the protest vehicle serves to attract segments of the population which might otherwise not be involved, or even interested at all, in politics.[38] Although at first the personal motive for such participation may be entertainment or social, they soon discover the functional and instrumental utility of this mode of political expression. As Etzioni argues, "demonstrations help to reduce the inequality among the member groupings of society in terms of their access to political tools; they add to the tools particularly appropriate to the middle and upper classes [e.g. lobbying], one which is especially suited to the under-privileged and young."[39]

Protest utility, however, is not merely a particularistic matter. Society as a whole may benefit. The problem lies in the dynamics of political organization development. Virtually all political systems are built to preserve and continue themselves as they were originally designed or formed. This refers to the overall ideology, the system's institutions, and the group(s) controlling the sources of power. It also involves the access to, and patterns of, communication within the system. "In other words," Coser elaborates, "the channels of political communication tend to be so constructed that they admit access only to those social forces that have succeeded in making their voices heard in the past. When new social forces appear in the arena they often find themselves blocked from these channels and hence remain unable to actualize their potential force."[40] Protest, then, communicates to the establishment the fact that new social forces have arrived and need to be incorporated *into* the system. As Zimmerman summed it up: "If protest and turmoil call attention to problem areas hitherto neglected and if they lead to solutions, they may be said to have beneficial effect. If (potential) dissidents gain access to institutional channels for expressing their protests, a better overall integration of the political system may result."[41]

Thus, protest as a form of political communication has not emerged to supplant traditional democratic institutions or activities. Democratic protesters are (usually) not interested in changing the system but, on the contrary, are demanding to be counted in. "Part of the causes of violence and the means for its prevention rests at the level of alternative modes of political expression,"

---

38 Ekkart Zimmerman, "Macro-Comparative Research on Political Protest," in Gurr, *Handbook*, op. cit., p. 235.
39 Etzioni, *Demonstration Democracy*, op. cit., p. 20.
40 Lewis Coser, *Continuities in the Study of Social Conflict* (New York: Free Press, 1967), p. 96.
41 Zimmerman, "Macro-Comparative Research . . .," op. cit.

asserts Etzioni. "They [demonstrations] are not to replace existing democratic instruments but to complement them."[42] In the end, therefore, protest does present a challenge to the establishment; but it is more in the nature of a call to expand the house and broaden the lines of communication, and not necessarily to remove the occupants or build the structure anew.

CONCLUSION

The problem of public protest as a result of political non-communication is not unique to Israel, although it apparently suffers from this more than most. In his book, *Politics as Communication*, Meadow notes that "the reasons for demonstrations and protest are many, but most important is the fact that they often are the only channels of communication available for demands (or support) to be articulated *in totalitarian systems*."[43] Israel can by no means be considered to be such a system, and the point of this essay is to highlight how a very open democracy (in many other ways) can suffer from being closed in one important respect.

At the end of their massive five-nation protest study, Barnes and Kaase arrive at much the same conclusion: "under a functionalist perspective these developments [protest, etc.] can very well be regarded as one possible response to ossified political structures that need to be cracked in order to accommodate and facilitate peaceful sociopolitical change."[44] If so, then the ever-increasing public pressure in Israel through protest[45] might eventually lead to a thorough-going reform of the political system. This is an optimistic way of viewing the matter, and as noted earlier, at least on the local level of government, the Israeli polity has shown an ability to transform itself institutionally. But one must inject a note of pessimistic caution here as well, for the rot at the central level has advanced for at least fifteen years without much being done about it. Arian noted that as early as 1969, despite the high level of political involve-

---

42 Etzioni, *Demonstration Democracy*, op. cit., p. 45.
43 Emphasis mine. Robert G. Meadow, *Politics and Communication* (Norwood, N.J.: Ablex Publishing Corporation, 1980), p. 79. More interestingly, he notes how political noncommunication can be used at times as an explanation by the government for public protest when the matter is really one of policy dissatisfaction. As a result, "symbolic reassurances of future access are offered in place of substantive concessions to defuse the situation" (p. 81).
44 *Political Action*, op. cit., p. 532.
45 A socio-economic breakdown of past Israeli protesters indicates that all else being equal, the number of protesters will increase in the future. See my "The Israeli Protester," *The Jerusalem Quarterly*, No. 26 (Winter 1982), pp. 127–38.

ment among Israelis, they were left with a low sense of political efficacy.[46] If anything, this gap is wider than ever before.

In the final analysis, therefore, it is incumbent upon the authorities to take notice of not only the sundry demands of Israel's multifarious protest groups, but even more important to focus on the fundamental message underlying the act of protest *qua* protest. The general environmental conditions in which Israel finds itself are not wholly under the Israeli government's control. Policy dissatisfaction is a natural problem endemic to all political systems, and in any case the deep-seated cleavages in Israel society cannot always be resolved by governmental acceptance of pressure group demands (since another group would then in turn be dissatisfied). However, restructuring the form of political communication is well within the means and capability of the political establishment — assuming sufficient political will exists.[47]

As Meadow points out, "historically, it has already been possible for regimes to operate without linkages to demands."[48] Thus, the issue here is not merely one of (decibel) level or type of public discourse. Rather, reforming the channels of political communication is ultimately a matter of the continued health and very existence of Israeli democracy.

46 Alan Arian, *The Choosing People* (Cleveland: Case Western Reserve University, 1973).
47 While a detailed discussion of possible prescriptive cures is beyond the scope of this study, several suggestions can be advanced in schematic form: 1) Changing Israel's election system to allow for some form of district representation which would give the constituency a specific electoral address for the redress of grievances or even merely for verbal unburdening. 2) Greater democratization of the internal nominations process within the political parties, so as to make the party more responsive to its grass-roots supporters. 3) Accelerating the movement towards decentralized, local decision-making and/or execution in a host of social areas: education, health, welfare, etc. Barring that, or in addition, the central government would do well to learn some lessons from the local authorities' successful systemic experimentation. 4) Expanding the mass media (especially electronic) and allowing bi-directional communications technology (e.g. two-way cable television) to develop and grow without the present innumerable government restrictions and prohibitions. Numerous "teledemocratic" experiments in the U.S., Sweden, West Germany, and New Zealand have already met with some success. (See my *"Demoskraty* in the Mega-Polis: Hyper-Participation in the Post-Industrial Age," in *The Future of Politics*, ed. William Page [London: Frances Pinter, 1983], pp. 221–9.)
48 *Politics as Communication,* op. cit., p. 83.

TABLES

Table 1 — Political Activity in Israel *

"Are you active in any way in the political or public sphere in Israel?"
1) Active party member (devotes time to party matters) —   3.2%
2) Active member in pressure group — a non-party group attempting
   to influence public issues —   1.9%
3) Active independent (write letters to the editor, to MKs,
   involved in community activities, etc.) —   3.8%
4) Non-active party member —   8.2%
5) Not involved at all —   82.4%
6) No answer —   0.6%

* The poll surveyed a representative sample of 1250 Israeli adults, excluding the
  kibbutz and the Arab sectors. It was conducted in December 1981.

Table 2 — Public Explanations for High Level of Israeli Protest

"Compared to other countries, Israel has a high level of public protest.
The interviewer shall read to you a number of possible reasons for this.
Choose up to three which you consider to be the most important reasons for
the high number of public protests in Israel."

1 — "In diaspora the Jews always protested against the authorities
    and continue this tradition today in Israel"   10.7%
2 — "The citizen does not have enough other means to express
    himself to the authorities"   49.7%
3 — "It is necessary to express protest because the government does
    not repond to the wishes and needs of the public"   40.9%
4 — "When cabinet ministers and members of Knesset want their
    point of view to be accepted they shout and use forms of
    protest, and this influences the man in the street"   35.1%
5 — "Living conditions in Israel are generally difficult, and this
    leads to protest against the authorities"   39.3%
6 — "Whoever protests publicy achieves something; it is one of
    the few ways of achieving something"   42.2%
7 — Did not answer   7.7%

Note: While the 7.5% difference between answers 2 and 6 may not seem overly
large, it is a substantial one given the method of response (the ability to
choose up to three answers).

GIORA GOLDBERG

THE STRUGGLE FOR LEGITIMACY:
HERUT'S ROAD FROM OPPOSITION TO POWER

INTRODUCTION

For many years, the Israeli political system seemed to be stable, static and even moribund. The 1970s, however, witnessed significant political changes, culminating in 1977 with the electoral defeat of the social-democratic Labour Party by the liberal-nationalist *Likud* party. Previous attempts at explaining these changes have invariably been limited to an analysis of voting patterns. This paper will argue the need for emphasizing long-range political processes which are often ignored, or at least underestimated. It will analyse one such process, the legitimization of the central component within the *Likud* — the *Herut* movement. The explanation of this process, it will suggest, is essential to an understanding of the political upheaval of 1977. Thus observed, the stability apparently characteristic of the 1950s and 1960s in effect becomes limited to election results. During these two decades there were other dynamic — even to some extent unstable — elements in the political system, and this was particularly true of the party system. A crucial cause was the legitimization of *Herut*.

As a process, the legitimization of *Herut* comprised three basic elements: a conscious-manipulative adoption of new party strategies by *Herut* leaders; changes in the inter-party strategy of the Labour Party with regard to *Herut*; and external events and processes, not directly related to the party system. Each of these three elements will be analysed below.

Herut was not the only Israeli party to undergo legitimization. To some extent, the ultra-religious *Agudat-Yisrael* and the Communist Party also underwent such a process. But, to use Duverger's concept, both remained permanent minority parties.[1] Various parties throughout the Western world have undergone legitimization, but the case of *Herut* is striking: although the party grew out of an underground movement which was outside the national consensus, remaining politically isolated for many years, it succeeded in gain-

1   Maurice Duverger, *Political Parties* (London: Methuen, 1967).

ing enough power to replace the dominant party as the governing party, with the former underground leader, Menachem Begin, becoming Prime Minister.

Legitimization was itself part of the broader process of party transformation. Defined by Wilson as "that type of party change that produces new styles, organization, tactics and inter-party relations",[2] party transformation has been found to have been generated by four factors: changes in the socio-economic setting, the political culture, the political institutions and the competitive situation. Wilson himself found the first and second to have had only a marginal impact (creating a "favourable milieu"), the third and fourth to be more influential; but the key factor is the action of party leaders. It is this which links the four factors to party transformation and serves as an intervening variable. The Israeli case of *Herut* appears to follow a similar pattern.

The main goal of the *Herut* leaders was to alter their image from a revolutionary, irrational and belligerent faction to that of a responsible and rational party. In so doing, they acted in accordance with the theory put forward by Sellers and Trilling — that party images play a crucial role in the transformation of party identification.[3] The shift in party image was successfully achieved. More importantly, this success and all it implies was accomplished without the introduction of basic changes in the nature and ideology of the party or in its system of symbols and myths. In other words, the change in party image was sufficient to achieve political goals. This seems unique to the Israeli case since most parties — primarily socialist parties — which have undergone legitimization through transformation have had to forgo many of their ideological principles. The German case of the SPD is the most relevant here, and that of the Italian PCI to a lesser extent.[4]

Herut did not sacrifice its ideological principles, but made other concessions — through inter-party alliances which contributed significantly to its legitimization. In this way, *Herut* ceded a large part of its parliamentary representation to its partners. These "shrinking" parties provided *Herut* with legiti-

2 Frank L. Wilson, "Sources of Party Transformation: The Case of France", in *Western European Party Systems*, ed. Peter H. Merkl (New York: The Free Press, 1980), p. 526.

3 Charles Sellers, "The Equilibrium Cycle in Two-Party Politics", *Public Opinion Quarterly*, Vol. 29 (1965), pp. 16–38; Richard J. Trilling, *Party Image and Electoral Behavior* (New York: Wiley, 1976).

4 For a discussion of the German case, see for example: William E. Paterson, "The German Social Democratic Party", in *Social Democratic Parties in Western Europe*, ed. William E. Paterson and Alistair H. Thomas (London: Croom Helm, 1977), pp. 176–212. For an analysis of the Italian case, see Ariel Levite and Sidney Tarrow, "The Legitimation of Excluded Parties in Dominant Party Systems: A Comparison of Israel and Italy", *Comparative Politics*, Vol. 15 (April 1983), pp. 295–327.

macy through parliamentary and electoral alliances, and were rewarded by parliamentary seats. Paradoxically, when *Herut* eventually emerged from its opposition status in 1977 it held only 19 parliamentary seats, just two more than it had held in 1959 and 1961, the last two elections in which the party had run independently. Let us now turn to an analysis of *Herut* party history as it relates to its transformation, and more specifically to its legitimization.

THE PRE-STATE PERIOD

The Revisionist movement emerged in the 1920s: its youth movement, *Betar*, was founded in 1923, and the Revisionist Party was established in 1925. Unlike other political movements, the Revisionist movement was founded and dominated during its early years by a single prominent Zionist personality, Ze'ev Jabotinsky, thus constituting a "party of personality". Accordingly, the Revisionist party was singular in that it was not the product of a specific social stratum. Other parties (Communist, Socialist, etc.), were based mainly on clear-cut social categories, while the religious and ethnic groups relied on other cleavages. When the Revisionists appeared on the political scene, parties representing all of these categories already existed. The Revisionists emphasized militant nationalism and adopted revolutionary means in order to achieve statehood. The priority accorded to uncompromising nationalism cut across social barriers. As a result, the Revisionist party emerged as the most heterogeneous party. Moreover, as a populist party, it posed an immediate threat to all the others. But the sharpest conflict emerged between the Revisionists and the Labour movement, since these were the two camps vying for political hegemony. Although they favoured different political styles, both tried to win the support of the same electorate. Moreover, the ferocity of their competition belied their relatively mild ideological differences. *Mapai*, the main arm of the Labour movement, implemented social policies which were basically no different from those demanded by the Revisionists. In their socio-economic programmes both were centre parties, supporting the model of a welfare state, and were basically in agreement — even on such issues as the relationship between state and religion. There were some ideological differences concerning foreign and defence policies but, once again, as in the socio-economic sphere, the gap between *Mapai*'s performance and the Revisionist ideology was relatively narrow. Deeper disputes existed within the Labour camp itself, with *Hashomer-Hatzair* (later *Mapam*) insisting on a bi-national state, a view which ran counter to *Mapai*'s basic concept of a Jewish state. Furthermore, *Hashomer-Hatzair* was basically "Eastern-oriented" in its foreign policy, while *Mapai* remained unaffiliated until 1950, with a slight tendency towards a

"Western orientation". While it would be misleading to argue that *Mapai* and the Revisionists were ideologically close, the differences in ideology cannot by themselves explain the psychological rivalry between them. The two movements created different political sub-cultures which accelerated the inter-party rivalry. They competed for the same resources through different organizational bodies, and it was this inter-organizational competition which was translated into a deep political rift. Both parties tried to justify their rivalry and hostility by sharpening the ideological gaps, thus contributing in part to the conventional wisdom which explains inter-party relations as an expression of deep ideological controversy.

The conflict between the two movements developed during the late 1920s and 1930s and, in accordance with the spirit of the times, took the form of a conflict between social-democrats and fascists. In fact, only one marginal splinter of the Revisionist party publicly identified itself as fascist. The mainstream of the movement completely rejected fascism, but most *Mapai* leaders preferred to label the entire Revisionist party as fascist. In another reflection of the period, both sides maintained party militias which clashed from time to time. However, compared to similar struggles at that time in Europe, the rise in political violence and bloodshed was relatively small. Another aspect related to the period, although not directly to the 1930s and 1940s, was the Jews' lack of sovereignty. In such a situation, neither movement was called upon to take full responsibility for policies in a wide range of areas. Only certain areas of policy were handled by the national institutions, while others, such as economic policy, were dealt with only on the ideological level. Thus, ideological controversies over various issues could develop without having to take the constraints of reality into account. It was only after the establishment of the State of Israel in 1948 that major areas began to be examined in terms of operative ideology — "principles which actually underlie policies and are invoked to justify them" — rather than in terms of fundamental ideology — "fundamental principles which determine the final goals and the grand vistas in which they will be realized".[5] What is important is that party development prior to the attainment of sovereignty may have served as an incentive for deep inter-party conflicts, as it was the ideological extremists and not the mainstreams which were dominant.

The most significant element in the conflict concerned legitimacy. The Revisionists sought to delegitimize Labour's claim to a monopoly over resources; but much more important was the strategy of the Labour movement, which attempted to delegitimize the Revisionist movement as a partner in

---

5 Martin Seliger, *Ideology and Politics* (New York: The Free Press, 1976), p. 109.

the Zionist camp. This conflict was exacerbated in 1935, when the compromise agreement reached by Ben-Gurion and Jabotinsky was rejected by the Labour movement. The Revisionists reacted by constructing a network of separate organizations. In 1934, they had formed a separate trade union — the National Workers' Association — which rivalled the *Histadrut*, Labour's powerful trade union. In 1935 the Revisionists left the formal institutions of the Zionist movement, creating a rival organization — the New Zionist Association. The Jewish Agency was another national institution whose legitimacy was challenged by the Revisionists. Later on they also formed separate military organizations — *Etzel* and *Lehi* — and in 1944 they removed themselves from the national institutions of the Jewish community in Palestine by refusing to take part in the elections to the fourth Elected Assembly. The Revisionist strategy of abdication reinforced the legitimacy conflict, with the dissenters rejecting the legitimacy of the Zionist institutions in Palestine and in the diaspora, as well as those of the *Histadrut* and the *Haganah* — the military underground led by the Labour movement.

Relations between the two movements reached two climaxes: The first occurred in 1933, on the eve of *Mapai*'s rise to the position of a dominant party, with the murder of Haim Arlozorov, a senior *Mapai* leader. This act was viewed by *Mapai* leaders as a case of political violence by the Revisionists, although it appears to be evident that the murder was not executed by them. The second climax occurred in 1944 when Ben-Gurion declared a new policy, known as the "Season", the essence of which was the persecution of the Revisionist underground movements. Begin's decision not to react was possibly based on two factors: his realistic perception of the superior strength of the Labour movement and his loyalty to the Jewish political tradition's abhorrence of the use of violence against fellow Jews.

To sum up, the pre-State period was characterized by an intense and multidimensional conflict over legitimacy between the Labour and the Revisionist movements. The Revisionists made desperate attempts to discredit the institutions dominated by the Labour movement, while the latter systematically tried to prevent the Revisionists from achieving the status of a legitimate party. There is no doubt that the Labour movement was more successful in achieving its goals. For that period, as Shavit states: "The history of Revisionism is a history of failure .... a history of a losing movement".[6] Whether this trend would continue after the establishment of the State remained to be seen.

---

6 Yaacov Shavit, *Me'rov Le'medinah* ("Revisionism in Zionism") (Tel-Aviv: Yariv, 1978), p. 308.

OPPOSITION IN PRINCIPLE

One day after the establishment of the State of Israel, Begin declared that the *Etzel* would be transformed into a political party called *Herut*. He promised that the new party would act legally and would accept the democratic rules of the game. But one month later, in June 1948, a severe crisis of legitimacy erupted. A Revisionist arms ship, the *Altalena*, arrived in Israel following certain negotiations with government officials. The government demanded that the arms be confiscated for the army; Begin requested that one-fifth of the arms be transferred to the *Etzel* forces in Jerusalem, which at that time was not formally annexed to the State of Israel. On the orders of Ben-Gurion, then Prime Minister, the army shelled the ship, killing fourteen Revisionists and wounding forty. Begin again decided not to react, although he himself remained on the ship, abandoning it only at the last moment.[7] Had Begin decided to use force against the army, civil war might have erupted, but once again he preferred to follow the basic value of the Jewish political tradition forbidding bloodshed among Jews. He was also realistic in his judgement that his movement would not have stood much chance in a direct confrontation. No less important was his refusal to obey the legal authorities prior to the shelling of the ship. Ben-Gurion justified his decision to use force by arguing that the Revisionists had tried to harm the unity and sovereignty of the state, its military capability and its international status. He called them "a terrorist gang", adding that the citizens, not only the army, had to take immediate action against them.[8] Five top Revisionist leaders were arrested following the "*Altalena* affair". Most political parties, not only *Mapai*, publicly denounced the Revisionists. The only outstanding exception to this was the old Revisionist party. This relatively moderate party continued to exist throughout the years of the underground revolt; in 1946 the party returned to the formal Zionist institutions and, on the eve of the establishment of the State, was recognized by the leadership of the *Yishuv* as a legitimate party. While *Etzel* and later *Herut* were not included in the pre-State institutions or in those of the new

---

7 Like other Revisionist leaders, he tended to believe that Ben-Gurion wanted him killed. As another Revisionist leader, S. Katz, testifies: "If Begin was killed in the process, well, so much the better from Ben-Gurion's point of view. A threat to Labor's domination of Israeli politics would have been eliminated". Frank Gervasi, *The Life and Times of Menachem Begin* (New York: Putnam, 1979), p. 261. Begin himself stated a few years later that Ben-Gurion had ordered that he be fired on with a cannon. *Ha'veidah Ha'reviit Shel Tnuat Ha'cherut* ("The Fourth Convention of the Herut Movement") (Tel-Aviv: The Herut Movement, 1957), p. 287.

8 *Moezet Ha'am Ha'zmanit* ("The Temporary People's Council") (Tel-Aviv: 1949), Vol. 1, June 23, 1948, pp. 4–7.

State of Israel, the Revisionist party was: its leaders were partners to the Declaration of Independence, although their request to receive a ministerial position in the temporary government was rejected.

The official foundation of *Herut* in August 1948 was an act of no confidence in the old Revisionist party. The two parties did conduct negotiations on the formation of a joint list for the 1949 national elections. *Herut* agreed to grant the old Revisionists every fourth place on the list, but opposed the inclusion of leaders who had collaborated with *Mapai*.[9] Consequently, the two parties ran independently in the elections. *Herut* won 14 of the 120 *Knesset* seats; the Revisionist party failed to gain even a single place. The direct implication of the victory of the *Etzel* leaders over the older and more moderate Revisionists was the sharpening of relations between the Labour and the Revisionist movements.

A few months after the elections the two factions agreed to form a united party. In fact, the veterans recognized *Herut*'s domination in the Revisionist movement within the State, although they continued to lead the movement outside Israel. Through this merger, specifically through the Revisionist party, *Herut* recognized the Jewish Agency, and in 1950 began to receive money from Jewish Agency funds, as did all Zionist parties.

Herut and the Communist Party were denied legitimacy by Ben-Gurion as potential partners in the government coalition. Actually, *Herut* itself was reluctant on this point, preferring to function as an opposition party. The intensity of its opposition was so great that in 1949 Begin considered the government's failure to adopt a constitution as an illegal act, calling the government an "anti-constitutional usurpation".[10] On the parliamentary level, *Herut* was isolated and was subjected to a boycott by all other parties, including the opposition parties. Y. Bader has described how the *Herut* legislators used to sit alone even in the *Knesset* cafeteria, adding that he did not try to negotiate with members of other parties, of whom he personally knew only three: one a relative of his, one from Poland and one who had spent some time with him in a British jail during the underground period.[11] When the *Knesset* celebrated its first anniversary, *Herut* and the Communist members remained isolated: "I approach them; let us fill glasses and drink together".[12] As the fourth largest

9 Yochanan Bader, *Ha'Knesset Ve'ani* ("The *Knesset* and I") (Jerusalem: Edanim, 1979), p. 20.

10 *Divrei Ha'Knesset* ("The *Knesset* Record") (hereafter, *Div. Hak.*), Vol. 3, Nov. 9, 1949, p. 21.

11 Bader, "The *Knesset* and I", op. cit., p. 26.

12 Ibid.

parliamentary delegation *Herut* was entitled to a Deputy Speaker, but the majority, led by Ben-Gurion, violated the rules by deciding to have only two Deputy Speakers — a decision which meant that *Herut* remained outside the Presidium.[13] When the committee chairmanships were divided among the various parties, *Herut* received the Committee of Social Services, the least desirable. They protested in vain.[14] A supreme education committee, nominated by the Education Minister, included only one *Herut* member, while the General Zionists (also in opposition at that time, and holding only seven parliamentary seats), received two places on the committee. Following intensive efforts, *Herut* was accorded an extra seat. The first *Knesset* delegation to the Inter-Parliamentary Union did not include a single *Herut* member. *Herut* threatened to send a separate delegation to Stockholm, and thus succeeded in cancelling the mission.[15] Ben-Gurion was so hostile towards Begin that he used to leave the plenum each time Begin started to deliver a speech. It was only about a year after the elections that Ben-Gurion first listened to one of Begin's speeches and, even then, his response was that Begin and his party had not changed, comparing them to fascists.[16]

Herut emphasized parliamentary initiatives on foreign and defence issues, neglecting other areas. This shaped its image as a one-issue party and precluded any chance of legitimization. During this period *Herut* was also preoccupied with issues related to its historical rivalry with the Labour movement, such as the failure to capture the Old City of Jerusalem during the War of Independence.[17] Among other issues raised by *Herut* were what they perceived to be discrimination against their daily newspaper through the distribution of newspapers in the army;[18] the demand that the period of exile served by members of the *Etzel* prior to 1948 be recognized as military service;[19] the protest against the location of a psychiatric hospital in the Acre fortress where *Etzel* soldiers had been executed by the British;[20] the demand that the official name of the army be altered from "Israel Defence Army" to "Israel Army",[21] thus omitting the name of Labour's underground organization ("Defense": *Haganah*). These examples illustrate *Herut*'s preoccupation with its rivalry

13 Ibid., p. 25.
14 Ibid.
15 Ibid., pp. 25-6.
16 *Div. Hak.*, Vol. 3, Nov. 21, 1949, pp. 125-6.
17 Ibid., Vol. 3, Jan. 23, 1950, p. 613.
18 Ibid., Vol. 3, Jan. 16, 1950, p. 511.
19 Ibid., Vol. 3, Dec. 27, 1949, p. 329.
20 Ibid., Vol. 2, Aug. 25, 1949, pp. 1392-3.
21 Ibid., Vol. 2, Sept. 8, 1949, pp. 1639–43.

against Labour, its focus on symbolic issues and its tendency to adopt an ideology rather than a policy orientation. This strategy served Ben-Gurion's interests well. Occasionally, he would himself initiate a parliamentary clash with *Herut*. In November 1950, for example, he described his decision to issue an ultimatum to the Jerusalem Etzel branch, sarcastically adding that the "brave *Etzel* heroes immediately gave up".[22]

Herut lost almost half of its strength in the 1951 elections, dropping from fourteen seats to eight. It was now only the fifth largest party, possessing less seats than *Mapai*, *Mapam*, the General Zionists and *Hapoel Hamizrachi* — the religious Labour-oriented party. Its position as the leading right-wing opposition party now passed to the General Zionists. *Herut* went into a deep internal crisis. Its two leaders, Begin and Meridor, decided to end their parlimentary careers.[23] The latter did so in November 1951. Begin signed a letter of resignation immediately after the elections, gave it to one of the *Herut* leaders, Ben-Eliezer, and told him to present it to the Speaker of the *Knesset*. Begin left for Italy on vacation, but Ben-Eliezer had not yet submitted the letter by the time of his return. Meanwhile, two other prominent leaders, Landau and Bader, were considering resignation. Begin refused to serve as the formal chairman of the party, and decided to leave the political arena entirely. He began studying for the bar examinations in order to qualify as a lawyer.[24] For five months he refused to take his oath of loyalty as a Member of *Knesset*; yet did not submit his letter of resignation.

It was the reparations agreement between Israel and West Germany which brought him back to politics. In January 1952 he decided to return to parliamentary activity. He took his oath the day the *Knesset* began discussing the agreement and delivered two addresses, one in the *Knesset* and the second at a mass demonstration in Jerusalem. The latter was a fiery speech in which Begin explained why the agreement with the West Germans should not be signed. He called Ben-Gurion a "maniac" and declared that his own followers would do everything possible to prevent the signing of such a shameful agreement only a few years after the Holocaust.[25] He compared the *"Altalena* affair" with the issue of reparations, stating that while in the former case he

22 Ibid., Vol. 7, Nov. 1, 1950, p. 148.
23 Bader, "The *Knesset* and I", op. cit., pp. 57-8; Aviezer Golan and Shlomo Nakdimon, *Begin* (Jerusalem: Edanim, 1978), pp. 196-7.
24 Bader has analysed this as part of Begin's "Cincinnatus complex". Begin told Bader that the Cincinnatus story had great pride and beauty. Bader, "The *Knesset* and I", op. cit., p. 17.
25 Ibid., p. 62.

had ordered self-restraint, he would now "give the order: yes". Begin marched to the *Knesset* with thousands of his followers. They surrounded the *Knesset* building, clashing with the policemen who used tear gas in order to halt the riot. Begin entered the *Knesset* as stones were being thrown by the demonstrators into the plenum, where one *Knesset* Member was hurt, but the discussion went on regardless. While the window panes were being shattered, Begin told Bader: "Mother would have been happy",[26] an indication of his satisfaction with what was going on outside. Begin then began his speech, which was interrupted by Ben-Gurion, who referred to the demonstrators as "your hooligans". Begin replied, "You are the hooligan", and refused to comply with the Deputy Speaker's order that he retract his words. The Deputy Speaker responded with the decision that Begin's speech be terminated, but the latter declared: "If I do not speak, nobody will speak".[27] At this stage, the Deputy Speaker declared a twenty-minute recess. Begin remained on the rostrum. Two of his colleagues, Bader and Landau, concerned that he would be attacked, hastened to Begin's side to defend him. Two female *Knesset* Members, one from *Mapai* and the other from *Herut*, joined the fight. Almost four hundred demonstrators were arrested during the riots, and approximately three hundred persons (93 of them policemen) were wounded. The Attorney General had to decide whether to bring the arrested demonstrators to court. Bader told him that it would be very desirable from *Herut's* point of view as a political-ethical confrontation, quoting Ralph Emerson's opinion that "good men should not obey laws too well".[28] All the demonstrators were released without further legal action. Begin was suspended from the *Knesset* until Passover, which meant a four-month exclusion from parliamentary activity.[29]

Herut continued to hold mass demonstrations against the reparations agreement. Extra-parliamentary activity was expanded. D. Shilanski, a survivor of the *Altalena*, was arrested holding a bomb in the Foreign Ministry building and was sentenced to jail.[30] Another activist, a reporter for the *Herut* daily newspaper, was arrested for possessing a bomb in the Haifa port, and was also sent to jail.[31] There were other arrests and police searches during that period

26 Ibid.
27 Ibid., p. 63.
28 Ibid., p. 64.
29 This decision was taken following Begin's behaviour in the *Knesset* and was actually a violation of the Immunity Law enacted in 1951.
30 Ibid., p. 65.
31 Ibid.

and, in Bader's opinion, the private telephone calls of the *Herut* leaders were all tapped.[32]

In May 1952 Begin returned to parliamentary activity. That same day *Herut* submitted its first motion of no confidence in the government. Although *Herut* failed to prevent the conclusion of the reparations agreement, it succeeded in rebuilding its image as a revolutionary opposition force. When the General Zionists joined the government coalition in 1952 *Herut* regained its position as the main opposition party. The split which occurred in *Mapam* in 1954 further reinforced this trend. The change in *Herut*'s strategy, adopting extra-parliamentary measures and becoming an opposition of principle, helped to strengthen the party apparatus. *Etzel* members returned to party activity, marking the end of the profound crisis within the party which had been reflected in the 1951 election results.

It would be misleading to argue that the emphasis on the reparations agreement was merely a case of political manipulation. For *Herut*, opposition to the agreement was indeed an ideological principle. However, considering the moderate means applied prior to the 1951 elections, it can be argued that *Herut*'s emphasis on the reparations agreement was not only an expression of ideological controversy, but also a new strategy designed to overcome the party's own crisis.

OPPOSITION IN TRANSITION

The 1955 elections constituted a turning-point in *Herut*'s history. The parliamentary delegation was enlarged from eight to fifteen members. For the first time, *Herut* became the second largest party and clearly comprised the principal opposition force. *Herut* leaders began to shape a new strategy which would eventually lead them to replace *Mapai* as the governing party. This new strategy consisted of a number of elements, all designed to help build a new party image. It involved:

1) Concentrating on the *Knesset* as the main arena for competition, relinquishing somewhat the use of extra-parliamentary means.

2) Adhering strictly to the rules of the parliamentary game, refraining from clashing with the government and violating the Procedural Code. This was reflected primarily in the adoption of a new political style.

3) Concentrating on a wide range of issues, not only those related to defence and foreign policy. At the 1956 party convention, for example, an overall

32 Ibid., p. 86.

economic programme was presented by Bader as the basis for further discussion.

4) Not instinctively rejecting the government policy *in toto*, but considering each policy individually, prepared to support the government if needed or to suggest an alternative policy.

5) Putting aside the historical rivalry between the Revisionist and the Labour movements. This involved an effort to rid itself of the image of a sectarian party constricted by the memories of the past. *Herut* tried to de-emphasize the symbols of the Revisionist sub-culture, and not to provoke emotional debates in the *Knesset* on past issues.

6) Constructing a party apparatus which would facilitate mass mobilization. The party convention of 1956 adopted a new organizational party structure designed to put an end to its underground period and to embark on the new stage of a political party based on a different outlook and organization.

7) Emphasizing grass-roots day-to-day politics and not only abstract ideas. This was expressed in attempts to engage intensively in local politics, as well as to enter the governing coalition in the Jewish Agency and the Labour-dominated *Histadrut*.

8) Attempting to form alliances with other parties at the electoral and parliamentary levels in order to build an alternative governing coalition.

At this stage, the party leaders were reluctant to make any ideological compromises, at least at the declarative level. They believed that the above-mentioned eight guidelines did not constitute an ideological transformation. But even these changes in strategy by the party leadership were opposed by devoted activists. However, the latter were not organized as a faction and failed to prevent the adoption of the new strategy. A. Achimeir, who was suspected of having been involved in Arlozorov's murder in 1933, stated at the 1956 party convention that only through political revolution by the *Herut* party would a change in government be possible.[33] D. Shilanski told the convention that *Mapai* was still "internal enemy number one", "Satan" — and it was not prepared to give up its control of the government. Hence, "the war against *Mapai*" should not be waged with "silk gloves" since *Mapai* used "iron gloves". He proposed reopening the debate against the reparations agreement.[34] Other activists criticized the moderate parliamentary behaviour of the party delegation, advocating revolutionary behaviour in the *Knesset*: ".... to

33 "The Fourth Convention of the Herut Movement", op. cit., pp. 204-5.
34 Ibid., p. 227.

prepare the masses for the possibility of rebellion against *Mapai*, and to use against the gangsters from *Mapai* the same methods they use".[35] Begin was criticized for being too supportive of the government in times of crisis. What had to be achieved was the total delegitimization of the regime's foundations through independent activity outside Israel in order to make the masses in Israel rebel against the policy of taxation. Begin tried to explain why such proposals were futile. *Mapai* was not an enemy but a rival: "The wall of hatred which surrounded us has been broken down";[36] the first stage, the emergence from moral isolation, had been achieved. It was now time to move on to the second stage — to break out of political isolation.

Ben-Gurion was well aware of the emerging threat and continued to delegitimize *Herut* by an *a priori* rejection of that party as a potential partner in the governing coalition. He viewed *Herut* as an irresponsible party and treated it in the same way as he did the Communist party. He continued to initiate parliamentary clashes with *Herut*, mainly by evoking historical controversies of the past. Moreover, he consistently refused to fulfil Jabotinsky's wish that a Jewish government reinter his remains in the State of Israel. Ben-Gurion was aware of the symbolic meaning and the dangerous implications of such a decision.

Some of Ben-Gurion's colleagues in the *Mapai* parliamentary delegation were less hostile towards *Herut*. Thus it was that the parliamentary leaders of the two parties could agree that *Herut* should support Y. Sprinzak, *Mapai*'s candidate for Speaker, while *Mapai* would support *Herut* in its demand for a Deputy Speaker. Indeed, in 1955 *Herut* was represented for the first time in the Presidium, and also won the chairmanship of the Economic Committee instead of the Social Services Committee.[37] In 1959, after Sprinzak's death, *Mapai* was defeated for the first time in a crucial parliamentary vote. Its candidate for Speaker, B. Locker, lost to N. Nir. This was not a total revolution. *Achdut Ha'avoda*, the party which Nir represented, was then in the coalition and an integral part of the Labour movement. What was significant was that *Herut* had co-operated with some of the coalition parties to break *Mapai*'s monopoly.[38]

Even more portentious was *Herut*'s co-operation with the General Zionists. Prior to the 1955 elections Begin had rejected any attempt even to discuss this issue. *Herut* was then still in its underground shell. Just after the 1955 elec-

---

35   Ibid., p. 278.
36   Ibid., p. 285.
37   Bader, "The *Knesset* and I", op. cit., pp. 95-6.
38   Ibid., pp. 117–20

tions, however, Begin initiated internal consultations in which he suggested that the time was ripe to form a united party with the General Zionists.[39] He wrote to P. Bernstein, the leader of the General Zionists, proposing negotiations on the possible unification of the two parties. Initial informal talks took place in the *Knesset*; they were followed by secret formal negotiations between Begin, Bader and Ben-Eliezer (for *Herut*) and Serlin, Sapir and Krinitzi (for the General Zionists). At one stage the two delegations discussed the issue of party leadership. The General Zionists demanded the position of party leader for themselves. Begin told his colleagues that he was prepared to agree to this, but they refused. The General Zionists conceded two of their pre-conditions: that the *Herut* ideology based on territorial expansion to the historical borders of the Land of Israel not be included in the platform; and that major decisions would be made only by a two-thirds vote of the united party institutions, which meant a veto power for both sides since equality had already been accepted as a basic principle for the united party institutions. In 1958 *Herut* decided to bring the negotiations to an end, accusing the other side of being too rigid on the organizational level, namely: their demand for the position of party leader; their desire to preserve both existing party frameworks in Israel and abroad; equality on the *Knesset* list, but maintaining the *status quo* on the lower levels, which would have meant an overwhelming majority for them; having two party chairmen, two general secretaries, and two parliamentary leaders; the annexation of the *Herut* daily newspaper by their daily, *Ha-Boker*, making the latter the central locus of the united press.[40] Although the talks eventually failed, they did result in *Herut* gaining a vast amount of legitimacy.

During the late fifties *Herut* had a partial agreement with the Jewish Agency on party financing through Jewish Agency funds.[41] The party now demanded that it be allowed to join the Jewish Agency executive, and achieved this goal in 1963, despite the opposition of the Labour parties.[42] Thus, *Herut* succeeded in penetrating an important political institution which controlled a large number of jobs and funds.

---

39 Ibid., pp. 109–13.
40 *Ha'veidah Ha'arzit Hahamishit shel Tnuat Ha'cherut* ("The Fifth National Convention of the Herut Movement") (Tel Aviv: The Herut Movement, 1958), pp. 34–7.
41 Ibid., pp. 78-9.
42 *Ha'veidah Ha'arzit Hashviit shel Tnuat Ha'cherut* ("The Seventh National Convention of the Herut Movement") (Tel-Aviv: The Herut Movement, 1963), p. 130; *Ha'veidah Ha'arzit Ha'shminit shel Tnuat Ha'cherut* ("The Eighth National Convention of the Herut Movement") (Tel-Aviv: The Herut Movement, 1966), pp. 141–3.

The next step took place in 1963, when *Herut* took a historic decision to join the *Histadrut* as a party. A similar proposal had been rejected by *Herut's* fourth party convention in 1956 by a vote of 140 to 7.[43] In 1961-62 the party's central committee devoted several sessions to this issue. This time Begin favoured *Herut's* joining the *Histadrut*, but was defeated by a vote of 34 to 27. Most of the opponents came from the ranks of the National Workers' Association headed by Shostak. But at the seventh convention, held in 1963, the proposal was carried by 324 to 257 votes. Begin exploited his unique personal position in the party, hinting just before the vote that a rejection of the proposal would lead him to "draw the necessary conclusions". This was in effect a threat of resignation, and paved the way for the adoption of the proposal. The Labour movement tried to prevent the implementation of this decision, but *Herut* won the subsequent judicial case and, in 1965, invaded the most powerful fortress of Labour dominance. By then, Ben-Gurion had resigned and had been replaced by Eshkol. Under the latter's leadership, Labour made only one further effort to continue the judicial process or to use other means in order to bar the Revisionists from the *Histadrut*.

First signs of co-operation between *Herut* and Eshkol had been apparent as early as 1961. *Mapai* and *Herut* had then reached prior agreement on the organization of and appointments to the parliamentary committees, causing the Liberals to criticize *Herut*.[44] Even more significant was Eshkol's decision to involve *Herut* in the government coalition negotiations of that year. He met with Bader, whom he knew well from their joint work in the parliamentary committees, and asked him whether *Herut* would join a *Mapai*-religious coalition. This was the very first time that such a question had even been put to a member of *Herut* (indeed, so novel was the suggestion that Bader was not authorized to give him an answer). When Bader reported to Begin on the meeting, the latter expressed dissatisfaction that Bader had not pressed Eshkol to make a concrete proposal.[45] Other steps soon followed: in 1963 Eshkol decided to fulfil Jabotinsky's wish by having his remains reburied in Israel. Carried out in 1964, this act proved to be a moral victory for the Revisionist movement and a symbolic turning-point in *Herut's* history. (The explanation for Eshkol's readiness to co-operate in certain areas with *Herut* lies beyond the scope of this discussion.) Another element in the legitimization process was

---

43 David Yishay, *Bein Kachol-Lavan Ve'adom* ("Between Blue-White and Red") (Tel-Aviv: Tchelet-Lavan, 1980).

44 Bader, "The *Knesset* and I", op. cit., pp. 153-4; *Div. Hak.*, Vol. 32, Sept. 4, 1961, pp. 13-4.

45 Bader, "The *Knesset* and I", op. cit., pp. 154-5.

the participation of *Herut* representatives from the early sixties in the Israeli delegations to the U.N. bodies.

Herut also tried to renew its negotiations with the General Zionists, who (following their merger in 1961 with the Progressives) were now called the Liberals. In the 1961 elections the Liberals had won seventeen seats, but this number had fallen to eight in the last elections in which the General Zionists ran independently. In 1959 and again in 1961 *Herut* won seventeen seats. Its leaders felt that the party would not be able to break the seventeen seat barrier, and were prepared to grant the General Zionists a larger share in a joint list in order to gain legitimacy and to build an alternative to *Mapai*. One of the reasons for the failure of the negotiations in the late fifties had been the attempt to form a united *bloc*, which would have meant the elimination of the historical parties. Some *Herut* activists had criticized the proposed merger in the fifties, viewing *Herut* as a different "tribe" or "race".[46] In the mid-sixties a reasonable compromise was found: both parties would remain independent, but would form a joint electoral list and, consequently, a single parliamentary delegation. Thus, each party would remain loyal to its own principles, and no attempt would be made to resolve ideological controversies.

The main problem during the negotiations was how to allocate the "safe seats" on the joint list. The Liberals demanded parity, as each party had won seventeen seats in 1961; but *Herut* objected, claiming that a possible split in the Liberal Party would accord *Herut* priority. In fact, the Progressive wing of the Liberal Party opposed the agreement with *Herut* and formed a new party — the Independent Liberals — while the majority joined with *Herut* to form *Gahal*. *Herut* demanded 17 places out of the first 26, while the Liberals demanded parity in the top 30 places. *Herut* agreed to allocate the Liberals 12 places among the top 30, but still they refused to agree. Begin proposed adding one safe seat for the Liberals, but this proposal was rejected by a vote of 8 to 7 in the *Herut* parliamentary delegation.[47] The Liberals continued to reject the proposal, and eventually achieved parity in the top 22 places (the first place was given to *Herut*) and in places 27 to 30. Places 23 and 26 were given to *Herut*, representing the only violation of the parity principle. *Gahal* won 26 seats in the 1965 elections, and 15.2% of the votes cast in the *Histadrut* elections also held in 1965.

The Liberals' readiness to collaborate with *Herut* had a significant impact on the legitimization of *Herut*. The image of the Liberals was that of a respon-

---

46 'The Fourth National Convention of the Herut Movement", op. cit., pp. 205, 240.
47 *Protokol Yeshivat Siat Tnuat Ha'cherut* ("Protocol of the Herut Parliamentary Faction"), January 18, 1965, Jabotinsky Institute, The Historical Archive.

sible party. They had participated in the governing coalition in 1952–55, and had been preferred as a coalition partner by Ben-Gurion in 1961 (although *Achdut Ha'avoda* joined the coalition at the last moment and the Liberals remained in the opposition). The Liberals were always within the bounds of the national consensus on defence and foreign policy. Their historical strength at the local-municipal level helped *Herut* to penetrate this grassroots dimension of politics. But in the short run *Herut* lost a certain amount of power, reflected in the shrinking of its parliamentary delegation from 17 to 15. One of the two seats lost belonged to the National Workers' Association, whose representation dropped from two seats to one. Its leaders also opposed *Herut*'s joining the *Histadrut*, and after the 1965 elections they began actively to contest Begin's leadership. They collaborated with some of *Herut*'s younger members, led by S. Tamir, and almost succeeded in overthrowing Begin in 1966. In 1967 the internal opposition split the party, resulting in the foundation of the Free Centre,[48] at a time when *Herut* had only 12 *Knesset* members. In fact, the death of a *Herut Knesset* member who was replaced by a Liberal (number 27 on the joint list), created a situation in which 12 Liberal members constituted a majority in the *Gahal* parliamentary delegation. Begin, however, was astute enough to perceive that an immediate loss of 35% in his party's parliamentary strength should be viewed as only a minor setback. Much more important would be the final breaking of the political isolation which surrounded *Herut* — the fulfilment of the second stage in Begin's plan which had been shaped in the fifties.[49] To this was added a sociological dimension. Through the institutional arrangement with the Liberals, *Herut* began to establish links with the upper-middle class, which was extremely important in *Herut*'s efforts to free itself of its image as a sectarian party. Furthermore, joining the *Histadrut* opened other possibilities for *Herut*: the development towns, populated mainly by immigrants of Oriental origin, were dominated by powerful political machines controlled by Labour. The new generation in these communities was eager to rebel against these manipulative political machines. As long as *Herut* remained outside the *Histadrut* it could not offer them any material incentives. However, once it joined the *Histadrut*, *Herut* no longer represented an alternative ideological political network. The new *Histadrut Herut* faction held special appeal for some of the Oriental immigrants. Most of the traditional Revisionist activists, many of them of east European origin, dominated *Herut*'s central

---

48 Giora Goldberg, *"Ha'oppositziah Ha'parlamentarit Be'yisrael (1965–1977)* ("The Parliamentary Opposition in Israel [1965–1977]"), unpublished doctoral dissertation (Jerusalem: Hebrew University, 1980), pp. 72-3.

49 "The Fourth Convention of the Herut Movement", op. cit., pp. 280-8.

and local institutions, but were somewhat reluctant to participate on the new *Histadrut* level. It was precisely there, however, that the Oriental party members could concentrate their efforts. New activists were mobilized and *Herut's* alliance with the Oriental communities began to be forged. The importance of this trend and the growing co-operation with the upper-middle class lay mainly in *Herut's* success — still limited — in imitating *Mapai's* pluralistic character.

On the parliamentary level, some limited co-operation between *Mapai* and *Herut* had become evident as early as the late fifties, mainly within the Finance Committee and principally on the basis of personal ties. Bader was the central figure in these relationships. When the "Lavon Affair" erupted, Bader and several others in *Herut* supported the opponents of Ben-Gurion, taking advantage of the rift in *Mapai*. In the mid-sixties, as new parties emerged— *Rafi, Haolam Hazeh* and the Free Centre — *Herut* began to be recognized as an integral part of the old party system by those who claimed to represent the younger generation. *Herut* was blamed for its collaboration with *Mapai*. This was to some extent desirable from *Herut's* point of view. In fact, the financial arrangements between *Herut* and the Jewish Agency were solidified, especially after *Herut* joined the Jewish Agency executive. *Herut* was one of the "old" parties which in 1966 decided to amend the Procedural Code of the *Knesset* in order to restrict the new activist parties. In addition, *Herut* began to moderate its militant political style, a trend which became increasingly salient as some of the new parties adopted an aggressive and militant style. *Herut*, influenced by the Liberals, tried to keep strictly to the rules of the parliamentary game, which some of the new parties often violated. There were also some signs of co-operation within the opposition between *Gahal* and *Rafi*, though this was not institutionalized. The legitimization of *Herut* was clearly approaching the final stages. For its completion, *Herut* needed to participate in the government.

HERUT PARTICIPATION IN THE NATIONAL UNITY GOVERNMENT AND ITS SUBSEQUENT FUNCTIONING AS A CLASSIC OPPOSITION PARTY

It is impossible to exaggerate the impact of the Six-Day War on the legitimization of *Herut*. During the three weeks of crisis prior to the war *Herut*, trying to emphasize its responsibility and maturity, did not criticize the government — despite the great temptation to exploit *Mapai's* vulnerability. Instead, *Herut* was motivated by a sense of responsibility, which is a necessary component of legitimacy. The party supported the government in parliamentary debates and in subsequent votes. Nevertheless, the government seemed incapable of handling Israel's most serious crisis since independence. The idea of altering the composition of the cabinet and of forming a national unity government was raised. Begin consulted with the leaders of Ben-Gurion's opposition party — *Rafi* — and with those of the National Religious Party — a coalition party. He proposed to Eshkol that he relinquish his position to Ben-Gurion, or at least appoint him as his Deputy or Defence Minister.[50] Eshkol refused, despite Begin's continued demands that *Rafi* be included in the government. Bader and Ben-Eliezer were reluctant to demand *Rafi*'s inclusion in the government. Bader told Begin ironically: "If I had known in advance that *Rafi* was so important in saving the state, I would have voted *Rafi*".[51] He insisted on grasping the opportunity to deepen the *Mapai-Rafi* conflict, but Begin stated that *Gahal* would not join the government unless *Rafi* was also invited to do so. Begin's insistence on the appointment of Dayan — a member of *Rafi* — as Defence Minister was successful. *Gahal* and *Rafi* joined the government on the eve of the war, and Begin and the Liberal leader, Y. Sapir, were appointed Ministers without Portfolio.

By joining a national unity government in a time of emergency, *Herut* undoubtedly removed several psychological barriers. Under normal circumstances, the move might have looked like a surrender to *Mapai*. Furthermore, *Mapai* would not have agreed to collaborate with *Herut* in a normal situation. Even during the crisis of May-June 1967, some members of *Mapai* opposed Begin's entry into the government, but public opinion and the media prevailed in their demand to place national interests above partisan politics. The formation of *Gahal* in 1965 also undoubtedly facilitated *Herut's* joining the government. Had *Herut* remained alone, it would not have been included in the national unity government. In fact, from a purely internal, political perspective, *Mapai* erred in consenting to include Begin in the government. *Herut* emerged as the true beneficiary from the formation of the national unity government, while *Mapai* was exposed as hesitant and incapable of handling the crisis, severely damaging its position of dominance.

Another implication of the Six-Day War was extremely favourable to *Herut*: in effect, a Labour government implemented the hawkish ideology of *Herut* by capturing territory from three Arab states. This was not simply a military necessity, as Labour subsequently began to justify Israeli occupation of the new territories in ideological terms. What had until then been a fanatic and dogmatic ideology became the operative policy of the Labour government.

---

50 Bader, "The *Knesset* and I", op. cit., p. 197.
51 Ibid.

The historical ideological gap between the two movements was thus shown to be quite narrow, and limited to tactics and phraseology.

Begin immediately adapted himself to his new role. His political style changed drastically. He rejected proposals to leave the government in the summer of 1967, agreeing to serve on several governmental committees; he also convinced Bader to participate in meetings of the coalition leadership — even though *Gahal* had not signed the coalition agreement. In 1969 Prime Minister Eshkol declared that Israel was not interested in remaining in the populated Arab areas of the West Bank, and that he would agree to negotiate with the leaders of the Palestinian terrorist organization *El-Fatah*. Several senior *Herut* leaders demanded that *Gahal* react by returning to the opposition benches, but Begin opposed them. On the eve of the 1969 elections *Gahal* collaborated with Labour on legislation concerning election financing, and even on a decision within the *Histadrut* dealing with the "political tax", signifying *Gahal*'s consent to receive funds from the *Histadrut* institutions. *Gahal* thus became an integral part of the establishment. In the short run, this limited its ability to exploit shifts in public opinion regarding defence and foreign policy. *Gahal* barely won 26 seats in 1969, the same number as four years earlier.

The next stage in the process of *Herut*'s legitimization was full partnership in a Labour government. In contrast to 1967, therefore, in 1969 *Gahal* signed the coalition agreement and received six ministerial positions (three of which were given to *Herut*) and several ministries (*Herut* held those of Development and of Transportation). While it had been initially convenient for *Herut* to join the government in a time of emergency, it now needed to convince public opinion that the party could take part in government even in normal times.

Having received three ministerial positions and two ministries, *Herut* was able to offer the position of Transportation Minister to General Ezer Weizman, one of Israel's brilliant military commanders. Shapiro argues that this was "a turning-point in Israeli politics", adding that "the members of the military-bureaucratic economic establishment, who had accepted the monopoly as a matter of course, understood that a new channel to the power elite had opened up; more of them began joining the *Gahal* parties ... *Gahal*'s newcomers decided to set up a more comprehensive electoral alignment and to form a counter-elite which would, in the eyes of the public, constitute a legitimate alternative to the Labour government".[52] Weizman's entry into the senior *Herut* leadership caused a bitter rift between Begin and Bader, since

52 Yonathan Shapiro, "The End of a Dominant Party System", in *The Elections in Israel — 1977*, ed. *Asher Arian* (Jerusalem: Jerusalem Academic Press, 1980), pp. 34-5.

the latter was consequently denied ministerial status. This is a noteworthy indication of how much Begin was prepared to sacrifice in order to obtain the legitimacy of himself and his party.

In the summer of 1970 *Herut* leaders were confronted with a new situation. U.S. Secretary of State William Rogers asked Israel to agree to his letter to the U.N. Secretary General calling for Israeli and Arab readiness to open negotiotions on a peace treaty. The majority of the government tended to support this preliminary step, but *Herut* opposed it, claiming that this could be interpreted as Israeli consent to territorial withdrawal. What probably led *Herut* to leave the government at this point was its leaders' belief that the process of legitimization had run its course. In order to replace Labour it was now necessary to return to the opposition. This issue, which was ideological in nature, was perceived as an ideal justification for leaving the government. Thus, as in May 1967, it was a major foreign policy and defence issue that led *Herut* to its decision. In reality, however, in both cases this issue served partly as a cover.

On the eve of the 1973 elections, *Herut* agreed to enlarge its electoral base as *Gahal* joined forces with the Free Centre, the State List and former Labour activists who supported the idea of a greater Israel.[53] All these groups, like the Liberals in 1965, obtained safe places on the *Likud* lists in in excess of their actual strength. *Herut* thus bargained parliamentary seats in exchange for legitimacy. The inclusion of the State List in the *Likud* was a historical turning-point. For the first time in Israel's history, a group of *Mapai*-rooted politicians left the Labour camp to join the rival camp led by *Herut*. Ironically, the State List had been founded in 1969 as a personal list by Ben-Gurion, who left politics one year later. His followers later joined forces with Begin in order to overthrow Labour.

Herut's opposition strategy in the years 1970–73 was even more moderate and responsible than it had been between 1965 and 1967. When Labour lost its position of dominance in 1973,[54] *Herut* sharpened its criticisms of the Labour movement, but these were mainly policy-oriented and accompanied by alternative policy suggestions. *Herut*'s political style became more refined and its historic rivalry with the Labour movement was largely ignored. This trend was reinforced by the emergence of a new generation of politicians for whom the historic rivalry between the two movements was only a marginal issue. In the 1973–77 period, *Herut* already made attempts to consolidate an

---

53 For a detailed discussion of the formation of the *Likud*, see Benjamin Akzin, "The Likud", in *The Elections in Israel — 1977*, op. cit., pp. 39–55.

54 Goldberg, "The Parliamentary Opposition in Israel (1965–1977)", op. cit., pp. 9–15.

alternative governing coalition through growing co-operation with the religious parties.

While the process of legitimization had in fact reached its conclusion in 1973, some remnants of it survived even after the political upheaval of 1977. Three examples can be cited: Begin's nomination in 1977 of Moshe Dayan, a Labour leader, to serve as Foreign Minister in his new government; the tendency to prefer the Labour-oriented senior administration officials over the emerging *Herut* members who wished to replace them; and Begin's stubborn efforts to achieve a peace agreement with Egypt, despite the fact that this caused a split within his party in the course of which several of his closest underground followers abandoned him. The 1981 *Knesset* elections were a turning point: *Herut* had totally freed itself from the need for legitimization. This was expressed in several ways: in the government appointments, especially that of Ariel Sharon as Defence Minister; in a clear attempt to build a *Likud*-oriented governmental bureaucracy; in a strong hawkish defence policy — particularly the 1982 war in Lebanon; and in the tendency to reopen the historic rivalry with the Labour movement reflected, for example, in the decision to set up a state committee of inquiry into the murder of Arlozorov. Moreover, an initial attempt, which goes beyond the scope of this paper, has been made by some *Herut* leaders to delegitimize the Labour movement.

CONCLUSIONS

The legitimization of *Herut* was a complex process. In fact, it involved not only the legitimization of a political party, but also of a political leader — Begin. In a movement that was founded and that has traditionally been led by a single leader, any distinction between the two elements would be misleading. The very essence of *Herut*'s success was its ability to achieve full legitimization without sacrificing either its ideology or its leader. In a sense, the leaders of *Herut* were not mere power-seekers, since not every political manoeuvre was exploited in order to replace Labour. When the voters preferred *Herut* in 1977, it was Begin who formed the government and tried to fulfil the original ideology of the Revisionist movement. The price that *Herut* had to pay in order to advance the process of its legitimization was to grant parliamentary seats to its partners in *Gahal* and the *Likud*. Later on these parliamentary seats were translated into ministerial positions. The first *Herut* government, formed in June 1977, included only one underground leader — Begin himself. The three central issues — foreign affairs, economy and defence — were entrusted respectively to ministers who were not members of *Herut* (Dayan and Ehrlich) and to Weizman, who joined the party only after the 1969 elections. Only later did Begin succeed in appointing his followers to these three senior positions. *Herut* was clearly the dominant force in the government between 1981 and 1984, but the Liberals are still overrepresented in the government and in the *Knesset*.

Theoretically, it is important to emphasize that party transformation may succeed even without a fundamental change in party ideology. The transformation of the party image may prove sufficient. The errors of the rival parties and external events and processes — the Six-Day War, which was followed by a shift in public opinion towards more hawkish positions — facilitated the process of legitimization and helped reshape the image of *Herut*. The case of *Herut* is striking because it was confronting a dominant party, which had for years enjoyed an almost total monopoly over resources as well as superiority in terms of political ideology.

Dahl's model of political opposition includes several components which might be useful in an analysis of the legitimization of an opposition party.[55] The co-operation between *Herut* and other opposition parties increased the *cohesion* of the opposition, as well as its *competitiveness* and its *distinctiveness*. *Herut* attempted to increase the number of *encounter sites* with the government. Of the four opposition goals mentioned by Dahl — change of government personnel, specific government policies, the structure of the political system, and the socio-economic structure — *Herut* carried out the first two, while its goals were changed with legitimization. The limitations of Dahl's model become apparent with regard not only to goals but also to strategies. He mentioned six strategies of opposition, some of which can be applied to the case of *Herut*. In general terms, *Herut* adopted a revolutionary strategy in the early fifties, but any analogy to Dahl's examples of the Nazis and the Communists in Weimar Germany would be misleading. What can be argued is that the weak revolutionary elements in *Herut*'s strategy totally disappeared in the late fifties. The party then began to adopt various elements of the other strategies mentioned by Dahl: concentrating on "entering into a governing coalition and gaining as much as it can by intercoalition bargaining" (the Italian case); "seeking to gain enough votes in elections to win a majority of seats and then to form the government" (the British case); hard bargaining in quasi-official organizations (the Swedish case), which can be related to *Herut*'s entry into the Jewish Agency executive, the *Histadrut*, and several local bodies. Dahl's contribution to an explication of the Israeli case is very limited.

55   Robert A. Dahl, "Patterns of Opposition", in *Political Opposition in Western Democracies*, ed. Robert A. Dahl (New Haven and London: Yale University Press, 1966), pp. 332–47.

Nachmias' discussion of *Herut* strategy is more fruitful.[56] Labelling *Herut*'s new strategy as "patterns of expansion", he argued that these were the formation of electoral and parliamentary alliances; a strategy of penetration (joining the *Histadrut*); and ideological moderation. This "conventional wisdom" argument regarding *Herut*'s ideological moderation has also been mentioned by Mendilow, who analysed the formation of different types of party clusters in Israel and in France.[57] We have tried to indicate throughout this paper that while such an ideological moderation was a part of the new image projected by *Herut*, in fact it did not occur.

Kirchheimer links de-ideologization to the emergence of catch-all parties.[58] In the case of *Herut*, neither de-ideologization nor the emergence of a catch-all party has occurred. To sum up, the process of legitimization undergone by *Herut* refutes any deterministic perception of political life. In other words, what seemed totally impossible in the fifties became a reality in the seventies. Leaders can change the course of history. Those who were in the past described as fanatic and irrational, were revealed as being politically highly sophisticated. Ideological fanaticism does not necessarily mean that one must be irrational in the use of the party tactics and strategy needed to achieve ideological goals.

56 David Nachmias, "The Right-Wing Opposition in Israel", *Political Studies*, Vol. 24, no. 3 (September 1976), pp. 268–80.

57 Jonathan Mendilow, "Party-Cluster Formations in Multi-Party Systems", *Political Studies*, Vol. 30, no. 4 (1982), pp. 485–503.

58 Otto Kirchheimer, "The Transformation of the Western European Party Systems", in *Political Parties and Political Development*, eds. Joseph Lapalombara and Myron Weiner (Princeton, N.J.: Princeton University Press, 1966), pp. 177–200.

EPHRAIM TABORY

PLURALISM IN THE JEWISH STATE:
REFORM AND CONSERVATIVE JUDAISM IN ISRAEL

Religious and political fragmentation has characterized Judaism intermittently since ancient times. Religious pluralism has been tolerated only when it could not be eradicated. Conflict between the Pharisees and the Sadducees, for example, even led to civil war during the reign of Alexander Jannai (103–76 B.C.E.), and to a request by the Pharisees for military assistance from the Syrians.[1] The fact that disagreements between the followers of Shammai and Hillel even erupted into physical violence is likewise one of the less proud — and often overlooked — facets of Jewish history.[2] *Ḥassidim* and their antagonists, the *mitnagdim* (eighteenth century), followed in the footsteps of Jewish history; each sought political assistance from the secular authorities in their efforts to outflank the other.[3]

One factor contributing to the evolution of dissent in the Jewish community has been the impact of secularization on Jewish life. The struggle between the Maccabees and the Hellenists (second century, B.C.E.), well demonstrates this. Sociologically, Jewish law, or *halakhah*, has often served as a wall-like barrier before non-Jewish society [4] and, indeed, between observant and non-observant Jews. Even today, requirements concerning the observance of the Sabbath and *kashrut* effectively limit intimate interaction with non-observant persons.

It is difficult, though, to prevent walls from crumbling. There is always

---

1 Solomon Grayzel, *A History of the Jews: From the Babylonian Exile to the Present*, second edition (Philadelphia: The Jewish Publication Society of America, 1969), pp. 80-1.
2 Shmuel Safrai, "Hapluralizm BeYahadut Bitkufat Yavneh" ("Jewish Pluralism in the Yavneh Period"), *Deot*, 1980, no. 48, pp. 166–70.
3 Max L. Margolis and Alexander Marx, *A History of the Jewish People* (New York: Atheneum, 1974), pp. 380 ff.
4 Some scholars, for example, believe that the Eighteen Decrees promulgated close to the time of the destruction of the Temple were based on political considerations, and were actually intended to segregate the Jews from the Romans and other neighboring peoples (see "Purity and Impurity" in *Encyclopaedia Judaica* [Vol. 13, col. 1409]).

someone prepared to trumpet for change. In recent times the tempo of modernization has been altered. Change is more rapid. Cultural lag, the gap between technological change and cultural patterns institutionalized in an earlier period, is greater. Those sensitive to change, those who wish to participate in it, those who want to be accepted as part of modernity are bound to demand, or at least argue for, rapid religious modifications in line with social and technological innovations.[5]

As a result of these forces, in "modern" times, Judaism has undergone a religious fragmentation. While religious change and development have characterized Judaism throughout the centuries, this is the first time that the majority of Jews are not observant, at least by the standards of Orthodox *halakhah*. (It is noteworthy that the emergence of Reform and Conservative Judaism has been most instrumental in the conceptualization of Orthodoxy as a separate entity.[6]) This is the first time that persons can identify themselves as religious, non-Orthodox Jews.

This article briefly surveys the development of the Reform and Conservative as alternate approaches to Judaism in Europe and the United States, and then focuses more specifically on the establishment of these movements in Israel. The social forces contributing to the widespread growth of the movements in the United States are examined in order to contrast them with the parallel forces in Israel. The problems of legitimization facing the movements in Israel are then analyzed, as are the reactions of the movements to their adverse political and legal situation. The analysis of the establishment of Reform and Conservative Judaism in Israel, and the manner in which these movements are accepted by the government and the public, is instrumental in understanding this latest development in Jewish pluralism.[7]

5　Stephen Sharot, *Judaism: A Sociology* (Newton Abbot: David & Charles, 1976) provides an excellent macroscopic survey of the social forces influencing Judaism historically, and of the impact of non-Jewish society on the development of Judaism.

6　The term Orthodoxy was apparently an epithet used against the "old fashioned," traditional Jews by the "modern" reformists, but it was adopted as a symbol of pride by those who remained faithful to the traditional religious practices. It is possible that the Pharisees, whose Hebrew name, *Prushim*, means "separatists," were similarly labeled as "outsiders" by the Sadducees and that they adopted this name as their own.

7　This research was initiated as my doctoral dissertation, *A Sociological Study of the Reform and Conservative Movements in Israel* (Unpublished Doctoral Dissertation, Department of Sociology, Bar-Ilan University, 1980). I have since continued this work, and take this opportunity to thank Bernard Lazerwitz for our many hours of discussions on this topic, and to the members and leaders of the Reform and Conservative movements in Israel who have extended to me their whole hearted cooperation.

THE RISE OF REFORM AND CONSERVATIVE JUDAISM

Historically, European Judaism prior to the Emancipation period was an isolated, ethnic religion. In medieval times, Jews were a minority group, and they lived in segregated areas by decree or by choice. European Jews, for the most part, spoke their own language — Yiddish — dressed distinctively, and ate distinctive foods. Though economic necessity led to trade with non-Jews, sociologically the Jews were not only a religious sect, but also a marginal sub-group of society.[8] Their beliefs and behavioral patterns set them apart from non-Jewish society.

While in the course of time Jews began to interact more widely with non-Jews, it was political emancipation in western and central Europe that drastically changed their social and economic conditions, and that had dramatic consequences for Judaism's religious development. The period of the Enlightenment also led to increased social interchange between Jews and non-Jews as equals, and many of the "enlightened" Jews, or *maskilim*, came to view the future of the Jewish society on the basis of the values of their national societies. They saw themselves as the pioneers and harbingers of Judaism's future, despite the fact that traditionalists regarded them as deviators and violators of religious propriety. Normative cultural patterns re-evaluated in light of the Enlightenment thus prepared the ground for the changes made necessary by political emancipation.[9]

The situation was ripe for a division between those Jews who desired to adhere to traditional forms of Judaism, and those seeking to introduce substantial changes in keeping with the new times. As noted by sociologists, religious change is often associated with social mobility and with change in the general social order. New values and social conditions subject old values to strain. There are alterations in personal religious needs and interests that result from such factors as intellectual development and social advancement.[10] Such, indeed, was the case for the Jews. Their traditional religious symbols, suitable for a closed, segregated sub-group apart from the mainstream of society, had to be modified in order for the Jews to adequately cope with their encounter with a new range of institutions and social patterns. In particular, many nineteenth-century German Jews were uncomfortable with their ambiguous status as Jews and as Germans, and with what they felt to be their

---

8 Jacob Katz, *Tradition and Crisis: Jewish Society at the End of the Middle Ages* (New York: Schocken Books, 1961), pp. 11–34.

9 Ibid., pp. 252–9.

10 J. Milton Yinger, *The Scientific Study of Religion* (New York: The Macmillan Company, 1970), pp. 232-3.

ancient, and stagnant laws. They viewed their religious services, in particular, to be incongruous with the needs of persons aspiring to the status of full members of the German nation. The enlightened Jews of the upper classes preferred to de-emphasize the national, cultural and ethnic aspects of Judaism and to define Judaism only as a religion. In this manner they could be nationalists (Germans, or in France, Frenchmen, etc.) of the Mosaic faith.[11]

It was in this context that Reform Judaism began as a movement of middle- and upper-class Jews who were dissatisfied with the traditional services which they saw as un-Germanic and un-Western.[12] Reform Judaism was suitable for many of those persons who wished to retain a connection with their religious heritage and yet attain respectable status in the national society. To be sure, theological considerations were not lacking in the development of Reform Judaism.[13] Of particular importance in this regard were the teachings of Abraham Geiger (1810–74). Geiger was most influential in laying the intellectual foundations of Reform Judaism, arguing that while the spirit of Judaism was sacred, like all living things, its form was subject to change. In its essence, though, the reform of traditional doctrine was only meant to bring it into accord with the needs of the era of emancipation.[14] At the very least there was an "elective affinity" between the desire for emancipation and social equality on the part of many Jews, and certain notions about the nature of Judaism that were current from the late eighteenth century until the middle of the nineteenth century.[15]

If Reform Judaism developed as a reaction to Orthodoxy, Conservative Judaism may be described as a reaction against Reform. Early exponents of this new approach, such as Zacharias Frankel (1801–75), a liberal German

---

11 Nathan Glazer, *American Judaism*, second edition, revised (Chicago and London: The University of Chicago Press, 1972), p. 27.

12 Ibid., p. 272. On the development of Reform Judaism in general, see W. Gunther Plaut, *The Rise of Reform Judaism: A Sourcebook of its European Origins* (New York: World Union for Progressive Judaism, 1963); David Philipson, *The Reform Movement in Judaism* (New York: Ktav Publishing House, Inc., 1976).

13 Philipson, op. cit., p. 3. The work of others, such as Leopold Zunz, was also instrumental in this regard. The *Zeitgeist* that affected his work also affected the scholarship of such persons as the Gaon of Vilna, Elijah, son of Solomon (1720–97), who believed that secular knowledge as well as Judaism could be helpful in understanding the world.

14 Joseph L. Blau, *Modern Varieties of Judaism* (New York and London: Columbia University Press, 1964), pp. 33–9.

15 Charles S. Liebman, *The Ambivalent American Jew: Religion, and Family in American Life* (Philadelphia: The Jewish Publication Society of America, 1973), p. 12.

rabbi, held that Reform had been too extreme in its innovations. A position labelled as "positive-historical Judaism" evolved, maintaining that the popular will of those who sought reform could be blended with the possibilities of progress inherent within Jewish tradition. This position was further developed in the United States and led to the establishment of the Jewish Theological Seminary, the theological center of Conservative Judaism.[16]

To the extent that the concepts of "church" and "sect" distinguish between open, wordly religious movements, and those that are inner-oriented, and segregated from the larger social environment,[17] both Reform and Conservative Judaism are basically "church" movements. Both developed as a result of a desire to modify traditional Judaism in line with modern social needs. What differentiated between them were the specific needs of the members of each of the movements and the unique religious "market" situation in which those needs developed.[18] What is common to both of them is that while they each had their origins in Europe, they flourished and greatly expanded in the United States. Data from a 1970/1 United States National Jewish Population Survey indicate that synagogue membership by religious stream was then 15% Orthodox, 50% Conservative, and 35% Reform. Among those who were not members of synagogues 8% said they preferred the Orthodox movement, 35% preferred the Conservative and 33% preferred the Reform. Twenty-five percent of the non-synagogue members had no movement preference. The minority position in which American Orthodoxy found itself is emphasized in the movement breakdown by generations. Forty-one percent of third-generation Americans preferred Reform congregations and the preference for Conservative congregations was 30%. Only 3% of the American third-generation Jewish population preferred Orthodoxy.[19]

16 For histories of the development of Conservative Judaism, see Simon Greenberg, *The Conservative Movement in Judaism: An Introduction* (New York: National Academy for Adult Jewish Studies, United Synagogue, 1955); Mordechai Waxman (ed.), *Tradition and Change: The Development of Conservative Judaism* (New York: The Burning Bush Press, 1958); Moshe Davis, *The Emergence of Conservative Judaism: The Historical School in 19th Century America* (Philadelphia: The Jewish Publication Society of America, 1963).

17 Benton Johnson, "On Church and Sect," *American Sociological Review* (Vol. 28, 1963), pp. 539–49.

18 This has been analyzed by Marshall Sklare, *Conservative Judaism: An American Religious Movement*, new, augmented edition (New York: Schocken Books, 1972).

19 Bernard Lazerwitz and Michael Harrison, "American Jewish Denominations: A Social and Religious Profile," *American Sociological Review*, vol. 44 (1979), pp. 656-66.

Given the division of American Jewry into three major religious streams,[20] it is important to note the mutual accommodation of Reform, Conservative and Orthodox Judaism in the United States. In principle, each of the three should view itself as the legitimate representative of "authentic" Judaism. At least this is what one might expect from *religious* movements. Indeed, only in Orthodoxy does one find a parent synagogue body identifying itself by its religious identification (the Union of Orthodox Jewish Congregations). The Conservatives are federated in the United Synagogue of America, and the Reform are incorporated in the Union of American Hebrew Congregations. *De facto*, if not *de jure*, the movements grant a measure of recognition to one another if not religiously, at least politically.[21]

The primary reasons for this, according to Marshall Sklare, are the ethnic functions that all three movements fulfill in the United States, and the separation of religion and state in that country. "Whatever differences exist between Jew and Jew, they share more in common than does any given Jew with any given Gentile ... whatever differences divide Jew from Jew, only a fellow Jew can be relied upon as an ally."[22]

Separation of religion and state in the United States has made it possible to bypass the divisive question of granting official recognition to a particular Jewish movement. Leaders in the three religious trends are able to work together on a political level (as in the Synagogue Council of America, and in the Conference of Presidents of Major American Jewish Organizations) because of their common ethnic basis. A fundamental acceptance of the "privatization" of religion facilitates this accommodation. It may be noted that the most divisive issues between the major Jewish religious movements in the United States relate to halakhic matters of a communal nature, such as conversion procedures and other questions regarding who is a Jew. Orthodox pronouncements regarding behavioral patterns on a personal level, such as calls for the strict observance of the *Shabbat*, have little impact on non-Orthodox Jews, or

20 The importance of Reconstructionism in American Jewish life is recognized, but it is not commonly considered to be on an equal par with Orthodox, Conservative and Reform Judaism. Nevertheless, Charles S. Liebman has called Reconstructionism the fourth major movement in American Judaism. See his article "Reconstructionism in American Jewish Life" in *American Jewish Year Book* (Vol. 71, 1970), pp. 3–99. There is one synagogue in Jerusalem, *Mevakshei Derekh* ("Seekers of the Path") which may be characterized as Reconstructionist.

21 During the early 1900s a Board of Rabbis, composed of Orthodox, Conservative and Reform clergymen was formed in New York, although religious issues did prevent many Orthodox rabbis from joining.

22 Marshall Sklare, "Jewish Religion and Ethnicity at the Bicentennial," *Midstream*, Vol. 21 (No. 9, 1975), p. 21.

their leaders. The only truly divisive issues relate to the mutual recognition of divorce and conversion procedures; and even this is problematic only when a converted or divorced Conservative or Reform Jew (or the offspring of such a convert) wishes to marry under the auspices of an Orthodox rabbi.

REFORM AND CONSERVATIVE JUDAISM IN ISRAEL

Whereas Reform and Conservative Judaism (as well as Orthodoxy) operate in a "liberal" environment in the United States, the situation in Israel is relatively more complex. While there is no official state religion in Israel, Orthodox Judaism is clearly the sole legitimate manifestation of Judaism on a state level.[23] The following section of this paper will survey the efforts of the Reform and Conservative denominations to establish a presence in Israel, and will describe the difficulties that they have encountered.

A. *Reform.* Reform Judaism in Israel dates its genesis to 1935, when Congregation Beth Israel was established in Haifa by Max Elk, a liberal rabbi who had recently immigrated from Germany.[24] Rabbi Elk also founded the Leo Baeck School in Haifa in 1939, which maintained a close relationship with Reform Judaism and came under the formal auspices of the World Union for Progressive Judaism in 1971. The principal of the school is hired by the World Union and part of the school's budget is also financed by that institution. Furthermore, the World Union has a decisive role in the formulation of the school's general educational aims through the Board of Directors it selects to oversee school affairs.

The first liberal congregation continued in that function for only a few years. The general anti-Zionist stand of Reform Judaism — a position that had developed as a result of the interpretation of Judaism as a religion and the de-emphasis of its ethnic nature — was one of the primary factors responsible for its dissolution.[25] Even liberal German Jews, who comprised the "natural"

---

23 On religion in Israel see, *inter alia*, S. Zalman Abramov, *Perpetual Dilemma: Jewish Religion in the Jewish State* (Jerusalem and New York: The World Union for Progressive Judaism, 1976); Zvi Yaron, "Religion in Israel," *American Jewish Year Book* (Vol. 76, 1976); Moshe Samet, *Religion and State in Israel* (Jerusalem: The Hebrew University of Jerusalem, The Eliezer Kaplan School of Economics and Social Sciences, 1979, Hebrew); Eliezer Don-Yehiya, *Hadat BeYisrael* ("Religion in Israel: Status, Organizations, and Services") (Jerusalem: Ministry of Information, 1975, Hebrew).

24 Max Elk, "The First Step," *Shalhevet* (No. 1, September 1969), pp. 9–12 (Hebrew).

25 On the change in the attitude of Reform Judaism toward Zionism see David Polish, *Renew Our Days: The Zionist Issue in Reform Judaism* (Jerusalem: The World Zionist Organization, 1976).

membership of the early liberal synagogues, were inhibited from attending these services.[26] In addition, as Alfred Gottschalk has pointed out, economic hardships handicapped the early congregations: they experienced difficulties in obtaining facilities in which to worship because of political pressures exerted by the Orthodox.[27]

It is clear that the success of the early congregations was short lived. A pamphlet describing Reform Judaism in Israel put out by a member of the Reform movement does not even mention its early pre-statehood history.[28] Aside from the Leo Baeck School, Reform Judaism in Israel had its "modern" beginning (i.e. after Statehood) in 1958 with the foundation of the Harel Synagogue in Jerusalem. The main thrust of expansion came during the 1960s, with the establishment of several new congregations. To date, there are 12 Reform congregations that conduct weekly services at least on Friday nights (most conduct services on *Shabbat* mornings too).

Services in all congregations are conducted in Hebrew, and follow a national Reform prayer book issued in 1982 (often with musical accompaniment). About half of the congregations possess full-time rabbis. The movement is now trying to attract additional rabbis to immigrate to Israel and serve its congregations; Conservative rabbis, too, have been asked to officiate in the Reform congregations.

Many of the congregations conduct a *kiddush* at the conclusion of services. Some also arrange weekly study groups, but these are generally limited to the congregations in Jerusalem, Tel Aviv and Haifa.

The findings of a survey conducted in 1978 show that there were about 900 members in the movement.[29] Almost 90% of these members were born outside Israel, principally in Germany (30%) and North America (8%). Eleven percent were native-born Israelis. Most of these latter persons came into contact with the movement through their North American spouses, or on visits to Reform congregations in the United States. Only 2% were natives of Asia/North Africa.

26 Ze'ev Harari, "Chapters in the History of the Movement for Progressive Judaism in Israel." Seminar paper, Hebrew Union College (1974, Hebrew).

27 Alfred Gottschalk, "Israel and Reform Judaism: A New Perspective," *Forum on the Jewish People, Zionism and Israel* (No. 36, Fall/Winter, 1979), pp. 143–60.

28 Shlomo Cohen, *Lo Lishlol Banu Ela Lislol* ("Not to Negate Have We Come but Rather to Pave the Way") (Ramat Gan: n.p., n.d. *circa* 1975, Hebrew).

29 For a detailed demographic picture of the members of the Reform and Conservative movements in Israel, see my article, "Reform and Conservative Judaism in Israel: A Social and Religious Profile," *American Jewish Year Book* (Vol. 83, 1983), pp. 41–61.

The Reform movement has also established a kibbutz, Yahel, in the Negev, and in 1982 plans were under way for the establishment of another kibbutz, Lotan. In 1982 Yahel had about 50 members. The establishment of the second kibbutz means that Yahel will not expand in the next few years, inasmuch as all new members are being recruited to the new kibbutz.

By affiliating with the national Scouts movement, the Reform movement has also established a national youth movement, comprised of several specifically Reform Scout "lodges." However, these contain only a few hundred members, most of whom do not come from a Reform background. According to movement leaders, their commitment to Reform Judaism "is a problematic issue."

The Hebrew Union College — Jewish Institute of Religion in Jerusalem constitutes the main center of Reform Judaism in Israel. Weekly services are conducted on its premises but these are attended primarily by tourists rather than by a contingent of permanent members. All Reform rabbinical students now reside in the Jerusalem Center for one year of their studies. A significant development for the Reform movement in Israel has been the registration of five native Israelis in the Reform rabbinical program. The Israeli students have won the right to undertake and complete their studies in Israel (without having to study in the United States). In addition to their rabbinical studies, the Israelis are also registered in a program of Judaic courses at the Hebrew University of Jerusalem. The first Israeli student was ordained a Reform rabbi in 1980. Two additional Reform rabbis were ordained in 1981.

B. *Conservative.* The first Conservative congregation was also established by a liberal immigrant rabbi from Germany, David Wilhelm. Rabbi Wilhelm founded the Emet Ve'Emuna Congregation in Jerusalem in 1937, although the congregation affiliated with Conservative Judaism only at a later date.[30] The Conservative movement's World Council of Synagogues sought to establish a presence in Jerusalem during the 1930s by constructing what is today one of Jerusalem's major and most prestigious synagogues, Yeshurun. The synagogue, however, followed its members' leaning and became a bastion of Orthodoxy. The only reminder of its original establishment as a Conservative institution is a plaque on its walls commemorating the construction of the building.

---

30 Although Rabbi Wilhelm studied at the Jewish Theological Seminary in Breslau and in New York, he sought financial assistance for his synagogue from the World Union for Progressive Judaism. His correspondence with the World Union is described in James Scott Glazier, *The World Union for Progressive Judaism's Participation in the Development of Liberal Judaism in Palestine, 1926–1948* (Ordination thesis, Hebrew Union College — Jewish Institute of Religion, 1979).

Today there are over 20 Conservative congregations that conduct weekly services (High Holiday services are conducted in an additional 20 locations). Most of the congregations were founded after 1970. The growth of Conservative Judaism appears to have commenced at precisely the time that that of Reform Judaism ceased. (The Reform have established only five congregations since 1970.)

In 1978 there were about 1,500 members in Conservative congregations. About 14% were native-born Israelis. Twenty-four percent of the members were born in North America, and 48% of all members were from English-speaking countries. One reason for the differential growth of the Conservative and Reform movements may be the nature of immigration to Israel. Immigration from Anglo-Saxon countries, particularly the United States, increased in 1967 and continued at a comparatively high level for several years.[31] There is an overrepresentation of Orthodox and Conservative Jews among American immigrants in Israel, and an underrepresentation of Reform Jews.[32] This implies that there are more persons who might join a Conservative congregation than there are Reform. Supporting this is the fact that at the time of the survey, the median year of immigration for the non-native born Reform members was 1944. Conversely, the median year of immigration of the non-native born Conservative members was 1965.

As is the case in the Reform movement, the vast majority of members of Conservative congregations are *Ashkenazim*. Only 2% emanated from Asia and North Africa.

The average age of the Israelis in each of the movements was 42. The average age of the non-Israeli born member in the Conservative movement was 55 (in the Reform movement it was 61).

Conservative services are always conducted in Hebrew. A few congregations use an Orthodox prayer book, but the majority use an American Conservative *siddur*. Efforts to publish the Conservative *siddur* used in the United States without the English translation have failed.

The Conservative services are essentially similar to those held in Orthodox synagogues, albeit somewhat abbreviated. Unlike the Reform service, which also abbreviates the reading of the *Torah*, the full weekly *Torah* portion is read at Conservative services.

31 Israel Central Bureau of Statistics, *Immigration to Israel 1948–1972. Part II. Composition by Period of Immigration* (Jerusalem: Special Series No. 489, 1975), Table I.

32 Bernard Lazerwitz and Arnold Dashefsky, "Success and Failure in Ideological Migration: American Jews in Israel." Paper presented at the 1979 annual meeting of the American Sociological Association.

The most obvious difference between Conservative and Orthodox services is to be found in the seating pattern. In Conservative congregations men and women almost invariably sit together, although in two congregations they do sit apart. In some congregations women are counted as part of the *minyan*, although in most they are not. Women are not generally called to the *Torah*, nor may they officiate as cantors. The attitude toward women in the Reform congregations is much more liberal: there, women are regularly called to the *Torah*, and some women have even read the *Torah* portion.

Several of the congregations conduct classes during the week, especially those that employ a full-time rabbi. While there are over a hundred Conservative rabbis in Israel, only about ten congregations possess full-time rabbis. This is due to the remote locations of the synagogues, to their limited membership, and to their consequent financial inability to employ a rabbi (even if one could be found who would be willing to reside in that area). Thus far, only one native Israeli has expressed an interest in becoming a Conservative rabbi, and enrolled as a rabbinical student (in 1983).

The Conservative movement has established a national youth movement (whose present membership runs to some 400), and appointed an American immigrant as its first director. Unlike the Reform youth program, the Conservative scheme is synagogue-based, with most of the youth being children of Conservative members. National programs are conducted every summer, and regional programs are held throughout the year.

The Conservative movement established its first kibbutz late in 1984. An American *gar'in* was formed, and immigration to Israel took place, as scheduled, in September 1983.

It is noteworthy that there is almost no cooperation between the Conservative and the Reform movements in Israel. Little dialogue takes place between them, although a joint colloquium was held in 1983 on the subject of conversion in *halakhah*, and was attended by several Conservative and Reform rabbis. However, there exist no joint study programs for members, nor do youth groups from one movement visit their counterparts in the other (although intra-movement visits are conducted by the Conservative youth movement).

CONTRASTING THE SUCCESS OF REFORM AND CONSERVATIVE JUDAISM IN ISRAEL AND THE UNITED STATES

To date, the Reform and Conservative movements have not gained many new adherents in Israel. The positive functions the movements serve for their present members is not to be denied. Neither Reform nor Conservative Judaism, however, have attained in Israel the widespread popularity that they enjoy in the United States. Attention will now be turned to the social factors that might account for this difference.

The most serious question the denominations face in Israel in their quest to gain adherents relates to the religious and spiritual needs of non-Orthodox Israelis. The basic question is whether Reform and Conservative can meet some unspecified need that is currently unmet by existing institutions. Do *masorati* (traditional) Jews in Israel require a separate religious denomination, or can their religious needs be met within the framework of existing Orthodox synagogues?

In this connection, Marshall Sklare has noted that the success of Conservative Judaism in the United States has not been in the religious sphere. Originally, it was hoped that a relaxation of religious requirements would lead to increased adherence to those requirements that were retained. In fact, Sklare maintains, Conservative Jews have essentially broken with *halakhah* as a religious system.[33]

Sociologically, the provision of a religious plausibility structure for their affiliate members is not one of the main functions of Reform and Conservative Judaism in the United States. Rather, Reform and Conservative synagogues appear to be religiously undemanding frameworks in which the individual can maintain an ethnic affiliation with the Jewish people. For many American Jews, the religious framework of Reform and Conservative Judaism appears to be a legitimate shield for an ethnic Jewish identification. While religiously secularized, the desire to retain such an identification with Judaism thus leads many American Jews to maintain an affiliation with a synagogue.[34]

There is, understandably, little need in Israel to affiliate with a religious movement in order to identify ethnically as a Jew. Other positive features contributing to the popularity of the movements abroad are likewise less important in Israel. The issue of greater equality for women in the synagogue and in Jewish life that has so affected American Judaism is not as pressing in Israel. Little pressure has been exerted in Orthodox synagogues to enhance the facilities for women, nor have there been large groups of dissatisfied women who have turned to non-Orthodox synagogues in order more actively to participate in synagogue services. Ostensibly, it is the absence of feminism

---

33 Marshall Sklare, *Conservative Judaism*, p. 271.
34 I have discussed this in an article co-authored with Bernard Lazerwitz, "Americans in the Israeli Reform and Conservative Denominations: Religiosity Under an Ethnic Shield?" *Review of Religious Research* (Vol. 24, No. 3, 1983).

as a pressing issue in Israeli life that has also prevented it from becoming an issue of religious life.[35]

In this context it is to be noted that the Conservative and Reform patterns of worship are very western oriented. They are quite alien to those found in the synagogues of Asian/North African traditions — the background of about half of Israel's population. It is unlikely that such persons would be attracted to the religious services of either the Reform or Conservative synagogues. Furthermore, even if these persons were to be motivated to attend western-style services for social reasons (as a manifestation of social mobility, for example), it is more probable that they would attend western Orthodox services (as many do) rather than synagogues that are perceived by many to be secular-ist-oriented.

The factors listed thus far contribute to an explanation of why the majority of the Israeli population is apathetic to Reform and Conservative Judaism. The list is not exhaustive, but it is always difficult to specify all the reasons why people refrain from joining a movement. One additional issue that is at times cited in order to explain the limited positive response to the movements in Israel is the discrimination against them on the part of the religious and political establishment. This issue of conflict is germane to an understanding of the lack of accommodation between the divergent religious bodies, and the limits of religious pluralism. For these reasons, the issue is here examined in greater depth.

POLITICAL REACTIONS TO THE ESTABLISHMENT OF REFORM AND CONSERVATIVE JUDAISM IN ISRAEL

The intertwining of religion and politics in Israel raises the question of the Reform and Conservative presence in Israel to a political level. Inasmuch as the Orthodox political parties seek to create a state in keeping with the principles of Orthodox Judaism, they cannot treat the presence of Reform and Conservative Judaism with indifference. Recognition of these movements might necessitate the establishment of a society that would not abide by Orthodox precepts on a state level. If all three religious movements were accorded equal legitimacy, what right would Orthodoxy have to demand that state laws be formulated in line with traditional *halakhah*? Political recogni-

---

35 See my article "Rights and Rites: Women's Roles in Liberal Religious Movements in Israel," *Sex Roles* (Vol. 11, 1–2, 1984).

tion of the movements of Reform and Conservative Judaism inherently carries with it an acknowledgement of their legitimacy as religious entities. The Orthodox parties do not want to grant such legitimacy because of their belief that such recognition is unwarranted, in line with their conception of Judaism.

There is another factor, however, that impels Orthodox political leaders in Israel to negate Reform and Conservative Judaism. Many Orthodox politicians have as their reference group — that is, the group of persons by whom they judge their own standards of behavior and whose opinions are important to them — Orthodox scholars and rabbis, especially those in the *yeshivot*. The latter are strongly motivated by religious ideology, and any breach of religious tenets carries with it the danger of denouncement by them. Personal inclinations that might lead to tolerance and compromise are therefore held in check.

To what degree have Reform and Conservative Judaism been discriminated against in Israel? Reform and Conservative rabbis are not granted blanket permission to perform weddings, nor may they sanction conversions. Reform and Conservative conversions performed abroad are likewise not recognized. Reform and Conservative rabbis are not permitted to serve as army chaplains, nor are they employed by local religious councils as community rabbis.

At times, Reform and Conservative congregations have had difficulty in obtaining premises in which to conduct services. Some establishments have been informed that their certificates of *kashrut* would be rescinded if they allowed non-Orthodox services to be held on their premises. Political coalition considerations have apparently led some mayors to refuse to allow state school facilities to be used on the sabbath for Reform and Conservative services. One mayor informed the chairman of a Reform congregation that he could not allow services to be held in a certain public building because it might lead to public disorder.

At times there has been opposition to the construction of Reform and Conservative institutions. The building of the Hebrew Union College in Jerusalem in the 1960s, which contains an auditorium for prayer services, was the occasion of marked political controversy. Reform leaders in the Tel Aviv area allege that approval of their plans to construct a synagogue in the 1980s has been delayed because of political considerations. They claim to have been told that they cannot build in a residential area because services might disturb neighborhood inhabitants, and they cannot build in a non-residential area, because services might disturb recreationers. Anti-Reform actions in Israel do not necessarily elicit the same negative reaction among the Israeli public that would have greeted similar acts occurring abroad (see Plate 1).

Orthodox politicians often attempt to besmirch Reform and Conservatism as "unauthentic," and "imported" manifestations of Judaism, that are only

183

suited for the Diaspora, or *galut*. Efforts are made to refer to Reform and Conservative rabbis by the English term "rabbis" even when speaking Hebrew, in order to stress their foreign nature, and their lack of authenticity. A Reform prayer book has been thrown to the floor from the podium of the

Plate 1: Source: The Jerusalem Post, March 7, 1977

Knesset by an Orthodox speaker, and a commission to print a Reform prayer book in Israel was thwarted because the Orthodox printer was informed that he is forbidden by *halakhah* to print a Reform prayer book (but this was not the only reason for the initial failure of the enterprise). In addition, the Orthodox rabbinate has appealed directly to all Jews to refrain from worshipping in Conservative synagogues (See Plate 2).[36]

הרבנות הראשית לירושלים והמחוז

THE CHIEF RABBINATE OF JERUSALEM DISTRICT

המועצה הדתית ירושלים

HALACHIC RULING

Many people have asked us the question: Is it permitted to participate in the High Holyday services arranged by the Movement of M'sorati Judaism ("Conservative"), which have been advertised in the Press. We wish to express our opinion — halachic ruling — (as we did in the press on the eve of Rosh Hashana, last year) that the Holy Tora forbids participation in these "prayers," and that one cannot fulfil one's obligations to pray by going to a Conservative congregation, either on the High Holydays or during the year.

In the same way, one cannot fulfil one's obligation to hear the blowing of the shofar, at the "prayer" houses of the Conservative Movement.

We therefore issue this only appeal to the public not to be tempted by the propaganda of this movement, not to participate in any of their activities and not to associate with them. Everyone can find a place at a synagogue where the form of prayers is the form used from generation to generation; there he may devote himself to the Creator of the world, and pour out his heart to Him who examines the hearts of all.

And may the Almighty bless us, hear our prayers, give us salvation, and with compassion and favour accept our prayers and grant the blessing of peace on all Israel and on Jerusalem,.

May you be signed and sealed for a good year.
May it be a year of redemption for us and all the House of Israel.

Shalom Mashash   Chief Rabbis of Jerusalem   Yaacov Bezalel Zolti

Plate 2: Source: The Jerusalem Post, September 5, 1980

Despite the negative actions here depicted, some of the congregations do receive some assistance. In some localities congregations have been offered

---

36　The fact that Reform synagogues are not mentioned in the advertisement (which also appeared in other years) suggests that the Conservative movement is perceived to be a greater danger to Orthodoxy than is Reform.

land for but a nominal fee on which to build a synagogue.[37] (The land for the Hebrew Union College in Jerusalem was granted for $1.) The Ministry of Religious Affairs has appropriated money to a few Conservative congregations for educational purposes. These sums come from "special" budget items that do not appear on the regular government budgets. In this way the congregations are inhibited from claiming lack of government support. At the same time, the government does not have to account for the fact that it dispenses funds to these congregations. (Conservative leaders have been divided over whether to accept these funds, inasmuch as they do not want to be "co-opted" for paltry sums.) In some communities Conservative rabbis have quietly worked out arrangements for the provision of religious services with the assistance of the local Orthodox rabbi. *Ḥametz* is transferred to them in their homes, rather than their offices, for example. Some community rabbis send Conservative rabbis circulars issued by the local religious council, but they address them to their private, home address, rather than that of their synagogue.

REFORM AND CONSERVATIVE REACTIONS TO POLITICAL DISCRIMINATION IN ISRAEL

Formal declarations deploring what the organizational forms of Reform and Conservative Judaism view as "discrimination" have been issued by both movements. The Israeli government has been petitioned to grant the same recognition and benefits to Reform and Conservative Judaism that it accords to Orthodox Judaism. The 29th World Zionist Congress passed a resolution calling on the State of Israel "as the homeland of the Jewish people to implement fully the principle of guaranteed religious rights for all its citizens, including equality of opportunity, equality of recognition and equality of government aid to all religious movements within Judaism." It is worthy of note, however, that at least until the 1980s protest was largely limited to ceremonial gatherings of the movements, such as annual conferences. In particular, the topic has arisen mainly at international conventions held by the Reform

---

37 The most recent instance is in Beer Sheva, where the allocation of land for a Reform synagogue was approved, although only after the National Religious Party arranged that it not be near the site of an Orthodox synagogue. The representative of Agudat Israel to the Beer Sheva Municipal Council was quoted as saying that "the approval of the construction of a Reform synagogue in Beer Sheva is a tragedy for the city and a misfortune for generations. Today the construction of a Reform synagogue was approved, tomorrow we will be asked to approve the construction of a Mission" (*Ha'aretz*, November 12, 1982, p. 3).

and Conservative movements.[38] There has been much less protest against the lack of recognition, or even interest in the issue, on a day-to-day basis.

There is, of course, the question of what pressure could be exerted to elicit recognition. The number of Reform and Conservative members in Israel (about 3,000) is too limited to constitute a powerful political constituency. State President Yitzchak Navon called for the large-scale *aliya* (immigration) of Conservative Jews so that they could lobby for religious rights from a more powerful political basis.[39] Members are also affiliated with a wide range of political parties, and opposition was expressed when a Reform leader who was a *Knesset* candidate on the Shinui slate sent a letter to Reform adherents asking them for their support for his party. The argument against this action was that religious issues should not become intertwined with politics. Indeed in a survey of the members of the two denominations in Israel, the overwhelming majority rejected the idea that a specific political party should be organized in order to seek religious rights for the movements.[40]

Occasionally there are calls for Diaspora Jews to withhold contributions from Israel, given the fact that the majority of donors are Reform or Conservative Jews, whose movements suffer from discrimination in Israel. Only 23% of the Reform and 16% of the Conservative members in Israel agree that such an appeal should be made to Diaspora Jews.[41] Israel's problems are its own. An Israeli Reform leader put it this way:

> I wouldn't want to tell them to exert financial pressure, because that isn't a proper way. It is blackmail. Then also, I don't want to tell them that we have differences here. I don't want to take away their joy in donating. It's like a rich uncle supporting a family and then the man says "my wife is no good" and she says "my husband isn't any better." It's not fair to take away his good feeling.

Even if members did seek to influence Diaspora Jews to exert their own influence on Israel, they might not be successful. Daniel Elazar notes that the American Jewish community is very closely bound up with Israel and it per-

---

38 The 1981 convention of the Central Conference of Reform American Rabbis, for example, which was held in Jerusalem, passed a resolution demanding the "disestablishment" of the official rabbinate in Israel and the granting of equal rights to Reform and Conservative rabbis (*The Jerusalem Post*, June 29, 1981, p. 3).

39 *The Jerusalem Post*, March 14, 1977, p. 3.

40 See my article, "Freedom of Religion and Non-Orthodox Judaism in Israel," in *Journal of Reform Judaism* (Spring, 1982), pp. 10–15.

41 Tabory, *A Sociological Study . . .* op. cit., p. 287.

ceives its own needs to be tied to the survival and success of the Jewish State.[42] Charles Liebman maintains that among non-Orthodox Jews in the United States, the commitment to Israel surpasses the commitment to their own denominations (which, itself, is quite limited).[43]

One activity that members do support is the recourse to legal action in order to enable non-Orthodox rabbis to carry out all the activities performed by Orthodox rabbis in Israel. The most recent Reform conference in Israel passed a resolution calling upon its leaders to take such action.[44] Two Reform rabbis, one of them ordained in Israel by the Hebrew Union College in Jerusalem, appealed to the Supreme Court in 1982 against the Minister of Religious Affairs and the Chief Rabbinate for recognition of the right to register marriages (in other words, to conduct weddings). That case is still pending before the court.

The Conservative movement in Israel has refrained from following in the footsteps of the Reform leaders. In general, Conservative leaders have been more complacent about their situation in Israel. Some of these persons feel that challenging the Orthodox establishment will only lend further credence to the charges by the Orthodox that the non-Orthodox are non-indigenous, "imported" movements and religiously "inauthentic." In addition, there is the pervasive feeling among some leaders in both movements that rights for the rabbis will not lead to a mass registration of new members or adherents. As the Dean of the Hebrew Union College in Jerusalem wrote in 1968:

> Frustrated by the slow growth of liberal Judaism in Israel, some of us prefer to think that the fault lies in the disabilities imposed upon the Reform rabbis of Israel. We delude ourselves that if only we were permitted to perform marriages and receive State funds . . . we would be free to rally thousands of Jews to the banner of Reform. This is a gross and pathetic fallacy. We will grow in Israel, not by gaining these privi-

---

42 Daniel J. Elazar, *Community and Polity: The Organizational Dynamics of American Jewry* (Philadelphia: The Jewish Publication Society of America, 1976), pp. 89 ff.

43 Charles S. Liebman, *Pressure Without Sanctions: The Influence of World Jewry on Israeli Policy* (Rutherford: Fairleigh Dickinson University Press, 1977), p. 115. Elazar (op. cit., p. 181) also notes that the United States Jewish "power structure" is mainly based on fund raising via local Jewish federations. This structure is not tied in to the American Jewish denominational organization. This means that those persons who could exert influence on Israel are not necessarily the same as those who are interested in the politics of religion.

44 "Protocols and Resolutions of the Sixth National Conference" (Zichron Yaacov: The Israel Movement for Progressive Judaism, 23–24,-10, 1981, Hebrew).

leges, but by offering a meaningful answer to the spiritual problems of modern man.[45]

The relative lack of success of Reform in Israel has indeed led its leaders to search for an identity that is not just a "watered-down form of Orthodoxy," in the words of one leader. To some degree, the Reform leaders have questioned the legitimacy of their own religious movement in Israel, and they have been struggling to provide a positive answer to what Reform Judaism in Israel actually stands for.[46] Such introspection has inhibited the Reform movement from undertaking a stronger challenge of the Orthodox rabbinate in the past. With considerable reservations, it may be suggested that it took the ordination of a native Israeli as a Reform rabbi and his later appointment as Director of the movement in Israel to move beyond this self-questioning phase. Such a person, born and raised in Israel, could be more amenable to "seeking rights in accordance with the 'rules of the game'" in Israel.

As mentioned earlier, some Conservative congregations have received some official and non-official assistance from the State. This considerably mitigates against the possibility of their raising charges alleging discrimination. In addition, such quiet assistance in the past has led some leaders to believe that they might benefit from greater assistance and even recognition in the future. Some leaders have thus come to believe that court actions would impose a wall between them and the Orthodox that would be difficult to surmount.

An additional factor affecting the Conservative movement, in particular, is the attitude of some of the leaders themselves toward Conservative Judaism. There is apparently a considerable number of persons who were members of Conservative synagogues in the United States, but in Israel attend Orthodox synagogues. These persons feel that in Israel this is the religiously correct thing to do. One Conservative leader explained that such persons are of the opinion that in Israel, *ma'alim bikdushah velo moridim* (one moves higher in holiness, and not lower). They feel that Conservative Judaism is essentially a compromise in the United States, "and here a compromise isn't necessary." Some of them actually question the legitimacy of Conservative Judaism and hesitate to seek greater recognition for Conservative rabbis because that would entail legitimization of some Conservative practices, especially those emanating from the Diaspora, with which they do not agree.

---

45 Ezra Spicehandler, "What Can We Say to Israel?" *Yearbook: Central Conference of American Rabbis* (Vol. 78, 1968), p. 235.

46 I have discussed this in "Reform and Conservative Judaism in Israel: Aims and Platforms," *Judaism* (Vol. 31, No. 4, Fall, 1982), pp. 390–400.

Then, too, Conservative leaders are reluctant to cooperate with the Reform movement in their attempt to seek greater recognition in Israel. There are two main reasons for this. First, Conservative leaders believe that by avoiding too close an association with the Reform, they will have a better chance of being recognized by the Israeli religious establishment. As one national Conservative leader put it, "here in Israel it doesn't make any sense to cooperate with the Reform movement, because if we did that we would lose any hope that we now have of recognition ... the ball game would be over." Related to this is the feeling that Conservative Judaism has a better chance of attracting Israel's traditional Jews as long as it remains apart from Reform Judaism. Persons holding such a view feel that affiliation with Reform would stigmatize Conservative Judaism as a non-religious movement.

The second point relates to the degree to which Conservative leaders believe in religious pluralism. Conservative leaders in Israel are hesitant about denying the legitimacy of Orthodoxy. Indeed, from their perspective, their relationship to Orthodoxy might be analogous to the modern Orthodox Jew's attitude towards ultra-Orthodoxy. They are less hesitant about denying the legitimacy of Reform Judaism. As one Conservative rabbi said in an interview, "we are a *halakhic* movement. One can argue *halakhic* points with the Orthodox, but the Reform are anti-*halakhah*." This affects the willingness of some Conservative leaders to cooperate with the Reform in seeking government recognition. As the same Conservative rabbi said, "cooperation would mean that we feel that our rabbis and their rabbis should be equally recognized, and we basically reject that position."

CONCLUSION

An examination of the state of Reform and Conservative Judaism in Israel suggests that the lack of official recognition is not the primary factor inhibiting native Israelis from joining Reform or Conservative synagogues. The problem faced by the movements is more one of apathy than hostility. Such a situation can produce a great deal of dissonance for those movement leaders who perceive the Israeli Reform and Conservative denominations as vehicles for legitimizing Reform and Conservative Judaism in general. For example, the Executive Director of the World Union for Progressive Judaism, Rabbi Richard Hirsch, has written that in the United States, "many Reform members belong to *our* synagogues because we offer the most palatable, the most aesthetic, and the easiest way to be a Jew. In other words, I suspect that the most influential factor in building American Reform Judaism has not been theology, but sociology."[47]

Since the social conditions that attracted Jews to Reform synagogues in the United States are so different in Israel, the widespread acceptance of Reform Judaism in Israel in the future (should it so develop) could be attributed more to purely religious factors. Indeed, Israel can serve as a testing ground for Reform Judaism as a religious movement. As Rabbi Hirsch writes:

> Israel offers a real test of our authenticity. For in Israel, there is no societal pressure or inner compulsion to join a synagogue in order to identify as a Jew. No Israeli Jew is subconsciously moved by the question "What will the gentiles say?"; and since when are Jews moved by "What will the Jews say?" ... The liberal Jew in America will never have a full and proper relationship to Israel until there is a liberal movement in Israel. Until then we shall always be considered as outsiders and therefore shall consider ourselves creations of the diaspora ... an American sect practicing a way of life which can flourish only in a gentile soil, aliens and oddities foreign to the authentic Judaism of Eretz Yisrael.[48]

Some Conservative leaders have likewise taken renewed interest in the success of Conservative Judaism in Israel. A Foundation for Mesorati Judaism has been established by Conservative leaders in the United States to support Conservative Judaism in Israel. According to some rabbinic leaders in the United States, the precipitating factor for this renewed interest was the attempt by the Israeli government once again to raise the issue of who is a Jew, and by the realization that a change in the Law of Return that would specify Orthodox *halakhah* as the principle by which Jews would be certified as such would constitute a severe challenge to Conservative Judaism as a religious movement.

It should be emphasized that not all Conservative or Reform Jews consider the success of their movements in Israel to be important for their religious identity. Indeed, it is probable that most do not consider the Israeli aspect at all. For the average Reform or Conservative Jew in such countries as the United States, there is legitimacy in numbers. Reform and Conservative Judaism so dominate the organized Jewish establishment, that they place Orthodoxy in a minority status (although it is probable that the theological nature of Orthodox Judaism provides its adherents with sufficient legitimacy to shrug off

---

47 Richard G. Hirsch, *Reform Judaism and Israel* (New York: Commission on Israel, World Union for Progressive Judaism, 1972), pp. 15–16.

48 Ibid.

any feeling of illegitimacy that might ordinarily derive from being in a minority status).

It is also to be noted that the failure of Reform and Conservative Judaism in Israel would not, in itself, prove that these are not religious movements. Different societies do have different religious needs. Nevertheless, inasmuch as Israel is central to Jewish identity, religious legitimacy in Israel is perceived by some to be central to the religious identity of their movements. This serves as one of the reasons for the efforts made to promote the success of Conservative and Reform Judaism in Israel.

Rather than predict how the relationship between Orthodox, Conservative and Reform Judaism will eventually evolve, a question of relevance might be speculated upon; can religion, in its essence, be pluralistic? The three Jewish denominations in the United States are able to operate in coordination with one another, or at least be tolerant of the others, because the exigencies of Jewish life in modern, secularized society undermine the importance of the theological distinctions between them. Cooperation on a political level is possible because there is no state mechanism that forces them to fundamentally challenge the religious legitimacy of the other religious movements. Theological considerations are important in Israel for the very reason that Israel is a Jewish state. How Israel relates to Judaism on a state level or religion and politics only complicates the issue in Israel, it does not create it *ab initio*. The question then perhaps should be rephrased: rather than ask whether religious pluralism is possible, the question should be, under what social conditions can religious pluralism be tolerated?

On a more restricted level, the question religious pluralism poses is what religious meaning is provided by the various movements. Charles Liebman distinguishes between what he calls a cultural religious-spiritual model of Jewish identity, that provides the adherent with an orientation to what life is all about, and to questions of ultimate concern, and a political-secular model of Jewish identity that takes the Jewish people as its starting point, and concerns itself with collective existence.[49] While Orthodox Judaism does ensure the preservation of the Jewish collective, its manifest and primary orientation is toward the former model. Reform Judaism is more primarily oriented toward the latter model, and Conservative Judaism more nearly overlaps both. It is no accident then that Reform and Conservative Judaism have been much

49 Charles S. Liebman, "Changing Concepts of Political Life and their Implications for American Judaism," in Sam Lehman-Wilzig and Bernard Susser (eds.), *Public Life in Israel and the Diaspora* (Ramat Gan: Bar-Ilan University Press, 1981), pp. 91–100.

more successful in the United States inasmuch as the maintenance of corporate Jewish identity is of central concern to Jews in that country. It is submitted that the Reform and Conservative denominations have not gained wider popularity in Israel, at least to date, because it is unclear what religious *Weltanschauung* they offer for the individual that cannot be accommodated by Orthodoxy in its present form in Israel.

Their future growth may depend on the manner in which they are able to develop as independent organizations (apart from their American counterparts), responding to the indigenous religious needs of those Israelis who cannot identify with Orthodoxy but who do wish for some alternative religious expression. To the extent that there is such a need for an alternative religious movement, or movements, this may lead to a more serious challenge to Orthodox Judaism as the sole "legitimate and authentic" embodiment of religious Judaism that it now perceives itself to be.

CHARLES S. LIEBMAN

THE "WHO IS A JEW?" CONTROVERSY:
POLITICAL AND ANTHROPOLOGICAL PERSPECTIVES *

The question "who is a Jew?" is not new. The Jewish status of particular individuals or groups has been of concern at least since Jews first returned from Babylonia 2,500 years ago. However, from the time of the enlightenment and emancipation (in the late eighteenth century) the question has become increasingly difficult to answer. Heretofore, the theoretical boundaries of Jewish society were clear. The problem had been to determine the characteristics of a given group (for example, the Ethiopians) or individual (for example, a Marrano), to see if they or he belonged within the boundaries. Only in the past two hundred years have the boundaries themselves been the subject of dispute. The contemporary controversy over "who is a Jew?" goes to the very heart of Jewish self-perception and identity in the modern era. It concerns Jews all over the world and it is not surprising that it should trouble the social and political life of Israel as well. But there are differences between the question as it arises in Israel and the Diaspora which help account for the sharper or broader form which the controversy assumes in Israel.

In the Diaspora questions about the nature of Judaism are posed in a literary, philosophical, speculative context. Answers, therefore, can be vague, ambiguous, or contextual, thereby satisfying a variety of parties. Furthermore, the answers do not have a compelling effect on an individual. In Israel the questions are posed in a legal-juridical context, and the answers must be clearer in formulation and less amenable to a variety of interpretations because they are legally binding. Even when the pronouncement is by a rabbinical court, that court speaks with the authority of the state. In addition, the resolution of the question "who is a Jew?" in Israel is a societal resolution. The government, the Knesset, the Supreme Court, or even rabbinical courts, speak in the name of the state and hence of its citizens. A citizen of Israel is not only bound by what the organs of the state declare, he is in some way also personally

---

* The first part of this article is a revised version of an essay "Who is Jewish in Israel" from the December 1970 issue of the *American Zionist*.

194

responsible for what they say. If a Reform rabbi should declare someone converted through criteria which he alone has established, the traditional Jew need not feel responsible. A quite different situation would arise if the Knesset decided to permit the registration as Jews of those who underwent Reform conversion.

The answer to the question "who is a Jew?" defines the boundaries of Judaism. To the extent that this question is determined in individual cases, to the extent that one must answer whether "x" is or is not a Jew, we are dealing with individuals who are marginal to the Jewish community and who want to be identified as Jews. It is a commentary on Jewish status in the Diaspora that this question most often turns on those of low social or economic status. High status groups and even high status individuals don't often claim Jewish membership, especially where such claims are open to challenge. Claims of low status groups and individuals tend to be muted and don't stimulate the interest which might arise from claims of high status groups or individuals. In Israel, where Judaism is the dominant culture, one is more likely to find high status individuals claiming Jewish membership. Indeed, there is one set of claims which was especially likely to come from high status or, at least, well-educated individuals before the government of Israel resolved the question in 1970; the claim to be accepted or registered as Jewish by *leom*, even though the claimant is not Jewish by religion. This was certainly true in the 1969-70 Shalit case, where the claimant, making demands on behalf of his children, was an officer in the Israeli Navy and a graduate student at the Hebrew University. (The term *leom* is sometimes translated as "nationality" and sometimes as "ethnic group." For purposes of Israeli law, however, the term "people" or "folk" is as adequate a translation.)

All residents of Israel, whether they are or are not citizens, must be registered with the Ministry of the Interior. Among the personal information which is recorded for each resident is his/her religion and his/her *leom*. Religion and *leom* then, are quite unrelated to one's status as a citizen. The problem of "who is a Jew?" until 1970 was a problem of defining the criteria by which one is registered as Jewish according to *leom* and/or religion. From 1970 the issue became, how does one become a Jew according to religious criteria?

Another difference between the "who is a Jew?" controversy in Israel and the Diaspora refers to the implications which the controversy may have for those who are indifferent to the question itself. Since Israel, unlike the Diaspora, can resolve the question authoritatively in terms of public policy, the controversy becomes a political issue. Individuals and parties adopt positions, make claims and promises, and invoke threats. The politicization of the conflict introduces secondary issues; new disputants are attracted, and virtually everyone in political life may eventually be involved. The National Religious Party, for example, threatened to leave the government in 1970 if the Knesset did not pass a law whose effect would have been to deny Jewish status to converts whose conversions were performed by a Reform rabbi. The potential consequences of the NRP's resignation from the coalition were believed to be enormous for the political life of the country and for national unity. Hence, the number of participants multiplied and public interest increased. NRP leaders and Moshe Dayan were on especially friendly terms and the young NRP element were among his enthusiastic supporters. Consequently, Dayan's other allies in the government were far more agreeable than his opponents to a compromise with the NRP on an issue which they considered secondary to questions of national security and leadership. On the other hand, within the NRP itself, or so it was believed, some individuals and groups adopted a hard or soft line toward "Reform Conversions" depending on whether they saw their own interests being advanced or impeded by the NRP's resignation. After all, not everybody in the party has an equal stake in its remaining in the government. For example, the resignation of the NRP would have meant loss of ministerial status, funds, and patronage by one group, thereby diminishing their influence within the party and enhancing the influence of others.

These examples suggest two things. First, as we noted, the "who is a Jew?" controversy in Israel is diffused into all sections of the population. It merits newspaper headlines and becomes a subject of intense interest among segments of the population who might otherwise not especially care about the main issue itself. It also creates side payoffs, even for the main disputants, which may also serve to moderate the controversy. "Who is a Jew?" cuts to the very heart of one's Jewish identity and self-perception. It is an ultimate issue and, to those who really care, it may easily become non-negotiable. But because the controversy is politicized it involves less interested participants and generates side payoffs which evoke other motivations even among the major participants. As politicians they have a variety of stakes in addition to the main issue itself. So far, this has served as an element of conciliation. Of course, there is no assurance that this will always be true.

The question "who is a Jew?" has led to governmental crises on a number of occasions. Following the 1958 governmental crises, after lengthy delays, indecision, threats, counter-threats and new elections, it was decided to let the Minister of the Interior decide who was or was not to be registered as a Jew. Since the Minister of the Interior was from the NRP, the resolution represented a *de facto* victory for the religious position. But the government never reached any decision on the merits of the issue itself, in this case, whether those not Jewish according to religious law could be registered as Jews.

In 1970 the question "who is a Jew?" was first raised with respect to *leom*. Could someone who was incontrovertably non-Jewish by religious standards, and did not wish to be registered as Jewish by religious standards, nevertheless be registered as Jewish according to *leom*? Can one be part of the Jewish folk or people without being part of the Jewish religion? The question ultimately rests on whether there is such a thing as a Jewish *leom* independent of the Jewish religion. This question formed part of the early constitutional debates in Israel. The unwillingness and/or inability of the government to resolve this question, their fear of bitterly dividing the country should they reach a decision one way or the other, was a prime factor in the decision not to formulate a constitution.

But the government was forced to decide the issue in 1970, at least in part, by an opinion of the Israeli Supreme Court in the Shalit case. Benjamin Shalit's wife, a naturalized Israeli citizen of non-Jewish parents rejected the idea of conversion and listed her religion as "none." The Shalits also registered their children as having no religion, but they did wish to register them as being Jewish under the category *leom*. The court upheld Shalit in a five to four decision on the technical grounds that, in the absence of legislation to the contrary, the Minister of the Interior had no authority to inquire into the veracity of a resident's statement; that the registration clerk's role was merely to record what the registrant claimed in good faith.

The court's decision forced the government's hand. By indecision it would confirm the court's opinion, thereby permitting separation of religion and *leom* as a matter of public policy.

The issue itself was a purely symbolic one. There are no consequences to a person's registration by *leom* nor did any group have an economic stake in Shalit's registration. The stakes, like the issue, were symbolic, which meant they were less amenable to compromise, more evocative of emotion. Herein was the great advantage of those who opposed the Shalit decision — the symbolic consequences for separation of religion and *leom* meant so much more to them.

Let us look at the matter from the point of view of the separationists — those who would separate religion and *leom*. The vast majority of them were not anti-religious. But they found it inconceivable to deny the symbolic status of Jew to one who was raised in Israel, would serve in its army, speak its language, form part and parcel of Israeli culture, but who, on grounds of conscience, would refuse to identify himself with, or undergo conversion to the Jewish religion. Many in this group also harbored certain feelings about the separation of religion and state and fears of government regulation in the field of religion. (This element of the population has internalized a number of Western, especially Protestant, notions about the relationship of religion, culture and nationality.) Only a minority of the separationists constituted a truly anti-religious element so hostile to the tradition that it refused to acknowledge the link between religion and nationality. Only a minority saw its identity as purely national, thereby severing it from the religious tradition of the past.[1] The great majority of the separationists, who may have constituted a majority of the country as well, did not see the issue of separating religion and *leom* in personal terms. In this respect, conditions have changed very radically since the debates of 1948 and 1949, when a much larger element would have asserted the independence of religion from *leom* because they themselves experienced their own sense of Jewishness as divorced from a religious consciousness. In 1970, by contrast, the majority of separationists were not personally threatened, their Jewish identity was not jeopardized if religion and *leom* were deemed inseparable. In this instance, then, they were really fighting the battle of others.

On the other hand, to those who opposed the separation of religion and *leom*, especially among the religious element who comprised the vanguard, the most vocal and probably the most numerous group, the issue was indeed a very personal one.

Most religious Jews in Israel care very deeply for the state. In fact, as a study by Simon Herman demonstrates, religious youth report greater readiness to place the state ahead of personal self-interest than do non-religious youth.[2] But the tie which religious Jews feel toward Israel is very much connected to their sense that Israel is part of the Jewish tradition, a tradition which is pre-eminently religious. In other words, many Jews in Israel (how many is difficult to estimate) are attached to the state because the state is Jewish and Jewish is religious. Should the state in some way choose to deny this relationship (and it is only symbolically that this relationship can either exist or be severed), then the whole set of ties that bind such Jews to the state will be altered. A decision to separate *leom* from religion, however symbolic and void of material consequences it may have seemed, vitally affected the emotions and national commitments of thousands of Jews. The Shalit decision, whose effect would have been to separate religion and *leom*, did not pose a religious threat to such Jews, it posed a threat to their national identity. The separationists may very well have constituted a majority of the population, but their stake in victory

---

1   For survey data in this regard see Charles Liebman and Eliezer Don-Yehiya, *Civil Religion in Israel* (Berkeley: University of California Press, 1983), p. 19.

2   Simon Herman, *Israelis and Jews: Continuity of an Identity* (New York City: Random House, 1970).

was so much less than that of their opponents that the outcome was no sur-
prise. The Knesset finally passed a law which defined a Jew as someone born
of a Jewish mother or a convert to Judaism who is not an adherent of another
religion.

The law, therefore, apparently defined a Jew by *halakhic* (religious law)
criteria and then specified that registration by religion and *leom* must be in
accordance with these criteria. Jewish *leom* was tied to Jewish religion. The
law, however, left open an important question with respect to the religious
criteria — how does one become a convert to Judaism? "Who is a Jew?" now
became "who is a convert?" More specifically, are non-Orthodox conversions
valid for purposes of registration? The law had tied *leom* to religion, the
question now became the *religious* criteria by which one's Jewishness was
defined.

The law itself was deliberately ambiguous on this point, referring only to
"conversions." The issue of non-Orthodox conversions in Israel almost came
to a head a few months later. Helen Seidman, born of non-Jewish parents,
had been converted by a Reform rabbi in Israel. She asked to be registered as
a Jew. The Ministry of the Interior refused and she took her case to court. It
finally reached the Supreme Court. A decision in Mrs. Seidman's favor was
anticipated and the NRP threatened to resign from the government unless
new legislation to prevent Reform converts from being registered as Jews was
adopted. A government crisis appeared unavoidable when Mrs. Seidman made
application for an Orthodox conversion. A special rabbinical court was con-
voked by the then Chief Rabbi of the Army, Shlomo Goren. Mrs. Seidman
was converted a day before the Supreme Court decision was to be announced.

In sumary, as far as the government was concerned, the Minister of Justice
announced that the government understood "conversion" to include non-
Orthodox conversions as long as they were performed outside Israel. But the
Minister of Justice also made clear that such recognition and consequent
registration of a non-Orthodox convert as a Jew would not bind rabbis and
rabbinical courts in Israel who would, presumably, continue to refuse to
recognize the validity of their conversion.

In the years following its passage (the law in fact was an amendment to the
Law of Return), the religious parties intermittently called for an amendment
of some sort which would stipulate that conversions, even when performed
outside Israel, must be in accordance with *halakhah* or performed by an
Orthodox rabbi in order for the state to recognize their validity.

The Orthodox parties have threatened, but never actually precipitated, a
government crisis. This is not purely symbolic, since recognition of non-
Orthodox conversions involves recognition of non-Orthodox rabbis. There are,

therefore, organized bodies within Israel, the Conservative and Reform movements, however small they may be, with a direct stake in championing the cause of converts such as Helen Seidman, or opposing changes in the law denying validity of non-Orthodox conversions outside Israel. There is also a group with a material stake in opposing them.

The controversy does not involve the kinds of basic national identity questions which were involved in the previous controversy, except perhaps for the non-Orthodox converts in Israel who are generally aware of the problems they face before they convert. The essential question, whether a non-Orthodox convert is a Jew, is in the last analysis a religious-political question. Obviously, having defined the state as *Jewish*, and having defined Jewish by *religious* criteria, one must now be more specific about the religious criteria themselves. Labelling the question religious rather than political in one sense begs the question. As long as religion is intricately tied to the Jewish state many religious questions are also political questions. Yet, in another sense, there is a difference between a political resolution to the question of whether leom is separable from religion (which involves, after all, a definition of *leom*) and resolving politically the meaning of religion.

The debate over the separation of religion and *leom* was heated, emotional, often puerile. It threatened a governmental crisis and disunity at a time when national unity was imperative. But it was a potentially ennobling battle as well. The combatants were materially disinterested, the stakes were symbolic, the ultimate decision-makers were the democratically-elected representatives of the people of Israel and the issue was one that touched on the central ideological questions of modern Judaism. The decision was a dramatic example of the renewed authority of the Jewish people, or a substantial portion of that people, to confront its existential questions in an organized manner through established procedures, and arrive at an authoritative decision. The issue of "who is a Jew?" in religious terms seems to me to have generated a different sort of dispute. Perhaps because Diaspora Jewry and the majority of Israeli political leaders are opposed to the change, its Orthodox proponents have resorted to political bargaining rather than public debate in order to obtain their ends. I, at least, am left with the feeling that the issue is no longer being considered on its merits and, as a consequence, religion is being in some way debased.

*

Viewed from a political perspective, the issue of separating religion and *leom* pits two segments of the population against one another and suggests that the religious segment is able to impose its values because it cares much more intensely about its values. An anthropological perspective may help us to understand why many non-religious Jews are not deeply committed to an anti-religious position on the "who is a Jew?" issue despite their opposition to clericalism, their reluctance to concede another symbolic victory to the religious parties, and their indifference to religious norms in the conduct of their own lives.

Let us begin by asking how Israeli Jews perceive their interrelationship. What, if anything, binds them to one another beyond their citizenship in Israel which they share with Israeli Arabs? The obvious albeit impressionistic answer is that Jews believe they ought to behave toward one another as they would to members of an extended family. The family symbol is very marked in Jewish interrelationships and Jewish conceptions of appropriate interrelationships. The phrase "our brothers, the sons of Israel" or "our brothers, the house of Israel" is a particularly meaningful metaphor in view of the reference (sometimes used sarcastically) to "our cousins" as a euphemism for Arabs. Religion, I would argue, provides the legitimating or charter myth for the sense of shared family.[3]

The central myths of the Jewish tradition, the stories of the Jewish past which are retold in order to convey group values and invest group membership with meaning, socialize Jews to a belief in their common origin and its importance. They commonly emphasize purity of descent. Conversions by groups of non-Jews in different periods of Jewish history are not incorporated into the mythology. The exception that proves the rule are the Kuzars. Although Jewish mythology acknowledges their conversion, it also tells of their destruction. Hence, no Jews today are descended from the Kuzars. The Jewish religion, because it is a religion (i.e. a system of beliefs and rituals related to conceptions of ultimate reality, to the metaphysical), also provides the mechanism whereby outsiders can be incorporated into the extended family (i.e. a common kinship group). Through the process of religious conversion the outsider transcends the biological distinction and is incorporated into the kinship group. By virtue of conversion, the rabbis insist, the convert may legitimately refer, in his prayers to "our fathers, Abraham, Isaac and Jacob." This explains why individual conversions, Ruth the Moabite is the most prominent example, are important mythic components of the tradition. The metaphysical transformation of an individual is found credible whereas transformation of a whole group of converts is dubious.

If we view religion as providing the charter myth for what is essentially an

3   Judith Nagata, "In Defense of Ethnic Boundaries: The Changing Myths and Charters of Malay Identity," Charles Keyes (ed.), *Ethnic Change* (Seattle: University of Washington Press, 1981), pp. 87–116, is most stimulating in this regard.

ethnic sentiment we understand the seemingly paradoxical attitude of "religiously" non-observant Jews in Israel toward conversion. Such Jews are indifferent to the religious behavior of other Jews since this has no consequences for their descent — a matter that is ostensibly crucial in defining Jewish identity. But if national affiliation or loyalty to Israel rather than descent were to become criteria for incorporation into the Jewish group, Jews would lose the sense of family tie that binds them to one another. Religious ritual becomes the necessary step in incorporating the outsider because it provides the instrument to symbolically overcome the boundaries imposed by descent from outside the group. Therefore, even many non-religious Jews have reservations about non-Orthodox conversions. The reservations stem in part from the fear that such conversions are "too easy." If converting is too easy it implies insufficient regard for the obligations which the convert assumes (treating other Jews as brothers) and the obligations other Jews assume toward the convert. Secondly, since incorporation into Judaism involves a metaphysical transformation of the convert's kinship group through religious ritual, the ritual must obviously be performed correctly. Such an interpretation of ritual implies that in the eyes of the non-religious Jews to whom we have referred, the ritual is really more properly defined as "magic" than as "religion." To the extent that one distinguishes magic from religion, I think this implication is quite appropriate.

The question is whether, over the long run, a sense of family buttressed by kinship myths will continue to bind Israeli Jews, and if this is the kind of tie which contributes to a nation-state's well-being? It may be the ideal. Ethnic sentiments evoke powerful resonances useful in mobilizing a group to activity. On the other hand, their very power may frighten some elements and provoke hostility among others. Ethnic sentiments projected at a national political level convey images of reality with consequences for treatment of other ethnic groups and relations with other states. I don't foresee the diminution of ethnic ties given the present constellation of forces within Israel and the nature of the challenges to Israel's security from abroad. On the other hand, one cannot dismiss the possibility that, in the long run, increasing numbers of Israeli Jews may view ethnic affiliation as a matter of secondary importance or, alternately, ethnic boundaries will be redefined. In that case, the tie between religion and nationalism will decline or new religious myths will be projected. But what I would stress is that the variable which maintains the importance of religion in Israeli public life in general and in the definition of "who is a Jew?" in particular, is the sense of Jewish ethnicity rather than religion itself.

ELIEZER DON-YEḤIYA

THE RESOLUTION OF RELIGIOUS CONFLICTS IN ISRAEL

Problems of religion and state are among the most divisive issues in Israeli politics: they reflect deep-rooted differences of opinion and ways of life within Jewish society in Israel.[1] Nevertheless, on the whole, the Israeli political system has managed to resolve religious conflicts by peaceful means, while preserving its stability and democratic character. The question to which this article addresses itself is how and by what means this has been accomplished.

To a large extent, the phenomenon can be explained by a pattern of decision-making and conflict management, defined by Arend Lijphart as the "consociational democracy" model. This refers to the settlement of conflicts in deeply divided societies by deliberate efforts to "counterbalance the immobilizing and unstabilizing effects of cultural segmentation" through cooperation, negotiation and compromise between the political leaders of the various segments in society.[2] Consociationalism involves "the settlement of divisive issues and conflicts where only a minimal consensus exists. Pragmatic solutions are forged for all problems, even those with clear religious-ideological overtones on which the opposing parties may appear irreconcilable and therefore may seem insoluble and likely to split the country apart".[3] Lijphart thus explains the phenomenon of such "fragmented but stable democracies" as Holland, Belgium, Austria and Switzerland.[4]

Through what means of consociational politics do the conflicting elites

---

1 For a discussion of the issue of religion and state in Israel see, for example: S. Zalman Abramov, *Perpetual Dilemma: Jewish Religion in the Jewish State* (Rutherford, N.J.: Fairleigh Dickinson University Press, 1976); Charles S. Liebman and Eliezer Don-Yehiya, *Religion and Politics in Israel* (Bloomington: Indiana University Press, 1984).

2 Arend Lijphart, "Consociational Democracy", *World Politics*, 1968-69, p. 212.

3 Arend Lijphart, *The Politics of Accommodation: Pluralism and Democracy in the Netherlands* (Berkeley: The University of California Press, 1968), p. 103. See Arend Lijphart, "Typologies of Democratic Systems", *Comparative Political Studies*, Vol. 1 (1968-9), pp. 3–22.

4 Ibid., pp. 17–19.

manage to overcome their rivalries, and what is their relevance to the resolution of religious conflicts in Israel?

THE COALITION PARTNERSHIP

One predominant consociational device is the system of cooperation in governmental coalitions between representatives of various and opposing segments and opinion groups in society.

Lijphart argues that William Riker's "size principle" (the tendency to form minimal winning coalitions)[5] applies solely to politically homogeneous cultures. In conflicts between subcultures in a deeply divided society, an attempt by the majority to impose unilateral decisions could lead to violent resistance and thereby endanger the unity and stability of the democratic system. Hence, in a consociational democracy there is a "deliberate resort to large majorities in a grand coalition, as the appropriate response for maintaining democratic stability in a fragmented system".[6] In Israel, only on rare occasions has a "grand coalition" been formed to include all the major parties in the country.[7] Lijphart's theory does however help to explain the stable coalition partnership between the Labor Party and the National Religious Party (NRP), which endured for as long as Labor remained the dominant party in Israel. This is evident from the fact that the Labor Party (or *Mapai* as it was called until 1968) could have formed a winning coalition even without the support of the NRP. Hence, at least until the *Likud* came to power in 1977, the almost permanent participation of the NRP in governmental coalitions was not due to arithmetic considerations of coalition formation. Rather, it reflected the application of the consociational model in Israel to the management of religious conflicts.[8] Because of the highly devisive potential of the religious cleavage in Israel, the major secular parties have always felt obliged to cooperate with religious parties in order to prevent a *Kulturkampf* which might endanger Israel's political stability and national unity.

Religious parties in Israel represent organized subcultures. They possess distinct values and lifestyles which are deeply rooted in the national culture;

---

5 William Riker, *The Theory of Political Coalitions* (Yale University Press, 1962), ch. 2.

6 Lijphart, "Typologies of Democratic Systems", p. 20.

7 On coalition formation in Israel see, for example: David Nachmias, "Coalition Politics in Israel", *Comparative Political Studies*, Vol. 7 (October 1974), pp. 316–33.

8 See Eliezer Don-Yehiya, "Religion and Coalition: The National Religious Party and Coalition Formation in Israel", in Asher Arian (ed.), *The Elections in Israel, 1973* (Jerusalem: Jerusalem Academic Press, 1975), pp. 255–84.

their members are prepared to fight for their beliefs. Because of the unique position of Jewish religion in Jewish history and culture, religious parties are also capable of mobilizing widespread support for their cause, both within Israel and abroad (i.e. among Jews not formally included in their political framework). On the other hand, the very fact that they are "camp parties", representing distinct subcultures with their own values and vital interests, is a powerful inducement to the religious parties to participate in governmental coalitions in order to defend the interests of their subcultures in the centers of power.

The pattern of a "stable coalition" between representatives of different and opposing subcultures is identified by Nordlinger as one of the salient methods of regulating conflicts in deeply divided societies.[9] Nevertheless, this consociational device of a "stable coalition", such as the "historical partnership" between Labor and the NRP, does not resolve all difficulties. Specifically, it does not adequately explain how the rival political elites manage to resolve their sharp antagonisms and maintain the stability of the coalition partnership, and of the political system as a whole.

Robert Dahl argues that "in general, conflicts involving subcultures rarely seem to be handled ... by the normal political process employed in other kinds of issues". These conflicts are too severe and divisive to be managed by such conventional methods of conflict regulation as winning elections and bargaining for the support of the majority in parliament.[10] Dahl enumerates six principal methods in which subcultural conflicts have been treated. Of these, three — "violence and repression", "secession or separation" and "assimilation" — are irrelevant to our discussion. They are incompatible with the consociational model, according to which leaders of the rival subcultures cooperate freely in a joint effort to settle their differences by peaceful means in order to maintain the stability of the political system while preserving its democratic and pluralistic nature. As Lijphart and Daalder point out,[11] the management of conflicts is more typically treated by the three other devices noted by Dahl — "proportional representation", "autonomy" and "mutual veto".

9 Eric A. Nordlinger, *Conflict Regulation in Divided Societies* (Cambridge, Mass.: Harvard University Press, 1972), pp. 21–33.

10 Robert A. Dahl, "Some Explanations" in R.A. Dahl (ed.), *Political Oppositions in Western Democracies* (New Haven: Yale University Press, 1966), p. 358.

11 Arend Lijphart, "Cultural Diversity and Theories of Political Integration", *Canadian Journal of Political Science*, 1971, p. 10; Hans Daalder, "On Building Consociational Nations: The Case of the Netherlands and Switzerland", *International Social Science Journal*, 1971, p. 367.

PROPORTIONALITY

Dahl points out that "proportional representation in the sense of representing groups more or less in proportion to their numbers can be applied in all kinds of agencies and organizations".[12] To this we may add that the principle of proportionality can also be applied in the allocation of financial and other resources among the various subcultures. In consociational democracy, proportionality replaces majority rule as the dominant mode of decision-making and resource allocation.

The proportional principle, known in Israel as the "party key system", was a feature common to the political systems of both the *yishuv* (the pre-state society) and the state of Israel. It was employed to settle conflicts in the allocation of financial aid donated by Diaspora Jewry, land for agricultural settlements associated with the various political movements, and even pre-state immigration certificates for supporters of the different political parties.[13] Today, one of the salient expressions of the proportional principles in Israeli politics is the system for the allocation of financial and other resources to religious institutions and services, as well as to educational and other bodies identified with the religious subculture (or "camp") in Israel.

The application of the proportional or "key" system in Israel has not been limited to relations between religious and secular political parties. However, it is in that sphere that the proportionality system is most meaningful and significant, and there that it is most rigorously applied. Principally, this is because of the religious sector's success in preserving its identity as a distinct subculture with its own way of life and highly developed network of institutions. The secular parties, by way of contrast, have failed to retain their former status as the representatives of distinct and organized political subcultures. Nevertheless, the proportional method cannot alone suffice to regulate all conflicts in this sphere. Indeed, it is a plainly inappropriate means for the treatment of many of the controversial issues in the field of religion and state. Disputes over the content and nature of education, for example, cannot be solved by resorting to the proportionality system.

AUTONOMY

Conflicts over education may be solved by the autonomy principle. Under this principle, which is also relevant to many other areas of conflict, the various

12 Dahl, "Some Explanations", p. 358.
13 See P. Horowitz and M. Lissak, *The Origins of the Israeli Polity* (Chicago: Chicago University Press, 1978).

segments or subcultures in the society remain free to adhere to their own values and way of life and to maintain their own set of institutions. The autonomy principle is most significant in the field of education because of the prime importance which religious and ideological groups attach to socializing their youth into their particular system of culture and values.

In Israel, as in such European consociational democracies as Holland and Belgium, the autonomy principle has been of great importance in resolving controversial issues between the religious and secular subcultures, especially in the field of education. In Europe, indeed, one of the principal achievements of the "politics of accommodation" has been the settlement of the "schools' problem". The methods employed have been consociational; religious schools have been granted both autonomy and proportional government support.[14]

In Israel, unlike the consociational democracies of western Europe, there exist major religion-state issues in addition to education. Of these, several cannot be resolved by resorting to those principles of autonomy and proportionality employed to solve the problems of education. It is important to note that one difference between religious political parties in Israel and their counterparts in western Europe is that Christian-democratic parties are primarily "parties of religious defense", whose major goal is the protection of religious institutions such as church schools.[15] They do not generally seek to enhance the influence of religion on the legislative and judicial systems of the state. Hence, the resolution of the schools' issue or other questions through the principles of autonomy and proportionality has greatly reduced the salience of church-state problems.

Religious political parties in Israel are not content to maintain a defensive role in the spheres of religion and state. They therefore cannot be satisfied with the attainment of autonomy and proportional support for religious institutions and education. On the contrary, they seek a central role for religion in Israeli cultural and political life. Two circumstances probably account for this phenomenon: one is the unique nature of the Jewish religion; the other is the very strong link between Jewish religion and national identity. Traditional Judaism seeks to extend the influence of religion over all areas of life and imposes a very broad and detailed system of obligations and duties on the individual and society. The identification of Israel as a Jewish state, together with the central role of religion in Jewish history and culture, ensures that it is not only religious Jews and avowedly religious parties who wish to maintain

14 Lijphart, *The Politics of Accommodation*, p. 118, 166.
15 See R.E.M. Irving, *The Christian Democratic Parties of Western Europe* (London: George Allen and Unwin, 1979), especially chs. I and II.

the influence of religion on public life. Many non-observant Jews in Israel also strongly oppose a total separation of religion from the political system.

This, however, does not preclude deep differences of opinion regarding the scope and nature of religious involvement in state matters. Many of these differences cannot be resolved by autonomy and proportionality. How can such methods be used, for example, to resolve the issue of "who is a Jew?", or the question of the jurisdiction of the rabbinical courts in matters of personal status such as marriage and divorce? Hence, the extensive use of the third method defined by Dahl as "mutual veto", which is known in Israel as the *status quo* solution.

THE *STATUS QUO* SOLUTION

Dahl defines "mutual veto in governmental policies" as a system which allows each of the opponents to "veto changes in the *status quo* involving his sub-culture".[16] The acceptance of the *status quo* by the opposing parties enables them to avoid decisions on controversial issues which might lead to sharp conflicts and severe crises in the political system.

In Israel the *status quo* has acquired an almost sacred aura. It functions in many ways as a constitution which no one fully understands and which lends itself to multiple interpretations. Nevertheless, it plays an important mythical role in projecting a belief that there exist firm criteria and a fixed process for resolving political disputes. Moreover, it implies that the maintenance of this process is more important than the advantage to be gained by any side in any particular controversy.

Because of its prime importance in the area of religion and state in Israel, the history of the *status quo* is really a history of the development of religion and state relations in the Jewish state. Much of the discussion which follows will therefore be devoted to this system of conflict regulation and its application to religious issues in Israel.

The genesis of the political reality to be maintained and preserved by the *status quo* principle is not easily described. In some instances, it has evolved "naturally", without any deliberate decision; elsewhere, an external factor was involved in the formation of whatever political reality became the basis for the *status quo* solution. In the case of Israel, the authority of religious courts on matters of personal status is largely based on the legal system first introduced into Palestine by Ottoman rule, and subsequently adopted by the British. Many other practices originated in the *yishuv* period and many are

16 Dahl, "Some Explanations", p. 358.

based on agreements achieved in negotiations between secular and religious political leaders in the pre-state period. These became part of the *status quo* system in the state of Israel.

As this example indicates, the *status quo* principle can be used to maintain and preserve political agreements by the implicit or explicit consent of the parties involved not to reopen them to debate and controversy. In this way, the *status quo* principle can be seen as complementary to other consociational methods of conflict resolution, helping to maintain and stabilize agreements based on these methods.

DEPOLITICIZATION

Sometimes new problems arise which cannot be solved by referring to the existing political reality, and yet the opposing parties avoid making decisions on the controversial issues. This is reflected in the strategy of "noninvolvement" or "depoliticization". According to Lijphart, "depoliticization" has been used in the Netherlands as a "method for neutralizing sensitive issues and justifying compromises to the rank and file".[17] In his discussion of conflict-regulating practices in divided societies, Nordlinger defines "depoliticization" as a situation in which "conflict group leaders agree not to involve the government in public areas which impinge upon the segments-values and interests".[18] Nordlinger cites the example of Lebanon in which "politicians consider it taboo to bring up any issues involving the religious communities in public". A more successful example is the separation of church and state in the United States. As noted above, "separation" or total noninvolvement cannot be accepted in Israel as a solution to the problem of religion and state. However, in its early years the Zionist movement did adopt a strategy of noninvolvement in cultural and educational matters in order to avoid severe internal conflict between religious and secular circles.

There are more limited and moderate forms of noninvolvement or depoliticization, such as the localization of controversial issues by transferring them to the management of local authorities. Dahl notes that in the United States "a great many questions are placed in the hands of private, semi-public and local governmental organizations".[19] In Israel, too, legislation on issues of Sabbath observance or *kashrut* has in many cases been handed over to the local authorities. In this way the opposing parties could agree on solutions which took into

---

17 Lijphart, *The Politics of Accommodation*, p. 129.
18 Nordlinger, op. cit., p. 26.
19 Robert A. Dahl, *Pluralist Democracy in the United States: Conflict and Consent* (Chicago: Rand McNally and Company, 1967), p. 23.

account the specific conditions and balance of power in the different local communities. The practice of localization can also serve to diminish the "load" of the national decision-makers. However, in Israel its main function is the neutralization of controversial issues by presenting them as local affairs, devoid of national significance.

The same goal was attained by the adoption of a number of parallel devices. One was the assignation of religious issues to the bureaucracy or the judicial system, thereby presenting them as "technical" or legal questions. Another was the tendency to regulate matters of religion and state not by parliamentary legislation but by ordinances issued by cabinet ministers or government administrators. Yet a third is the practice of settling religious issues by informal interparty agreements. Even when such issues are brought by the government to the *Knesset*, the tendency is to avoid detailed and clear-cut legislation. The proposed laws are phrased in language both general and ambiguous, leaving them open to different interpretations. Alternatively, the procedure adopted is the legislation of *ad hoc* laws, which limits their validity to specific conditions and circumstances.

In this way, even parliamentary legislation can be accorded the character of administrative regulations or informal agreements which tend to be of a rather limited and specific nature. As will be noted, such methods of conflict regulation have been used widely in matters concerning the organization of the system of religious services, or the election and status of the rabbinical authorities in Israel. Even when the contending parties feel obliged to make decisions on controversial religious issues, they try to do so in such a way that these decisions will not be considered binding on fundamental issues, and will not be open to public criticism.

Religious services constituted an area in which difference of opinion between the religious parties and *Mapai* centered on the organization and composition of the religious councils, the organs responsible for such matters as *kashrut* supervision and marriage registration. Although unable to reconcile their differences by compromise, the contending parties avoided recourse to permanent parliamentary legislation. Instead, they enacted *ad hoc* laws, which were periodically renewed. Furthermore, even those laws were phrased in deliberately general terms and left many important issues to be resolved by administrative regulations in informal interparty agreements. Only after numerous delays, and not until 1967, did the *Knesset* regulate the issue of the religious councils in a permanent law. Significantly, even that legislation was not voluntary. Rather, it was forced on the coalition parties by high court jurisdiction which invalidated governmental ordinances concerning the religious councils issued by the Minister of Religious Affairs.

THE *STATUS QUO* SOLUTION — THE DYNAMIC DIMENSION

The acceptance of the *status quo* in Israel does not prevent actual changes in the sphere of religion and state; it merely precludes the legitimization of such changes by formal acts of legislation. Thus, the term *"status quo"* is something of a misnomer. In fact, the system is dynamic; it allows for changes and developments by adjusting itself to new conditions and circumstances. Rather than precluding political changes, the *status quo* enables the contending parties to ignore them by denying them official and public recognition.

The *status quo* solution in Israel does not preclude conflicts over religious issues. Indeed, the interpretation of the *status quo* may itself become a source of conflict between the opposing parties. In many public controversies between religious and secular political forces in Israel, the injured party (and sometimes both) appeals to the *status quo*, maintaining that the other side is violating its provisions. Such was the case during the controversy over television broadcasts on the Sabbath and the "who is a Jew?" issue. Nevertheless, the *status quo* principle is usually effective in regulating religious conflicts. These it helps to moderate and mitigate, thereby making it easier for the conflicting parties to negotiate and compromise. Lijphart has noted a similar structure in the "rules of the game" of Dutch politics, where a "frequent tool of depoliticization is the resort to legal and constitutional principles".[20] This enables the parties involved to handle sensitive issues by "the skillful resort to a generally approved constitutional principle", which allows them to formulate such an issue in legal rather than ideological terms. Very much the same can be said of the quasi-constitutional nature of the *status quo* in Israel. It allows the religious and secular parties to present their controversies as differences of interpretation concerning the application of the *status quo* principle to specific cases. This practice does not prevent conflicts; but it does make them more negotiable and manageable.

As we have noted, the "avoidance model", which is reflected in depoliticization and in the *status quo* can be found in various political systems. However, its application seems to be particularly prevalent in the area of religion and state in Israel. To this day, Israel has no written constitution, mainly because of the desire to avoid fundamental decisions, particularly in the area of religion and state. Even the enactment of straightforward laws in this area often seems to be a difficult and sometimes almost impossible task.

This can be explained by two facets of the Israeli political culture, both of which can be traced to the earlier Jewish political tradition. The first is the

---

20 Lijphart, *The Politics of Accommodation*, p. 130.

tendency to insist on principles and to attach great importance to ideology. The second is a strong sense of Jewish solidarity and a deeply-felt need for national unity and political stability. These facets are often at odds. The first makes it difficult to negotiate and compromise on fundamental issues such as problems of religion and state; the second, on the other hand, induces Israeli Jews to cooperate in an effort to overcome their antagonisms and to preserve internal peace and unity. The avoidance model allows them to neutralize the divisive potential of controversial religious issues without being forced to "betray their principles".

There are, however, cases in which Israeli political leaders feel obliged to make clear-cut and public decisions on religious issues, and accord them the status of parliamentary legislation. Such is the case with novel and complex problems. These cannot be solved by resorting to the *status quo*, but, because of their complexity and importance, neither can they be handled by specific and ambiguous *ad hoc* decisions or informal agreements. Matters of personal status, for example, are regulated by fairly rigorous parliamentary legislation, which also defines the structure and authority of the rabbinical judicial system in this area. In this context, note must also be taken of those cases where the Supreme Court has denied the validity of government ordinances or of local by-laws on religious matters, thereby compelling the parties to agree to the process of parliamentary legislation. One such instance was the "who is a Jew?" controversy, when the Supreme Court denied the validity of ordinances issued by the Minister of Interior, thereby obliging the government to rule on the matter through *Knesset* legislation.[21] In such cases, controversies are regulated by compromises, which are often the result of hard bargaining and lengthy negotiations. But once an agreement is achieved it becomes part of the *status quo* system, which then helps to maintain and stabilize it.

CRISIS AND CHANGE IN THE CONSOCIATIONAL SYSTEM: THE EDUCATION CRISIS [22]

Changes and developments in the political system and its environment may, however, give rise to new circumstances. These prevent the *status quo*, or any other consociational device, from acting as an effective preservant of national

---

21 See Charles S. Liebman, "Who is Jewish in Israel?", *American Zionist*, December 1970.

22 The discussion of the case study of the education crisis is based on research done for my unpublished Ph.D. thesis: "Cooperation and Conflict between Political Camps: The Religious Camp and the Labour Movement and the Education Crisis in Israel" (submitted to the Hebrew University of Jerusalem, 1977).

unity and political stability. Such was the case in Israel, where major changes occurred in the social and political system during the first years of statehood. These resulted in intensive conflicts, which could not be managed by the traditional consociational devices of the pre-state period. Rather, and particularly during the crisis over religious education, they posed a severe threat to the stability of the new political system. It was this situation which induced the sides concerned, mainly *Mapai* and the religious parties, to cooperate in an effort to resolve their differences by negotiated agreements. The resultant settlements have become the basis of a new *status quo* in the area of religion and education.

The Israeli case seems to suggest the need for some revisions or elaborations of the consociational model. That model, as presented by Lijphart and others, is predominantly static in nature. It minimizes possible changes in the social and political system, and barely considers the likely impact of such developments on the nature and effectiveness of the consociational arrangements. This is probably because the size and social composition of the populations of the countries of western Europe, which have been considered to constitute prime examples of "consociational democracies", have indeed been quite stable. Such demographic stability has there enabled the use of consociational devices for maintaining the balance of power between major social groups. These, in turn, have helped to preserve the prevailing consociational system as a whole.

During its first years of statehood, Israel did not enjoy these conditions of relative socio-political stability. The period witnessed the mass immigration of Jews from all over the world, which brought about profound changes in the size and social composition of Israel's society and political culture. These developments threatened to shatter the prevailing societal balance of power, and generated fierce controversies between the various political parties, which could not be resolved by recourse to the traditional consociational methods which had adequately coped with religious and ideological differences in the relatively stable pre-state society.

The sheer magnitude of the immigration, which more than doubled Israel's population within three years, induced the parties to compete intensively over the political socialization of the newcomers. The political leaders of the day were quick to appreciate that whichever party gained the support of the new immigrants would be in a position to dominate Israel's social and political system. Consequently, each party set out to bring the immigrants into its own organizational and ideological network. Exacerbating the fierce competition which ensued were two further considerations. First, many of the newcomers, if not all, were totally unaquainted with the democratic system of government.

Secondly, however, they were dependent on the veteran political establishment for the supply of their basic means of livelihood. Each of the parties exploited these conditions, principally by urging the newcomers to join its own network in return for party-conferred material benefits. The stakes, on all sides, were very high indeed. Hence, the parties were not ready to retain their commitment to those consociational methods which had regulated their contests during the pre-state period.

The failure of the pre-state consociational system to cope with the new situation was most starkly manifest in the area of education. On that issue, the application of the methods of autonomy and proportionality was dependent on the principle of the parents' right to determine their child's education. But this principle could hardly be applied in the case of the newcomers. Many of them were totally unfamiliar with the ideological differences between the various political movements and their affiliated educational systems. Many, too, were induced to prefer a particular educational system because of their dependency on its parent party for their means of livelihood.

Of all the parties concerned, it was *Mapai* which was most inclined to violate the self-determination principle and other established consociational rules in the sphere of education. Many, if not most, of the newcomers were observant Jews from oriental countries. Had they been given full freedom to exercise their right to determine their children's education by themselves, they would naturally have been inclined to opt for religious education. Political and educational activists in the labor movement appreciated that this possibility, if realized, would bring about the loss of the political and cultural hegemony which their parties had hitherto enjoyed. Hence, they attempted to prevent the establishment of autonomous religious schools in immigrant settlements. Where such schools were established, parents were coerced or tempted to send their children to the rival secular-labor schools by means of economic and other pressures or inducements.

The religious parties reacted forcefully to these actions. Their leaders went so far as to threaten their opponents with "civil war" unless a stop was put to the "anti-religious inquisition". Their campaign, accompanied by strong public condemnations from within Israel and the Jewish diaspora, induced labor leaders to change their tactics. The attempts to withhold religious education from immigrant children ceased. Religious schools were established for the newcomers. However, these were to form part of the labor trend in education and hence to be controlled by *Mapai* and the labor movement.

Labor's new educational strategy was denounced by the religious parties as hypocritical and as a violation of the *status quo* agreements, which conferred on the religious parties alone the responsibility for providing and directing religious education. The conflict between *Mapai* and its religious coalition partners generated a cabinet crisis, as a result of which the Government resigned in February 1951, and early general elections were called for the second *Knesset*.

The behavior of the parties involved in the education crisis leaves no doubt that the main issue at stake was political power in the sphere of education, rather than the religious or secular content of the curriculum. As long as responsibility for education was divided between contesting ideological-educational subsystems, controlled by rival political movements, the intensive conflicts over the educational and political socialization of the mass immigration could not be regulated. The realization of this fact ultimately induced *Mapai* and the religious Zionist parties to negotiate a new agreement and thus permit the reestablishment of their coalition partnership. Its legislative expression was the State Education Law of 1953, which transferred power and responsibility in the educational sphere from the political parties to the state agencies. The system of "trends" controlled by parties was abolished, and replaced by a state-controlled educational system which included an autonomous religious subsystem.

The State Education Law has become the basis of a new *status quo*. It has embraced, albeit in a different form, the pre-state consociational principles of autonomy, proportionality and self-determination in the area of education. A development which contributed to the successful resolution of the education crisis was the deceleration, especially after 1952, in the rate and scope of immigration. This development exerted a restabilizing effect on Israel's social and political system, since it helped to restore and preserve the political balance of power in society. In this way it contributed to the reconstruction and reconsolidation of the consociational settlements in the area of religion and education.

The picture must not, of course, be distorted. The State Education Law has not resolved all differences and controversies in this sphere between religious and secular parties. Disputes have continuously arisen over the nature and scope of the autonomy of state religious education and over the allocation of resources between the two trends in education. Similarly endemic have been differences of opinion concerning the role of religious tradition in the "general" (i.e. non-orthodox) state education stream. Invariably, however, such conflicts have not been of an intensive nature. Related to the interpretation and application of the existing legislation, they have usually been resolved by discrete bargaining and negotiations, conducted within and between the administrative divisions of the Ministry of Education and Culture. Once concluded, these negotiated settlements have become part of the prevailing *status quo* in the area of religion and education. As such, they can serve as a basis for regulating further controversies in that sphere.

Even in its new form, the *status quo* in education established in 1953 has been dynamic in nature. It has proven sensitive to changes and modifications, although its basic principles have remained intact. Most of the developments which occurred in the sphere of education since 1953 have been favorable to the religious parties, a prominent example being the inclusion of religious secondary schools within the autonomous religious subsystem of state education in 1962.

The rise of the *Likud* to power in 1977, which increased the political influence of the religious parties, helped to enhance the religious standpoint in education. For the first time, a religious party representative, Zevulun Hammer of the NRP, was appointed to be Minister of Education and Culture. While in office, Hammer utilized his authority to increase the role of Jewish religious tradition in the non-orthodox state stream. Nevertheless, the changes which occurred in the wake of the *Likud*'s rise to power did not portend a departure from the *status quo* system. Significantly, Hammer did not even try to introduce major educational changes, since he knew that to do so would arouse strong opposition from both within and without the coalition.

CHANGES IN THE RELIGIOUS *STATUS QUO*: THE CASE OF SABBATH PUBLIC OBSERVANCE

Changes in the religious *status quo* have not always been favorable to the religious public and its parties. A salient example is the decline in the public observance of the *Shabbat*, evident in the increased tendency to operate cinemas, theaters and restaurants on the Sabbath, or to run public transport on that day. In many cases such actions have violated municipal by-laws or agreements and conventions of considerable age. The widespread decline in public observance of the *Shabbat* is related to the growing opposition on the part of non-religious people to any interference in their work and leisure activities. In large part, this attitude prevented the enactment of a national *Shabbat* law, despite promises given to the religious parties by their coalition partners to do so. In turn, the absence of a *Shabbat* law made it easier to violate or by-pass local *Shabbat* observance practices and regulations.

Significantly, the *Likud*'s rise to power did not reverse this particular trend. Admittedly, in some cases the political upheaval of 1977 did lead to a more rigorous insistence on the application of *Shabbat* observance regulations. The prominent example is the El-Al controversy, which resulted in the cessation of *Shabbat* flights by the Israeli national airline. But that seems to have been an isolated case. Probably more instructive is the Petach-Tikvah controversy over the desecration of the *Shabbat* in that town. That case indicates that violations of *Shabbat* observance practices and regulations continue on the local level, even under *Likud*'s rule on the national level.

The Petach-Tikvah affair also appears to demonstrate the validity of our assertions concerning the nature of the *status quo* system of conflict regulation in the area of religion and state in Israel. The intensity of the conflict in Petach-Tikvah cannot be explained merely by the fact of the opening of a cinema in that town on *Shabbat* eve. A considerable number of cinemas and theaters have similarly begun to operate on the Sabbath in several other localities. None have provoked the kind of fierce reaction on the part of religious circles as was the case in Petach-Tikvah.

The intensity of the religious reaction in Petach-Tikvah is due mainly to its wider context. The opening of a local cinema on *Shabbat* was connected with an attempt by the Labor-led municipal council to enact a by-law allowing the mayor to permit the operation of cinemas, theaters and restaurants on the Sabbath, despite earlier by-laws barring such practices. Religious circles have therefore interpreted the action to be an open and outright attack on the *status quo* principle and the legitimization of its violation. It seems to have accorded legal sanction and formal recognition to deviations from established norms and practices in the area of Sabbath observance. That would seem to explain why the mayor's plan has also been condemned by many secularists, including leaders and members of his own Labor party. They regard his action as an open violation of the *status quo* principle, to which they continue to be committed even while being in opposition. The Petach-Tikvah affair has resulted in the failure to bring about change in the local Sabbath legislation. Moreover, even the Petach-Tikvah cinema in question has been closed (ostensibly for redecoration) despite the continuous operation on the Sabbath of cinemas and theaters in other localities, where no attempt was made to accord the action legal sanction. The Petach-Tikvah case, then, provides further evidence of the dynamic nature of the Israeli *status quo*. It allows for effective changes and modification in the social and political system, but prevents the legitimization of such changes, by means of legal or public recognition.

CONCLUDING REMARKS

Our study indicates that political developments which affected the position and power of the religious parties did not exert a profound influence on the prevailing *status quo* system. Indeed, this system seems unlikely to be seriously affected by such developments as the formation of the government of national unity in 1984. Primarily, this is because the *status quo* principle constitutes part of the wider consociational pattern of conflict regulation, which itself reflects the perceived need for cooperation and compromise in order to overcome divisions and cleavages in the socio-political system. In the area of religion and state, this pattern of conflict management will be adhered to in Israel for as long as the major political parties continue to acknowledge the need for cooperative efforts in the settlement of divisive religious issues, in order to maintain the stability and national unity of the Jewish state.